THE LIFE OF
ROBERT NOBLE BURGESS

Dear Marv,

with thanks for your invaluable help at Golden State University in 1997!

Best

J Moore
Sept, 2019

THE LIFE OF
ROBERT NOBLE BURGESS

JAMES ROLPH MOORE, JR.

Alive Book Publishing

In memory of Kevin Starr,
my friend and writing coach,
without whom this book would never have happened.

CONTENTS

ACKNOWLEDGEMENTS

Many people helped in the creation of this book. Particular thanks are due to the staffs at the Museum of the San Ramon Valley, the Contra Costa County Historical Society, the Bancroft Library at the University of California at Berkeley, the Pleasant Hill Public Library, the San Francisco Public Library, the Crockett Historical Museum, the Walnut Creek Historical Society, the Concord Historical Society, the California State Law Library, Sacramento, Ca, the California Genealogical Society, the Martinez Historical Society, Contra Costa County Vital Records, the Bohemian Club archives, San Francisco, Ca., and the National Archives in San Bruno Ca. and in Kansas City Mo. Individuals who rendered great assistance include David Mackesey at the Diablo Country Club for his excellent help on the Burgess-Hearst partnership at Diablo, Sheila Starr and Kitty Lamprecht for their outstanding proofreading assistance, Pat Keats at the Society of California Pioneers in San Francisco, Ca, the Honorable John Devine for his helpful legal research into RN's Los Angeles years, Seth Adams of Save Mt. Diablo for his wide knowledge and perspective on Mt. Diablo and its history, and Janet Stapleton and Daniel O'Connell at the Contra Costa County Historical Society for their invaluable assistance with the arcana of digital photography. And finally, I am indebted to my daughter Mercedes Devine who acted as my outstanding research assistant and my wife Sharon for her tireless editing, counsel, and patience.

INTRODUCTION

For to the Puritan, a contemner of the vain shows of sacramentalism, mundane toil becomes itself a kind of sacrament. Like a man who strives by unresting activity to exorcise a haunting demon, the Puritan, in an effort to save his own soul, sets in motion every force in heaven above or in the earth beneath...For it is will- organized and disciplined and inspired, will quiescent in rapt adoration or straining in violent energy, but always will-which is the essence of Puritanism, and for the intensification and organization of will every instrument in that tremendous arsenal of religious fervor is mobilized.

—Richard Henry Tawney[1]

This book is both a story of America and of California. It is a study of character, of ambition, of will, and of a life that reflected the larger spirit of the times in which it occurred. It is a story about a commitment to a life of work and self-improvement, of success and failure, and of tremendous drive and need to achieve. Robert Noble Burgess was my maternal grandfather; he was the fourth child of a Presbyterian Minister and was descended from Scottish Presbyterian and Puritan stock.

Burgess (he was "RN" to his family and associates) lived a long life, dying just short of his 87th birthday. During his final years he wrote his *Memoirs*; it was his story, meant for family, some friends, and a few local historical societies. He was not a writer in the sense that the term suggests being a stickler for the rules of punctuation and style; he was a man of action, a deal-maker, a man of overar-

---

[1] Richard Henry Tawney, *Religion and the Rise of Capitalism*, (New Brunswick, New Jersey, Transaction Publishers, 1997, Orig. Pub: New York, Harcourt Brace and Company, New York, 1926)), 199-201.

ching ambition and drive. The writing style in the *Memoirs* reveals a man with an eighth-grade education, but it also reveals an autodidact who employed his ambition in the service of financial creativity, business acumen, and risk-taking, ultimately assembling one of the largest private landholdings in the history of Contra Costa County.

I wrote this book because, on detailed exploration of the *Memoirs*, I found a fascinating character with whom I could identify on a very personal level. His striving, his need to ascend in his world, to belong, and to achieve, were all themes that resonated with me. In addition, I became fascinated by what I read as a very American story, of hard work, of social and financial success followed by ignominious failure and banishment by his business associates and professional friends, and then of redemption, all characterized by an almost congenital need to work and to pull himself up in the world. To me, Robert Burgess personified the American character of the late 19th and early 20th centuries. A hard-working, disciplined, and frugal young man, RN embodied what we think about when we think of the Protestant Ethic; as an immigrant in California, he was an outsider seeking to be accepted as an insider; as a driven, talented young man with nascent leadership abilities, he was something of a lone wolf, preferring, as he described it, to operate on his own. As an outsider, he had a keen sense of social awareness in his new milieu and probably selected his mate with that in mind. His story touches on major episodes in the history of the western United States, largely in land development in the San Francisco Bay Area but also in areas as diverse as shipbuilding in Port Chicago, sheep ranching in New Mexico, and financing movies in Hollywood.

I've looked at his life in the context of the most significant events that formed it. It starts in rural, agrarian New Brunswick, Canada, then moves on, via a transcontinental rail trip in 1884, to San Francisco, and then to Danville, California, each move initiated by his father's "calls" to minister at Presbyterian churches. His working life began as an eight-year-old in a farm house that still stands in Danville and continued for almost 80 years, his final task the creation of his memoir. In many ways, this is the story of two lives, of an arc of accomplishment broken in mid-life by a bankruptcy in which he lost virtually everything and of a long, slow, and only partial recovery complicated by the great depression and the war which followed it.

RN was a man with an inborn talent for business and an intuitive grasp of economics that was part of his makeup. The activities of his life were an expression of this element in his character. Because of that this book has much to do with economics and includes periodic references to the larger economic backdrop against which his life occurred. These are included to add context, setting the larger stage on which he operated from his earliest years as a teenage businessman. During the first half of his life, national economic conditions were for the most part salutary; during the second half much less so, creating the circumstances for the largest challenges he faced.

A biography based as heavily on primary source material as this one is of course subject to serious limitations. The *Memoirs* were privately published with a limited production run. His caveat in the second paragraph of the *Memoirs* should not be taken lightly. In it he cautioned that in places where his memory failed him, the gaps should be filled in with imagination. He advised his readers that, "imagination works like an electric spark jumping between two electrodes. If the distance is too great there is no spark. Should you come across any 'sparking' just put it down to imagination." His comment acknowledges his age and his difficulty in recollecting the detail of many of the events in his life and can be interpreted as counsel to not apply rigid standards of truth too rigorously. An autobiographer is painting a picture of his life as he wants his audience to see it. As his biographer, I've tried to interpret his writings in such a way as to produce a more objective picture. Such a picture is not always flattering, but flattery has not been my goal. I've tried to understand the character of an obviously accomplished but also flawed man of many dimensions. I've tried to paint him as a real person with human attributes reflective of his frailties as well as his many strengths and accomplishments.

CHAPTER I

Origins

St John, New Brunswick in February of 1887 must have been cold. The city is roughly the same latitude as Portland, Oregon, but has considerably cooler average annual temperatures presumably due to the proximity of the Atlantic Ocean. St John, located on the western shore of the Bay of Fundy, is affected both by the tempering climate of the Bay and the more extreme temperatures of the inland areas it abuts. With temperatures averaging around 17 F in January, RN's early years were spent in a climate much less friendly than he would know in California.

RN Burgess came into a family not unacquainted with sadness; four years before his birth, his parents had lost one child, Isabella, at three years of age. Born on February 10, 1878, he would ultimately be one of nine children, six of whom survived to adulthood. He was the fourth child, the third boy, following two older brothers, William and John, who were playmates and mentors. RN was followed by two younger brothers, Gordon McGregor and Arthur Penryn Stanley, both of whom died in infancy. Two sisters followed, Marie Louise and Helen Hortense, and finally a brother, Malcom Stuart.

The family's home in St John, consisted of two distinct communities in the 1870s, the East Side, on the east side of the St John river, and the West Side. The Burgess home was in Carelton on the West Side, a working-class neighborhood at the time of the founding of the community in 1785.

The Protestant Ethic, a phrase made popular by German sociologist Max Weber in the 1930 publication in the US of his earlier book *The Protestant Ethic and the Spirit of Capitalism (1904)*, must have described well the environment of RN's childhood household.

Weber's text, a founding work in the history of sociology, suggests that the economic performance of certain northern European countries can be attributed to the Protestant Reformation of the 16th century and that the Calvinist ethic and related ideas strongly influenced the development of capitalism. In Calvinism, an individual's salvation was uncertain during life and various attributes of character were deemed to be demonstrative of election. These characteristics included self-discipline, hard work, and frugality.

What kind of a childhood did Robert Noble Burgess have? What was it like to be a child in St John New Brunswick, the son of a Scottish Calvinist Presbyterian Minister? The sect was nothing if not strict, reflecting the ideology of John Knox's brand of Protestantism with its emphasis on a life of hard work and frugality in the face of uncertainty as to salvation.

At the time of his third son's birth, Father Joshua Chase Burgess was eight years into the first of four clerical appointments he would ultimately hold in the Presbyterian Church. In 1870, he became Minister of the West Side branch of the Presbyterian Church of St. John, New Brunswick. Later, he served in similar capacities in First Presbyterian Church of San Francisco, First Presbyterian Church of Danville, CA, and First Presbyterian Church of Healdsburg, CA. Father Burgess was educated at Dalhousie University in Nova Scotia, Canada (1868) and at the Presbyterian Church College in Edinburgh, Scotland (1870).

RN's father was not as forbidding and uncompromising as his title and his time suggest. In the *Memoirs* RN relates an anecdote about the St John fire of 1877 in which much of the city burned. The city fathers appointed the Reverend Burgess and the Catholic Priest, "Father John," to supervise the distribution of the charitable relief funds which had been sent to the city. Father Burgess later said that he was initially inclined to view Father John as a heretic, having himself been brought up in the Calvinist Presbyterian faith, but after working with him on the project, they "were great friends, and he came to the conclusion good men were where you found them, regardless of their choice of road to heaven." This suggests a more tolerant side to Joshua than might be expected given his

Edinburgh training.

Nonetheless, the Calvinist tradition and the Protestant Ethic seem to have been imprinted on RN. In a paragraph early in the *Memoirs*, he talks about his lifelong commitment to work. "Always having to work and meeting the issue willingly probably accounts for the fact that my sister Marie and I always wanted to work – it became a habit – and working was of great comfort to us, and we shared the reward from our labors freely with our family."

It was during these years that RN's character was formed and it seems probable that his ambition, drive, and independence in later life were the result of these experiences and of the environment of Father Burgess' household. A father who was often absent on weekly preaching assignments in rural New Brunswick and preoccupied with ministerial duties when at home, and a mother who had her hands full with other children and was burdened with the sadness of loss of a child so early in her married life, must have produced a child characterized by self-sufficiency, stoic resilience and loneliness.

In a revealing insight about his character and upbringing, he relates an anecdote about his business relationships during the period when, as a very young man, he was managing the 10,000-acre Hookston Ranch in Contra Costa County. On one occasion, he ran afoul of one of his former principals, Arthur Castle of Castle Brothers, one of the largest dried fruit and nut dealers in San Francisco. Castle Brothers were not his current employers at Hookston. He had purchased fruit for them in his prior employment and they telephoned, asking for a favor. They needed dried silver prunes and, as the fruit was in short supply at the time, asked if he might locate two cars. RN was successful, found and contracted for the fruit, only to discover that the order had been cancelled by Castle, and that his failure to stay in daily touch with his buyer had left him with a financial loss far beyond his means. In describing the episode, and the dressing down he received from his principal, he suggested that, "I am not good at working with others and get along better going it alone." He attributed his predilection for "going it alone" to childhood experiences when he was reprimanded for making excuses for lack of performance.

It seems clear that RN was a loner, something of a self-drama-tizer, and, as a third surviving child behind two older brothers, craved a measure of attention and recognition which was not often gratified in a busy, industrious household. His relationship with his mother was his closest, certainly not an unusual circumstance but a significant one in his case because of his tendency to go his own way. His affinity with his younger sister Marie later in his life was unique, in both its intimacy and its duration, throughout their lives. With his brothers and his father, he reports perfunctory and distant relationships, but he describes a close and special relation-ship with his Mother. In his telling she was the only person he could relate to in a quiet, non-verbal way; she seems to have been a reservoir of calm acceptance and understanding for him during his childhood.

***

The Reverend Joshua Chase Burgess married Mary Helen Noble, daughter of Isaac and Mary Buist Noble in St. John, New Brunswick in January of 1872. The Burgesses in the Maritime Provinces of Canada are descendants of Thomas and Dorothy Burgess, Puritan arrivals in the 1630s to Sandwich, Massachusetts. RN's father-in-law, Isaac Noble, was the owner of a wholesale fish market, which bought, freeze-packed, and shipped fish to the in-terior – as far west as Chicago.

The Burgesses of Nova Scotia and New Brunswick descended from what were known as the New England Planters, a group of some 8,000 farmers and fishermen from various parts of New Eng-land who responded to an offer of land grants by the English Crown in the late 1750's. In consequence of the forced expulsion by the Crown of some 11,000-12,000 French Acadians during the Seven Years War between 1755 and 1764, the lands formerly inhab-ited by the French were offered to the Colonists. The Acadians had been adept farmers, cultivators, and irrigators, creating a system of dykes on the ocean shore which allowed enough salt-water incursion to produce very fertile farm land. Particularly in the Cornwallis Valley of Nova Scotia, on the northwest shore of today's Province, large plots were offered in 1759-1760.

A review of the Burgess Genealogy reveals that Seth Burgess, five generations following Thomas and Dorothy, married Abigail Howe on June 5, 1757 in Massachusetts and moved from there in 1760 to Cornwallis Nova Scotia. [1] One of four children born to them was Benjamin Burgess who married Abigail Hovey. In turn, one of their sons, John Newcomb Burgess, was RN's paternal grandfather. An update of Reverend Burgess' 1865 Burgess genealogy prepared by Katherine W. Hiam, his great-great granddaughter, in 1997, states that Thomas Burgess was a Mayflower descendant, although how or through whom is not clear as there were no Burgesses' on the Mayflower roster. [2]

The economic environment in The Maritime Provinces of Canada in the last third of the 19th Century was largely characterized by mining, agriculture, farming, forestry, and fishing. Joshua Burgesses' parishioners would have been struggling with challenging economic conditions in Nova Scotia in the years of his childhood. In addition to his duties at the church in West St. John, Father Burgess was an itinerant preacher. He rode his horse on Sundays and Wednesdays to preach in outlying communities. Such activity was physically difficult, and, after almost a decade and a half of it, the family began to think about a change of circumstance.

RN was born near the end of what was known as the "Long Depression," the economic downturn produced by the world-wide effects of the Panic of 1873. The proximate cause of this major economic contraction was a sharp decline in bank reserves in New York City in the fall of that year resulting from numerous factors, both domestic and global. The causes were complex, but the world-wide effects were economically devastating and included a significant decline in economic growth, an increase in unemployment,

---

[1] Burgess, Rev. Dr. Ebineezer, *Burgess Genealogy*. Doe Library, U.C. Berkeley, 1865.

[2] Katherine W. Hiam, *Burgess Genealogy*, (New England Historic Genealogical Society, Boston, 1997) 3.

reduction in credit availability, reduced trade, and price deflation, all continuing throughout the decade of the 1870s and contributing to a population decline in St John of almost 10 per cent in the decade ending in 1881.

The Canadian Maritime Provinces, with their economic dependence on natural resources, did not escape the ravages of the Panic of 1873. Earlier, during the mid-nineteenth century, the area had experienced a spurt of population growth in what has been described as a "Golden Age" of economic development, unusual for this long underperforming region of Canada. During the 1850's and 1860's, the Maritimes were one of British North America's largest manufacturing centers and the seat of a large, international shipping industry with rich timber resources providing the raw materials for a thriving shipbuilding industry. The growth in wealth during this period was not equally distributed throughout the population, however. It was concentrated in the highest tiers of society, positively effecting only the lives of the top ten per cent of the urban elite population. The rural areas within which Reverend Burgess worked saw little of this wealth filter down to a population struggling at the margins of a difficult existence.

Most households, consisting of farmers, fisherman, craftsmen, and laborers, lived close to poverty. In this environment, merchants, bankers, mine owners, ship builders and owners, and mariners prospered. RN's family would have been in this top tier of society with the father working in the Presbyterian clergy, although wages to clergymen were not such as to create wealth. His mother, Mary Helen Noble Burgess, came from a family that did participate in the growth, however. Her father, Isaac Noble, in the wholesale fish-shipping business, purchased, stored, and transshipped large catches of fish from the Grand Banks, a business that would have put him safely within the higher ranks of society.

In the economic history of the Canadian Maritime Provinces, the two decades of the mid-nineteenth century were the only relatively strong period in what was otherwise a protracted period of underperformance. Historians differ as to the causes of such poor economic performance but the geography of Canada explains some of it. During an age of sailing ships and colonial trade, the Maritime Provinces were well positioned to participate in the exporting of farming and mineral extraction products so important to trade. As sail turned to steam, however, and as railroads gradually established interconnections between the Atlantic coast and larger, growing population centers throughout the inland provinces, the economic center of gravity shifted to the west. In addition, newer, faster and larger steam-powered ships were less likely to stop at the lower population centers of Halifax and St John, instead favoring larger commercial centers like New York, Boston, and Montreal.

Adding to these causes, in 1867 Canadian Confederation occurred and the three British colonies of Canada, Nova Scotia, and New Brunswick were united into the federal Dominion of Canada, bringing changes inimical to robust economic growth in the Maritimes. A twelve-year old policy of lowered trade barriers between the USA and Canada was rescinded in 1866 by the US, partially out of resentment for British support of the Confederate States during the Civil War. In the following year, Canadian Confederation occurred on July 1 with Canada's first Prime Minister, John A. Macdonald, initiating trade policies characterized by protective tariffs. These tariffs, in combination with the depression of the following decade and the completion of the Inter-Colonial Rail Road (between the Maritimes and Central Canada), resulted in a reorientation of Maritime trade patterns from New England and Britain to interior Canada, resulting in the relative economic disadvantage of the Maritime Provinces to Central Canada.

Life in St John was thus challenging, characterized as it was by a rigorous climate, limited economic opportunity, and very little apparent chance for improvement. Three thousand miles away in California, the railroads, having just completed expensive investments in land rights, equipment, and track-laying, were eager to sell the promise and opportunity lying to the far west. In 1884, the year Benjamin Cummings Truman, a publicist for the railroads in California, published his *Homes and Happiness in the Golden State of California (San Francisco, 1884)*, there were a million residents in the

State and the recently completed railroads were eager to expand this population. Truman's book paints a picture of opportunities in California that must have been persuasive indeed to the hard-working and hard-pressed family of a Presbyterian Minister in the cold climates of Canada's Maritime Provinces.

Truman wrote that California could be a home for "well-disposed, industrious people who desire to better their conditions in life, to come to California and help settle her vast territory and make for themselves comfortable and happy homes – to dwell under their own vines and fig trees – not only in the land of promise, but in the land of real fruition." This was persuasive salesmanship and the decade of the 1880's saw the largest increase in California's population since the gold rush of 1849, growing from 865,000 to 1.2 million.

California historian Kevin Starr has written that the promotional literature about California at the turn of the 19th century was dominated by the theme of a return of the middle class of America to the land. After decades of post-Civil War industrialization and the urbanization which resulted, the prospect of a return to a simple and healthy life in agriculture had undeniable appeal. New and supposedly scientific methods of farming were now available and a new way of life seemed possible.

Starr suggested that, "Central to this emerging lifestyle was the raising of fruit. As an agricultural pursuit, orchards bespoke stability, patience, a high yield per acre, a reasonable workload – and beautiful surroundings." And, "Fruit ranching took time. One planted and then waited some years for a return. Hence, orchardists tended to look for a long-range capital investment rather than a scheme to get rich quick." The values implied here seem consistent with the world-view of a Protestant Minister seeking a better life and better opportunity for his young family.[3]

There is no evidence that either Joshua or Mary received or read any of this promotional literature. Indeed, in the *Memoirs*, RN suggests that his family's relocation was due to health factors, citing

---

[3] Kevin Starr, Americans and the California Dream 1850-1915, (New York: Oxford University Press, 1973), 201-203.

Father Burgess' arduous itinerancy lasting some fourteen years, and the resulting deterioration in his health. But it is difficult to believe that no one in an extensive family of both Burgesses and Nobles, all living in the Canadian Maritime Provinces, did not see or hear of these publications urging consideration of what must have been a promised land, and suggest the possibility of a change.

In any event, Joshua began to explore the opportunities, journeying to California early in 1884 and meeting with the Presbyterian leadership in San Francisco. A call to that ministry would follow and Joshua Chase Burgess was named Minister of First Presbyterian Church of San Francisco. The Burgess family of six would join the thousands of other "Pullman emigrants" on the overland journey to a new life in California.

George Mortimer Pullman, a 19th century industrialist in Chicago, developed the railroad car named for him, bringing luxury travel to the country in time for the great migrations to California in the 1880's. The selection of one of his cars to serve as transport for the body of assassinated President Lincoln in 1865 was a signature event for his company and, within a decade, Pullman cars ran on most of the rail lines connecting the major centers of the West. The fancy new cars were expensive, costing more than five times as much as traditional passenger cars, but they opened up rail travel for the masses in substantially more comfort than had been available earlier.

When RN's family of six, including the three boys, infant sister Marie, and the parents, made their trip in 1884, the cars were not connected by a vestibule. A year or so away at the time, such a convenience would have made possible indoor movement from one car to another. Nor did the family make this trip in the luxurious cars available to wealthier travelers. Dining cars were unavailable to them and they "lived out of a tiffin basket" supplemented by milk and coffee whenever Joshua was able to obtain it at stations along the way.

One can only imagine the wonder in the mind of a six-year-old boy during this adventure. Spending seven days in the same car, travelling through some of the largest cities of the United States and seeing some of the crowds and characters (RN described them as "rough") in the many stations along the way must have been a memorable experience. The journey took them from St John, New Brunswick to Boston, to New York City, Cleveland, Chicago, Omaha, Salt Lake City, Reno, Benicia, with its ferry to Port Costa, and finally to the Oakland pier where they boarded another ferry for San Francisco's Ferry Building Terminal.

In the *Memoirs*, he described arguing with his older brother, John Albert, about who would get the privilege of sleeping in the top bunk. RN won the argument after John could not make it through the night without a bathroom break only to discover that his original lower bunk was preferable because of its views of passing scenery and eastbound trains. He described in detail the workings of the individual car braking system, revealing his fascination with the mechanical underpinnings of things, an absorption which would fill the pages of his autobiography and characterize his life.

A six-year old boy was thus exposed to the wonders of a much wider world than he had known in New Brunswick. He had visited New York and Boston, two of the largest cities in America at the time. He had seen the wide open western states and the seemingly endless potential of a new, young nation. He was about to be introduced to one of the wildest and scrappiest of America's younger cities, a community where he would spend the next two years of his life, San Francisco.

RN at 25-30 years of age, 1903-1908.
Courtesy Contra Costa County Historical society.

RN's mother, Mary Helen Chase Burgess 1851-1920.
Courtesy Burgess Family collection.

RN's father, Joshua Chase Burgess 1842-1935.
Courtesy Burgess Family collection.

CHAPTER 2

San Francisco in 1884

L ate 19th century America was preoccupied with business and economic prosperity the sociological underpinnings of which were expressed by the Protestant Ethic and the embrace of Social Darwinism. This was the America that RN came to as a Canadian immigrant in 1884. The added dimension, so critical to his new environment, was that he came to California. He did not emigrate to New York City, Chicago, or any of the cities in the Deep South still in their Reconstruction phase. Californians, their state just thirty-four years into statehood, were still trying to assess who and what the idea of California represented. On the one hand, it implied in the popular mind a road to quick riches, but by the 1880s this was fading and the excesses of its frontier days were becoming a memory. The promotional activity of the railroads offered a vision of a new life, a new start, to many Americans struggling to find a place in the post-Civil War industrialization of the decades following that conflict.

In the first third of the 19th century, Alexis de Tocqueville suggested that commerce would flourish under the new democratic experiment in the United States. By the last third of that century his prediction was coming to full fruition. Almost a full century after Tocqueville's visit, President Calvin Coolidge would suggest in 1925 that, "The chief business of the American people is business." [1] At the same time, the science of Charles Darwin was being absorbed in intellectual circles throughout Europe and in the United States. Perhaps predictably, Darwin's science was warped somewhat as it was absorbed into the culture. It was not a great

---

[1] Calvin Coolidge, Speech to the Society of American Newspaper Editors, 17 January 1925, Willard Hotel, Washington D.C.

leap in the minds of many ambitious, hungry, and urgent Americans to apply his theories of natural selection among the lower forms of animals to the human species. Herbert Spencer's earlier description of the survival of the fittest, in his argument of inexorable human progress, adapted fairly easily to Darwin's thinking and a context for American business was created.

California, with its gold-rush background, its enormous population increases in a few short years in the early 1850s, its aura of being a source of fast riches (the reality notwithstanding), its ample land and natural gifts, was, as historian Starr suggests, a natural home for the ideas embodied in Social Darwinism. San Francisco, a young city, but already with a distinctive personality, itself began to experience the growth during the decades between 1860 and 1880 that would render it recognizable to its twentieth century residents. New neighborhoods were formed in the Western Addition, the Haight Ashbury, and the Mission. Golden Gate Park opened in 1887, providing recreational opportunities to almost a quarter of a million residents and cable cars made their appearance as mechanisms of transport among the elaborate and ornate homes of Nob Hill. Visitors from the east also brought a degree of culture previously unknown to the residents of a city barely removed from the chaos and disorder of its Vigilante and Gold Rush past. Mark Twain, Bret Harte, Ambrose Bierce, Rudyard Kipling, Robert Louis Stevenson, and Oscar Wilde all visited at various times during the decades of the 1870s and 1880s. The St. Francis Hotel opened during the Gold Rush days of 1849. In 1875, its latter-day competitor, the Palace, opened. In 1878, the San Francisco Public Library opened. And in 1880, a small daily newspaper was deeded to California Senator George Hearst in payment for a gambling debt. In what would prove a portentous development for RN Burgess, Hearst Senior gave the property to his son, Harvard undergraduate William Randolph Hearst, in mid-decade.

In 1873, Mark Twain penned the *"Golden Age: A Tale of Today."* It was intended to highlight the substantial disparities between the conspicuous wealth enjoyed by a few fortunate Americans and the vast and deep poverty existing among the laboring classes. The industrialization following the Civil War spawned rapid and widespread economic growth and, because wages were higher in America than in Europe, vast numbers of immigrants arrived with high hopes for a fresh start in life. These hopes were destined to be met in some cases, but certainly not universally, and Mark Twain's book highlighted the disparity between upper and lower classes. San Francisco in the 1880s had its share of wealth emanating not just from the gold fields but from businesses created to support and profit from the prospecting activities in the foothills of the Sierra Nevada to the east. Its Nob Hill homes were every bit as ostentatious, garish, and opulent as anything on Park Avenue in New York.

In this context, the idea of the self-made man, a term used first early in the 19th century in a speech by Senator Henry Clay, flourished. The words by Richard Henry Tawney quoted in the Introduction to this book invoked the Protestant ethos of hard work, frugality, and perseverance, which must have been a salient part of Father Burgess' teaching to his young sons. RN was thus a man of his times, a man who was raised to be eminently well-suited to the challenges confronting him. He was determined to make something out of himself, was presented the opportunity by his times, and had the skills, the attitudes, and the ambition to do so.

***

When a young boy from the Maritime Provinces of Canada stepped off the train ferry into 1884 San Francisco his first impressions might well have been shocking. Accustomed as he was to the more restrained atmosphere of St John, New Brunswick, with its economic deprivations, declining population, and more rural orientation, San Francisco, a bustling city of more than 230,000 residents, retaining much of the raw energy of its recent Gold Rush past, must have been an eye-widening experience to such a boy. His *Memoirs* are sparse as to his impressions of the almost two years the family spent in the city, but the historical record paints a picture of a place starkly in contrast with what they had left behind.

In the early 1880s, San Francisco was beginning to recover from the effects of the world-wide depression which may have figured in the Burgess' decision to leave Canada. Louisa Locke, a doctoral student in history who later went on to write fiction stories set in late 19th Century San Francisco, described the basic economic conditions that affected the city at that time. [2] Blessed with a good natural harbor and with relative proximity to the gold fields inland, it became the port of entry and exit for extensive commercial activity early on and had a virtual monopoly on seaborne trade into California up until the development of Los Angeles later in the century.

The city developed as a manufacturing center after statehood in 1850, responding to the needs of the mining and shipping industries. The trend towards local manufacturing was further supported in the early 1860s as the Civil War reduced normal cross-continental trade and demand for manufactured goods throughout the west continued to grow.

The completion of the transcontinental railroad in 1869 also stimulated demand for consumer goods in rural markets throughout the west to which the city responded, further enhancing its status as a viable commercial center. Railroad construction in the 1860s had attracted a large labor force of immigrants from Asia and Europe that, when the work was completed, became surplus and wages declined accordingly. The panic and depression of 1873 did not spare San Francisco, but cheap, available labor contributed to its growth as a manufacturing center. A double-edged sword, the availability of cheap labor after completion of the railroad became the source of significant unemployment during the depression of the 1870s, exacerbating its effect on the local economy.

By the time of the Burgess' arrival in September 1884, San Francisco was well on its way to recovery ranking 9th, according to Locke, in value of manufactured goods among US cities. San Francisco boasted strong participation in the major industries of the time, meat packing and processing, sugar refining, shoe making, heavy metal and machine making, the manufacture of men's clothing, and tobacco and cigar making.

---

[2] Locke, Louisa M. "What was San Francisco Like in 1880? The Economy." (blog), 17 June 2012.

San Francisco also became the financial center of the West, with the headquarters of almost all the major financial institutions located there. Later in his life, it would be these financiers, who initially saw RN as a young man of promise, potential, and ambition, who would ultimately participate in his undoing.

RN's San Francisco days were brief, with scarcely two years passing before the family was on its way again, this time to Danville, RN's home for the next nine years. The Burgess residence during this period was in a flat on 1914 Broadway Street, situated between Octavia and Laguna. RN described planked and locked wooden sidewalks built so as to control the shifting sands so prevalent in a city built upon sand dunes. He said little of his neighbors and friends, but did remember one or two who would be associates later in life, figuring prominently into his business career and later financial challenges. One of the directors of the Presbyterian Church of San Francisco was also a displaced Canadian, a family friend from RN's early childhood days in Carlton, New Brunswick. Joshua's call to minister in the First Presbyterian of San Francisco was signed by, among others, Director Robert Balfour, who had preceded the Burgesses to California, arriving in 1883. Balfour was from the London firm of Balfour, Williamson & Company, a world-wide insurance firm. When his father died, he became Lord Balfour, head of the firm, and a business associate, lender, and insurer of RN's companies for over half a century.

RN also remembered the Lipman family, with two of whose sons his life intersected decades later. One son was involved with Castle Brothers, one of RN's earlier fruit shipping customers in the mid-1890s; another son, Fred Lipman, later became head of Wells Fargo Bank and would be a valuable source of guidance for RN during his most difficult days in the lending crisis during the World War I period.

An amusing anecdote that resonates in the ear of a biographer trying to understand his subject's character and orientation to economics involves RN's conduct on his twenty-three-block walk to church. Taking different routes, each of the three brothers sought to attend to differing priorities, Will to his girlfriend, John to a school chum's home, and RN to the candy store. Upon arrival at the store he would purchase two sticks of penny candy, using the nickel he had been given for the Sunday School offering, "thereby reducing the Church's share to three pennies," but assuaging his guilt with the knowledge that three pennies tossed in the collection plate made substantially more noise than a nickel. One has the impression that such calculations were an almost constant neural activity for young Burgess.

San Francisco in 1884; Powell Street,
looking north from Market Street.
Courtesy Society of California Pioneers.

*This is the Port Costa Train Ferry in 1879 and would
have been RN's first view of Contra Costa County when
he disembarked five years later in September, 1884.
Courtesy Contra Costa County Historical Society.*

CHAPTER 3

A Young Farmer

Thank God every morning when you get up that you have something to do that day which must be done, whether you like it or not. Being forced to work and forced to do your best will breed in you temperance and self-control, diligence and strength of will, cheerfulness and self-content, a hundred virtues which the idle never know.

—Charles Kingsley

The decade of the 1890s, the decade in which RN came of age, was a turbulent time in American politics and economics. Not only was it characterized by a very serious depression, initiated by the Crash of 1893, but also by the election of 1896, in which the national political landscape changed dramatically. In that election, William McKinley, running against William Jennings Bryan, defeated his opponent by 51% to 47% of the popular vote. What the numbers masked was the bitter contest between so-called free-silver populists supporting Bryan against the gold-standard favoring Republicans supporting McKinley.

The depression exacerbated the bitterness and multiple splits within each of the major parties. The farmers were interested in moving from a gold standard to silver, as it was plentiful and would have the inflationary effect which they saw as beneficial with farm prices suffering during a deflationary economic contraction. With a candidate who excelled at oratorical rhetoric and had a commanding political presence, the appeal to farmers and other, poorer working-class people who were suffering in the depression, was seductive as Bryan invoked biblical references to stir up his supporters.

McKinley won in California, but by a narrow margin. He got

49.2% of the vote to Bryan's 48.5%, in a result that reflected Republican strength in urban counties around San Francisco, Los Angeles, and the lumber interests in the far northwest counties. Contra Costa County, RN's home, went for McKinley with a strong 56% to 42% majority. Less populated areas of the State were fairly solidly in the Democratic camp.

The economic contraction stimulated by the panic of 1893 was too early in RN's life to have had an effect on his own business, but the local economy, which meant primarily farming and farm prices, was affected by national trends. During the decade of the 1890s central Contra Costa County was an almost totally agrarian economy and local farm prices followed national trends, putting pressure on shippers trying to serve eastern markets with produce grown locally.

***

August Hemme, a leading citizen in the San Ramon Valley and an elder in Father Joshua Chase's Danville Church, was born in Hanover, Prussia in 1833. Attracted by descriptions of opportunity in America by his older brother's letters, he left Prussia for New York in 1846. Arriving in New York, he secured employment in his brother's store as a retail clerk and stayed for three years until the lure of the California gold fields drew him west. Once in California, Hemme headed for the Feather River gold mines and was successful enough that he was able to relocate to Danville after several years, finally settling there in 1852 at 19 years of age. He married Minerva Elizabeth Ish of Alamo four years later in1856.

After farming in Danville for almost a decade, he was ready for a change and moved to San Francisco in 1863 where he started an assaying company serving the needs of miners. He also speculated successfully in stocks and started a piano manufacturing firm. He and his wife retained their Danville land and added to it during their time in San Francisco. Financially quite successful, he was also a man of great public spirit and generosity. He was a significant financial supporter of the Presbyterian Church, both in San

Francisco and later in Danville. In San Francisco, he acquired the land for and funded the construction of the Central Presbyterian Church in 1869, furnishing it and purchasing a library of some 5,000 volumes.

In 1882, just two years prior to the Burgess family arrival in San Francisco, he moved back to Danville, and continued the expansion of the land holdings that would one day make him one of the largest landowners in the valley. His large farm on today's San Ramon Valley Boulevard, just south of Alamo, with its beautiful house and outbuildings, was indicative of his financial successes, and admired by all. He also affiliated with the Danville Presbyterian Church, becoming the fifth elder named in that congregation, and it seems quite probable that his was a key role in in arranging for Father Burgess to relocate to Danville from San Francisco in 1886, both providing some of his own land and building the Burgess home.

Later in his life, Hemme played a major role in bringing the Southern Pacific Railroad into the San Ramon Valley, providing a needed mechanism for local farmers to transport their produce to the larger markets west of the hills. Unfortunately, Hemme's earlier successes in finance and business did not survive the Panic of 1893. He had borrowed money from some local farmers, in connection with his efforts to obtain the railroad right of way, and, with the depression, was unable to service those debts. He declared bankruptcy in 1898 after moving to Berkeley, and died there in 1904. [1]

In the fall of 1886 Hemme facilitated the Burgess move from San Francisco by selling the family a twenty-acre portion of his own ranch and building a new home for them. The home, named "Bonny Vista" by RN's Mother because of its good views of Mt Diablo, still stands today, though not in the original location. It was moved a mile or so north and expanded in the 1980s closer to present Danville.

---

[1] Irma McGinnis Dodson, "The Impact of August Hemme on Nineteenth Century Agriculture and Cattle Ranching with an Analysis of His Economic Failure" (Master's Thesis, June 1972)

RN was eight years old in the summer of 1886 when the family moved to Danville and the environment into which he moved could not have been more different than what he left on Broadway in San Francisco. He came into a rural, agriculturally-based economy, leaving behind the urban shipping and manufacturing center of the City. His natural predilection to economics would ultimately be given expression through farming, and he would learn business and finance through that activity, with plenty of long days and hard work. He would also learn the trading mentality so prevalent among farmers.

Farming, specifically the planting of fruit orchards supplemented Father Burgess' meager salary for his ministerial duties. He was paid $1,000 per year on which he needed to support a family of six initially, later growing to eight. In today's dollars this equates to roughly $28,000 annually, not a comfortable cushion by any means, and all the children were expected to contribute their labor to the effort.

Initially too small to engage in the heavy work of fruit farming, RN would be his Mother's helper in the family kitchen for the first four years or so on the farm. With Father Burgess engaged in a new ministerial assignment, the work fell to Mary Helen Burgess and her three oldest children. RN reported long days, beginning at 4:30, with his first daily responsibility the preparation of breakfast, ready for the older boys and hired hands by 5:30. Then he helped with dish washing, wood cutting and hauling, washing clothes in the old "strong-arm washing machine," cooking, canning fruit, putting up jelly and fruits, as the canned goods of later years were not yet available.

As he grew in stature and strength, his farming responsibilities became a larger part of his daily routine. The business of the farm was planting, cultivating, and harvesting fruit for sale to local packers and shippers. The new Danville land had to be planted in orchards to get it started and RN played a role in this. In the *Memoirs*, he described in detail the procedure for planting almond, apricot, Bartlett pear, and prune orchards. He learned to plant the fruit trees in efficient geometric patterns maximizing the number of trees on the available acreage. He learned to plant, prune, bud, graft, spray and harvest, all under the tutelage of his older brothers Will and John, as Father Burgess, busy with his congregation, had little time or interest in farming.

RN finished his formal education in Danville. It is likely that he also had at least one and possibly two years of school in San Francisco, before moving to Contra Costa County. The Danville school had grades one through eight, so he was able to attain eight years of formal schooling before graduating in December of 1893, two months prior to his 16th birthday. There were six grammar schools in the San Ramon Valley in the decade of the 1890s and he attended one located in Danville on today's Front Street. It was a one-room schoolhouse and an 1894 photo shows a teacher, Mr. A.J. Young, and forty-one students with RN in the back row. Among other subjects, he would have studied reading, writing, composition, and arithmetic.

Because of his influence on RN, some attention to Albert Jefferson Young, his teacher in the Danville Grammar School between 1886 and 1893, is instructive. Young was not only a teacher, the only formal educator in RN's life, but he was also a clerk and elder of the Danville Presbyterian Church for over fifty years. He thus knew Father Joshua Chase Burgess, and, in all probability, his mother Mary Helen Noble Burgess. With a reputation as a tough taskmaster, both in the classroom as well as in his Sunday School sessions, it is probable that Young's mentoring role was one of the largest influences on RN as a child.

A.J. Young was a pioneer himself. A man of great respect in his community for his contributions over decades of time, he began teaching in Danville in 1868, and, with the exception of a two-year term in the State Assembly in 1877-1878, continued to teach in the community until his retirement in 1900. Young was born in Independence, Missouri in June 1841, attended grammar school there, and relocated to Council Bluffs, Iowa for his high school years, graduating in 1859. As a high school student in Council Bluffs, he met and spoke with Abraham Lincoln when Lincoln visited the home of a local citizen. Young served as Deputy Clerk of the

Circuit Court of Jackson County, Missouri for two years until ill health persuaded his doctor that he should emigrate to California. This he did, leaving Iowa in May and arriving in Sacramento in September of 1862. After living and farming in Napa with his brother for several years, Young moved to Danville in 1865.

In 1886, he was appointed to the teaching position that he held until 1900. Accounts from his students portray a no-nonsense instructor. In an oral history, William Albert Shuey suggested that "he was a martinet, oh he was a rough one." Marianne LaBarree Johnson reported that in teaching a wide range of students ranging in age from 6-7 up to high school age, "He drilled the thunder out of us. When you had spelling, you had spelling, and when you had mental arithmetic, you had mental arithmetic!" Local historian, F.J. Hulaniski wrote that Young's influence for good has molded the character of many of the best citizens of the San Ramon Valley." Beverly Lane of the Museum of San Ramon Valley noted that "Mr. Young was a devoted and strict teacher and, if you were a Presbyterian and attended one of the grammar schools, he kept you in line six days a week. He was known as a stern taskmaster."

It is hard to imagine that this combination of daily strict secular instruction and weekly moral and devotional study was not an important element in RN's early development. With the Reverend Burgess occupied with the needs of his parishioners, A.J. Young clearly played a larger role in his development than otherwise might have been the case.[2]

What kind of a student was he? He was spare in his written remarks about school days, other than to mention that his overwhelming, constant hunger often drove him to tardiness because he would stop on the way to school in the morning and fry a batch of frogs caught in the nearby creek, begging the question of how he managed to carry a frying pan in his school kit. He seems to have had a quick and agile mind, however, and his scholastic results probably varied with his effort. Both older brothers, Will and John Albert, went on to extensive additional formal education in

---

[2] Collection of Materials and Articles of Albert Jefferson Young. Courtesy of the Museum of San Ramon Valley, CA.

law and mining engineering respectively, and had careers requiring considerably more formal education than RN received. RN seems to have been more pragmatically inclined, fascinated with the way things worked, in particular mechanical things, and his interest in serious academic subjects might have reflected those predilections. In any event, his agility with numbers, and his creativity and comfort with abstract concepts, became apparent in later years as he turned to real estate finance.

Within his peer group, RN was one of a small group of boys who were habitually engaged in pranks and stunts to confuse and stymie the teacher. Blocking the venting of the pot-bellied-stove in such a way as to drive everyone out of the schoolhouse was one such stunt and RN described the flailing he and the other perpetrators received as a result. In another episode, he described taking on a bully who had earlier thrashed him, hitting the boy so hard with a one by six board that he was knocked unconscious. Mr. Young, whom RN suggested was afraid of the bully, did not intervene, apparently happy with RN's version of equity under the circumstances.

The evidence is that RN began his outside working life very early. While not in class, he raised vegetables and squabs and, with the money earned, bought his first property. A.J. Young must have had confidence in him because he loaned him $700 to purchase 20 acres of hay-growing land immediately adjacent to the Burgess property. RN, not being of age at the time, could not sign for the purchase. Young not only lent the money, but also carried the property in his own name until RN could own it legally. In what must have been his first serious foray into business, sometime in his fourteenth or fifteenth year, RN also bought a "Buckeye Hay Mowing Machine" and a horse hay rake, both essential to the harvesting of hay.

Another chore was the slaughter, cleaning, and transport to market in Oakland, of shoats, young hogs. In vivid, descriptive language, RN described going into the hog pen with a long knife, selecting one, flipping it on its back, slitting it from throat to heart and then, after affixing the hog to a spreader, dipping it repeatedly into a barrel of boiling water to cleanse it of the hair, preparing it for market. The twenty-two-mile drive into Oakland was made at two in the morning with a wagon and four-horse team. RN described the discomfort and cold attending this activity during the winter months, sitting on one hand and then the other in an attempt to maintain warmth while holding the reins with the free hand.

In his childhood, RN met many local farmers and ranchers who were pioneers in Contra Costa County history. August Hemme, Robert O. Baldwin, and Seth Cook, and numerous others are named in the *Memoirs* and often featured in anecdotes the point of which is sometimes explicit and other times unclear. His purpose in relating a dispute between August Hemme and Robert Baldwin, both elders in Father Joshua's Danville parish, about an unpaid debt is not clear. It might have been to demonstrate Hemme's attitude about his own conscience, telling Baldwin's wife, when she came to demand payment on a delinquent obligation and challenged his integrity in the process, that he left his conscience on his bedside chair when he went to bed, and thereupon slept soundly through the night. Recalling that Hemme, as an elder, had been instrumental in Father Burgess' coming to Danville, however, this is curious because the portrayal of Hemme is not at all flattering.

The Danville farm experience seems to have been formative in that RN assumed progressively more responsibilities as years passed, land under cultivation increased, and older siblings left to pursue their educational and professional choices in life. In the spring of 1894 or 1895 (the dates are unclear in the *Memoirs*), RN's parents returned to New Brunswick to assist in estate matters related to the death, some ten years earlier, of Mary Helen's father Isaac Noble. Around this time additional acreage was rented. Sixty adjoining acres, the property of the Boone and Close families, were added, increasing orchards under cultivation from twenty to eighty acres, and the workload accordingly. These fields were "rented on shares," an arrangement under which the proceeds from the sale of the crop would be shared by the landowner and the tenant, reflecting the Burgess family need for additional income.

Ranch operations were initially overseen by RN's oldest brother, William Crochton, five years his senior. William left the ranch in the early-1890s to enroll at the San Rafael Military Academy in Marin County from which he went on to U.C. Berkeley, ultimately graduating from the Boalt School of Law on that campus. On Will's departure, John Albert, born two years before RN, became head of ranch operations for a short time before leaving to attend high school in Hayward and then moving on, also to U.C. Berkeley, to study mining engineering.

With Father Burgess only marginally involved, it fell to RN to assume responsibilities and leadership duties that seem heavy in a modern context for a boy of his age. He possessed effective leadership skills, however, even as a young man. With 80 acres under cultivation, soon to be increased by his own purchase of twenty acres of adjoining hay land, he must have been challenged directing the work of hired hands and managing the process of plowing, planting, cultivating, and harvesting an estate of this size on his own.

His efforts were soon supplemented, however, by the arrival of relatives from Canada. Isaac Noble's widow Mary Helen Buist Noble, her daughter Hattie, with three sons, Noble, Marious, and Teddy, decided to come to California and take up residence on land across the road from Bonny Vista in Danville. Joshua, absent in St John, wrote RN instructing him to arrange for the purchase of a one-acre plot, to prepare plans, and to arrange to have a home constructed for their occupancy.

In what must have been his first experience in a career of home building, in accordance with his father's instructions, he drew up plans for a three-bedroom house and took them to the Hayward Lumber Mill for pricing. He learned upon returning that they had barely modified his plans, finding it necessary only to increase the headspace in the stairway, an impressive start for a fifteen-year old boy with no prior experience in preparing building plans. Father Burgess, on receipt of the plans, sent a check by return mail with instructions to buy the land and begin the construction. RN then contracted with Neil Harrison, a neighbor, to build the new Noble house.

One source of labor for the farm that RN managed were men who had left employment as seamen on ships sailing in and out of Port Costa which RN described as the "largest export grain port in the world." Many gained illegal entry into the United States by jumping ship there and traveling into the interior seeking work wherever they might find it, often turning up at the Burgess farm not far south in Danville. He characterizes them as ranging in aptitude, ability, and usefulness between criminals and very good, hard working and dependable men. His ability as a teenager, to give direction, manage, and terminate, if necessary, men of such wide experience, background and origin, so different from his, speaks to the leadership skills he brought to his role. A hard worker from earliest childhood himself, his example must have set the tone for operations under his control and gained him the respect he needed to accomplish his mission on the farm.

It was during the Danville Farm period of his life that RN encountered Seth Cook whose land would figure prominently in his later attempts to acquire large tracts of acreage throughout Contra Costa and Alameda Counties. From his home at Bonny Vista, then two miles south of Danville, he could see Mt Diablo clearly and, in particular, he could see the land known as the Cook Ranch. This property, some forty-five hundred acres which later came to be the site of the community of Diablo and the Diablo Country Club, was to become one of RN's most significant purchases, but not for another eighteen years. The Cook Brothers are described by RN as rough, but friendly to the young Burgess brothers, RN and John. He recalled that Seth Cook often gave them $20 gold pieces to pass on to their Father. His story in the *Memoirs* about an interaction with the brothers during his childhood and being advised that his father was "the best Goddamned preacher I ever knew," could not have happened as he described it because Dan Cook died in October of 1882, prior to the Burgess family arrival in California. The relationship, with Seth Cook, while good for earning the Burgess brothers the right to engage in two of their favorite activities, hunting and shooting on the Cook acreage at the time, was not productive in getting RN in a position to buy the property years later. But it apparently sparked an idea in his mind of the possibilities in-herent in the land on which he acted when he had the capacity to do so.

RN's fascination with guns and the power and status they con-veyed is a theme appearing throughout his life. During this period in his early experiences as a straw boss, he managed a payroll and was responsible for getting his various crews paid on the desig-nated pay-days. He described often carrying six or seven hundred dollars in gold and silver coins in his pocket which necessitated his being armed. The dramatic effect of this was not lost on him, "I must have been a sight - a kid of sixteen rushing around with a .44 caliber six shooter strapped to my hip." He recounted a shooting exhibition he put on in which he successfully shot at a rolling can at a rate of fire of one round per second, all on the mark. "It was intended to help get the word around that I not only carried a gun, but could use it as well."

The Danville Farm period of RN's life extended from the fam-ily's initial move there from San Francisco in the fall of 1886 until his seventeenth birthday, February 10, 1895, when he left home to go into business for himself. His final year at home was a transition year as he began to assume serious responsibilities for other, non-family associates and to develop new contacts that would serve him throughout his career in agriculture.

An early mentor was J. Z. Anderson, in his late seventies, knowledgeable in the fruit packing business but increasingly slowed by age and illness. RN described Anderson's role as han-dling the "green fruit," boarding at the Burgess farm, and working long days from planting time in the spring until harvest each fall. He had his own team of pickers, supervising them from his wagon seat with RN at the reins. Occasionally, he would direct his young helper to jump off and prod a slow worker. Anderson, with RN's help, would supervise the selection and picking, and then the del-icate job of packaging and loading on the refrigerator cars operated by Anderson's clients, the California Fruit Express, and The Earl Fruit Company. In late 1894, advancing age and failing health began to concern his clients. Worried about his ability to complete the summer's work, they asked him for recommendations as to a replacement. Anderson unhesitatingly recommended RN, saying "I have coached him from picking the fruit to packing it, and as to whether it goes into a refrigerator car or a ventilator, and he has been making out all my manifests of late." Shortly thereafter, the California Fruit Express representative offered RN the job at $3 per day.

In a harbinger of many such negotiations related by RN in the *Memoirs,* he responds "Nothing doing. You paid Mr. Anderson $10 a day and a flat fee of $125 a car. Ten dollars per day, or do it yourself." The parties ultimately agreed on $9 per day (and presumably the same rate per car) and within a short time thereafter RN's business expanded with the addition of Castle Brothers and Rosenberg Brothers, respectively the two largest dealers of dried fruit and nuts in San Francisco. A smart and aggressive sixteen- year-old was getting his start in business, largely on the strength of his hard work and talent for getting things done. This reputation would grow in the coming years as would a stable of contacts and influencers, all of whom would play a role in the ascendency of this young man.

Emblematic of a talent for accomplishing difficult tasks, he persuaded Robert Baldwin, a much older man and another elder in Father Burgess' church, therefore presumably known to RN, to devote 300 acres of his substantial holdings to sugar beets. RN accomplished this difficult mission (there was considerable resistance on the part of local farmers to plant sugar beets at the time) at the behest of a man representing the California Beet Sugar Refining Company, Mr. A. S. MacDonald. The Company had been trying for some time without results to obtain agreement from a number of local owners to put some of their land in sugar beets.

RN described the visit to Baldwin, with MacDonald along, in which he argued, after Baldwin's refusal, that he (RN) was "one of the men who went for (*sic*) the Grange to the Alameda County Sugar Refinery to present your plan for a refinery here so you could raise beets and diversify your crop. Now along comes a group of men from the Islands who spend a million on a refinery and they have the necessary water to operate it, and need a little encouragement. Is there any reason in the world why you can't put that lower 300 acres in beets?" Baldwin, either impressed by RN's argument, or embarrassed by his challenge, acceded to the request and the incident so impressed MacDonald that RN was soon hired by The California Hawaiian Beet Sugar Refining Company.

The association with the California Hawaiian Beet Sugar Refining Company would blossom into a rich source of work and attendant contacts in the years ahead. R.P. Rithet, the President of the firm, "decidedly a man of affairs" in RN's terminology, was a former member of the Canadian Parliament and a partner in the shipping firm of Welsh and Company. He offered RN a job as their agent with instructions to secure the approval of local farmers to plant sugar beets on their land. RN did this with great success, reporting that he obtained 3,000 acres of contracts to raise sugar beets in the months of late 1894 and early 1895, in the process cementing a relationship with one of the area's largest refiner of sugar beets.

Sometime in the late 1890s, RN began to get insight into his father's financial condition, which was precarious because, as RN put it, "We had been living for years beyond our means - living on the expectation of the income from the orchard which had not come into production in time." Joshua had previously mortgaged the Danville home as security for a loan of $4,500 from his wife's family's estate back in New Brunswick. This note was due on the final settlement of the Noble estate which would occur on the death of Mary Buist Noble (she ultimately passed in February of 1899 in the home that RN helped build for her in Danville) and RN saw a crisis approaching some years in advance of that date.

In the *Memoirs* RN wrote of himself as a young man always bearing some level of financial responsibility for his family. He mentioned both older brothers, with their focus on their school commitments, sisters Marie and Hortense intending to attend Mills College (with financial assistance from RN), and his mother and father, with "father not too well." In a decision taken in late 1894 or early 1895, he reported that, "I made up my mind that I would have to leave and make an effort to get into a position to help them. This responsibility, I believe, ruled the lives of my sister Marie and me." What he meant by this is not entirely clear. Joshua lived another forty years and, other than the explanation of the rationale for leaving Canada, and an illness during the holidays of 1896, there is no other mention in the *Memoirs* of his being ill. Was RN framing himself as the family's last best hope on the financial front? Perhaps, but it is difficult to see how he alone could make much of a difference in the living and educational costs of five siblings in addition to making a meaningful contribution to the basic household living expenses. In reading this passage, and numerous others in his book, one gets a sense of his tendency to cast himself in a heroic mode, emerging as the family enabler, providing solutions to all manner of problems. What his contribution actually was is of course impossible to say; it seems clear, though, that he fancied himself in this way.

Late in 1894, at Christmas dinner with fourteen friends and relatives around the table, RN announced his intention to wrap up his then current business relationships, leave the family, and go into business for himself. This intention was initially greeted with sarcasm, on the part of one or more of his younger relatives, but he explained that it was his intention to leave on the occasion of his seventeenth birthday, February 10, 1895. His mother's brother, Aaron Edward Noble, forty-one years old that year, twenty-four years RN's senior, had agreed to go into business with him in the establishment of a fruit packing house in Concord.

This partnership would last barely two years. RN described the meager resources of the pair, "He had $320 and I had saved $320 from my summer's work. That was all our capital. He was depending on my contacts and knowledge of the fruit business as well as my ability to build the warehouse and install the processing machinery." Beyond his $320 it is not clear what Ed Noble was bringing to the partnership and his later conduct seemed to indicate that age and a bit more maturity was the extent of it.

As a reader one hundred sixteen years later thinks of this portentous, and probably cold February morning, RN's boldness and courage are striking. Other than his mother, he was not close to anyone in his immediate family and almost expressed arrogance when he describes their reaction to his departure announcement: "I think some of the drones who were always there to be fed, but were not handy helpers, realized I meant what I said." His mother, though, was the exception. She "was the only person I knew whom I could go to when troubled, and I would just sit down, perhaps not say a word. I knew she would understand." Joshua told her not to cry, as "Robbie will soon be home again." But Mary Noble Burgess knew her son better than did his father, telling her husband, "Joshua, that is the son you do not understand. He has darkened your doorway for the last time." In recalling that moment, RN reported that, "In those few words she had changed the rubber in my back to steel. When the going got tough, and I might at least have gone to her for comfort, I pulled in my chin, stuck out my chest, and said, 'Mother expects me to succeed, and I will not fail her.' "

He described his father, on the morning of his departure, as "bewildered," when he suggested that the $320 that RN had saved from his summer work legally belonged to him (Father Burgess). RN acknowledged the law, but said he would not give his father the money; instead, he promised to stop at the grocery store in Danville on his way through town and deposit $300 on his father's grocery bill, thus providing food for the family for the next year.

He made one more stop before leaving for Concord and a new life in business. Mrs. Laura Flournoy, a neighbor, had insisted that he come by her home for his final goodbye. When he did so, she gave him a $5 gold piece, increasing his wealth to $25, after the grocery expense. In his mind, the important part of this goodbye was not the money, but her words; "Robbie, always remember, that regardless of rumors, I will always believe in you and you will be welcome here." What "rumors" she had in mind are not clear. Was she anticipating some rough spots in his business relationships in the future? If so, she was correct as his story turned out to have more than a few.

*RN's childhood home in Danville, named Bonny Vista by his mother.
Courtesy Contra Costa County Historical Society.*

*RN's class at the Danville Front Street school. He can be seen in the back
row, just to the right of center. His teacher, A.J. Young is on the left. Although the photo has an 1894 date, RN wrote that he graduated from the
eight-grade in December of 1893.
Courtesy Museum of San Ramon Valley*

*RN's childhood home today. Known as the Podva House,
it was relocated to the north of its original location.
Courtesy Author photograph.*

CHAPTER 4

Burgess & Noble

On February 10, 1895 a seventeen-year-old RN Burgess went into his first venture as an independent business-man with very little financial capital but with other assets of not inconsiderable value in his pursuit of wealth. In the 19th century, Protestant ministers were valued and respected members of their communities. Father Joshua Burgess was no exception. RN's social contacts within his new milieu were substantially stronger than would have been the case had Joshua been a small farmer, tradesman, or shop-keeper. In a word, while meager in financial capital, RN began his business career with considerable social capital.

When, it came to real money, however, the partnership had very little; between RN and his uncle Ed, they had $345. With this very limited amount, he needed to lease space along the railroad track for his facility, to design and build a warehouse and a barn, and to acquire the necessary equipment for the fruit drying and packing operation they envisioned. All of this he did essentially on credit and on his ability to convince a lumber yard operator, Mr. Carman of Port Costa Lumber Company, that he was a worthy credit risk with plans for a business that would prosper. The lumberman was in the process of selling his business, a position which would not allow for the extension of credit to anyone let alone a young, untested neophyte. RN's presentation of his plans and of the extensive relationships he was bringing into the new venture, were enough to convince Carman to take the chance and he got a six-month loan for the price of his materials, $1,500. RN seems to have appreciated the risk Carman was taking and the gesture he made by extending such credit to an untested newcomer. "I had met one fine man...he certainly gave me a boost."

This record is suggestive of RN's ability to convince older, more experienced men of his potential and would be repeated time and again during the first several decades of his life. Some combination of boldness, communications skill, reputation for getting things done, and an honest face, worked in his favor, enabling a convincing argument and success where others failed.

Obtaining the money was, of course, only the beginning. There was much additional work to be done to launch Burgess & Noble and RN's skill was the key ingredient. Ed Noble's only working experience was as a cowboy, working on a ranch in Gilroy for several years before setting out in this new venture. RN brought the necessary skill as a carpenter into the partnership, and watched Ed's confidence in him grow as he selected and sized floor joists, lay out rafters with ridge cuts, notched, and hoisted them, and finally cut in and braced doorways and windows.

On completion of the framed and sided building, RN assigned Ed the job of shingling the roof while he headed to San Jose, a distance of 60 miles, in a buckboard on a mission to obtain the mechanical equipment essential to the business of fruit drying and packing. For the work contemplated, they needed a "double prune dipper, a steam boiler, a steam engine, elevator, and prune grader." The credit to purchase these materials was forthcoming from the seller, Anderson and Barngrover, because they knew RN's buyers and other principals in the fruit buying houses in San Francisco. The relationships formed during his farming experiences on the Danville ranch proved essential to building a network of men who had capital, trusted RN, and would provide the necessary credit for him to realize his goals.

Burgess & Noble was in the business of buying fruit directly from farmers, then drying and packing it for shipment to large shippers, mostly in San Francisco, who would then reship it to eastern markets. They also bought wheat and barley, sugar beets, and sold sacks and twine to their farm customers covering an extensive portion of what today we know as the East Bay. The farmers they bought from were situated between Concord in the west and Knightsen in the east, and extended south to San Jose. In addition to fruit and grain buying, RN wrote insurance contracts on crops for farm customers. The insurance business derived from his former relationship with long-time family friend Robert Balfour and the insurance firm bearing his name, Balfour-Guthrie. The sugar beet business, which was to become his main activity within a year or so, came from contacts made on the Danville farm.

RN and Ed ran a low overhead operation, situated on a track siding of the Southern Pacific railroad in Concord, with an office in the warehouse and living quarters for RN and Ed upstairs. Two bachelors, they did their own cooking and cleaning, occasionally enjoying a meal of duck provided and prepared by a neighbor for a $1 fee. As RN related the living arrangements, "Our rule was cleanliness and neatness, and we were good at it, for we tried to make our living pleasant."

In one incident, descriptive of his aggressive approach to business as well as the quality of the relationships he formed, he describes his liveryman calling him with a warning about a competitive buyer trying to get business from one of his customers. The liveryman, loyal to RN, had loaned the buyer one of his slower horses and given him directions to the long route to the customer's farm, thus protecting RN's business. He also had a fast horse, hitched and ready for RN, enabling his getting to the farmer first and securing a three-carload order of prunes. The would-be competitor subsequently wrote RN a note saying that he had made a serious error, indicating that "I promise you I will recognize Contra Costa County as your home territory and keep out of it."

The fact that the liveryman would take the time to not only warn him, but to also send the competitor on a long route on a slow horse, speaks to the quality of Burgess' relations with his associates and the loyalty engendered. The would-be competitor, a Mr. Luning, headquartered in Suisun, in fact became a customer, when, later, he had an urgent need for three cars of prunes. This order, from a man who had tried to cut into Burgess & Noble's business, resulted in a payment large enough to pay off the $1,500 note to Mr. Carman at Port Costa Lumber Company.

RN's initiative and ability to get things done also came through in his relationship with the station agent with whom he contracted for shipping multiple cars of fruit. Fruit and nuts were shipped under an agreement that all cars would be shipped by October 31st of the year. In 1896, RN was running a three-shift operation when his night foreman became sick, necessitating RN's working about seventy-two hours without sleep. The shipping agent, doing RN a favor, asked him how many cars would not be ready by the October 31 drop dead date. RN's reply was that five or six cars would not make the date, whereupon the agent wrote up the bills of lading in advance and gave him four or five extra days to meet the deadline. The cars all shipped within the extended time period, each marked as shipping on October 31st.

Burgess & Noble had a significant competitive advantage over most of their competitors. The Balfour-Guthrie firm in San Francisco was providing working capital in the form of what would be called a credit line today. In the farming business of the late 19th century, most farmers sold their crops on consignment to an agent for a larger shipper. The agent would have contracted with the shipper to locate and acquire the produce on its behalf. The farmer retained title to the crop, thus accepting all risks of loss or damage up until the time of final payment. A packing house that could buy, pay cash, and take title immediately had a true edge, an edge which RN exploited profitably.

The relationship with Balfour, characterized by the confidence and trust that would have attended knowledge of the Reverend Burgess' household and his family for years, resulted not only in a market for RN's insurance contract sales, but also as a source of ready short-term financing for a young business. The details of his arrangement with Balfour put him in a very advantageous position for dealing with his farmer suppliers. "Where credits were satisfactory, Balfour Guthrie permitted me to draw on them to the extent of $20,000 a day for three days..." RN wrote that "This was *not* the regular arrangement with buyers...and it turned out to be a happy move for my principals as much trouble had come to the farmers by consigning their products. They literally flocked to me".

RN characterized this advantage as being derivative of a philosophy he acquired through reading a book while still at home in Danville. The book, *"Small Talk About Business,"* written by a retired banker in Maine, suggested that as a businessman, one should "never build up your principal at your expense. Be sure you are building the reputation of both," suggesting that, "if you had the capacity to operate a business, it was best to purchase in your own name and sell the product." Sound advice, doubtless, as was the implicit idea that business success, without attendant character and reputation, is a hollow accomplishment. In relating these facts of his business life, RN was highlighting traits very consistent with the Protestant ethic under which he was reared from childhood. A more nuanced view of matters would suggest that his early relationships were also key considerations in the successes he enjoyed. It takes nothing away from his own very considerable native talent and competence to suggest that he brought relational advantages to his business unavailable to many others.

The business must have prospered because RN described one trainload of some eighty cars, all loaded with his dried fruit, nuts, grain, and sugar beets. Feeling justifiably proud, as a train that size had never before been loaded at Concord, RN was shortly deflated by his bookkeeper who said that the profit on a train of eighty rail cars loaded with his produce was only $1.40. At about this time, the fall of 1895, their first year in business, he began to have doubts about his relationship with Uncle Ed Noble. He described Ed as an efficient buyer of farm product, knowledgeable about the local market, its physical layout, customers, and all the routes between and among the farms. In addition, he was well-liked by his customers, but RN complained that, if not constantly supervised, he was not good, "he slumped."

In the following year an incident occurred that ended the partnership for good. The departure of the trusted bookkeeper prompted RN to dig into the accounts himself and upon doing so he recognized irregularities in the numbers, discovering a less than anticipated balance. Upon discussion with his partner, he learned that Ed himself was responsible, having written several checks on the company account for his personal needs. Attributing Ed's actions to an overestimation as to the actual amounts of cash coming through the business (a charitable construction, certainly one putting the best face on the circumstances) as well as "getting involved with questionable company," RN gave him an ultimatum: his name must come off the Bank Signature Card, and, on an agreed valuation of the firm of $5,000, either RN would buy him out (for $2,500) or Ed would buy out RN for the same amount. In either event, the partnership was over.

Ed demurred however, saying "I will not agree to that. I know a good meal ticket when I see it, and am going to keep it." Exactly how this arrangement ended financially is not clear in RN's telling, because he suggests that he told Ed, somewhat ambiguously, that he (Ed) could use the packing house, "but if he (presumably Ed) became involved, the packing house and business would have to be sold." Also, Ed is portrayed as never having any money and his ability to come up with $2,500 seems suspect, so it is likely that RN just let the situation ride but got out of active participation himself.

There is additional evidence that Ed Noble stayed in the fruit packing business for at least another five years, with not always good results. Correspondence from the Penniman family in the summer of 1901 records dissatisfaction with Ed's service and his grading of their prunes. He was apparently still operating under the Burgess & Noble banner, with RN's awareness and at least tacit approval. From the evidence reviewed, it looks as if RN had severed the business relationship with Ed Noble long before the time of the Penniman difficulties, but continued to allow the business to use his name. By that time, he was involved with bigger and more challenging assignments.[1]

Ed Noble's domestic situation had changed since he and RN began the business in early 1895. In early 1897, his sister, RN's Aunt Hattie, left the Burgess home in Danville, with her three sons, and moved in with Ed in a rented house in Concord. Later, on hearing

---

Letters of Mary Pennimen to Bessy Pennimen Johnson, 12 July 1901, 30 August 1901, 10 September 1901, 29 October 1901, Collection of Materials and Correspondence of Mary Pennimen. Courtesy of the Walnut Creek Historical Society, Walnut Creek, CA.

complaints from Hattie about Ed's conduct, his irresponsible behavior, and lack of financial responsibility, RN decided to formally wrap up the Burgess & Noble business, advising Ed that it would be necessary to sell the warehouses and equipment. He sold the business to Alden Anderson (son of RN's early mentor J.Z. Anderson), but within a year fire destroyed the improvements and RN's first major business was gone.

After almost two years in business as Burgess & Noble, in December of 1896, RN was contacted by K.G. Raaf, the General Manager of Ranches for the California Beet Sugar and Refining Company, a large refiner of sugar beets with a plant in Crockett, Ca. During the Burgess & Noble days, he had stayed in touch with his former principals in that business and they offered him a new proposition. Interested in expanding acreage under cultivation in sugar beets in Contra Costa County, they had earlier arranged for RN to lease five thousand acres in the Hookston area (today's Pleasant Hill) and now wanted him to double that acreage. More importantly, they were seeking a full-time manager of the operation and offered RN the job.

While he was reflecting on the CBS&R offer, RN and Ed accepted an invitation from RN's mother to come south to Danville for Christmas dinner. Father Burgess was away in Canada and was experiencing some illness, leaving the family concerned about his condition. Against the backdrop of what RN called "the saddest Christmas I ever spent," he provided a description of the day and evening of Christmas 1896, which provides additional insight into his character. The two partners made the fifteen-mile buggy-drive from Concord to Danville in cold, dense, foggy conditions, typical of that time of year. After a meager Christmas dinner, and a grab-bag game of fishing home-made gifts out of a barrel, they began the return trip to Concord.

On reaching Walnut Creek both men, by this time quite cold, felt a need for a drink, and Ed suggested "Bob, let's have a hot toddy. You hold the purse, so you will have to treat." RN reply's that "…before I left mother's I had put $20 on her mantelpiece." To which, Ed responded, "That was the right thing to do, they needed it." The result, however, was that they had no money left and, at RN's suggestion, they headed to the Rogers Hotel, encountering Rogers himself, who must have thought well of RN because he volunteered, "Robert, you can have anything we have, even a little cash if you need it." RN's request was a little more modest, "All I wish for is hot toddies for two and two Christmas dinners." These were provided and the trip to Concord resumed.

Shortly thereafter, on receipt of the bank statement from the Bank of California, RN discovered an unexpected and unaccounted-for extra balance of $1,000. On inquiry, he was advised by the cashier of an erroneous deposit in that amount and a corresponding obligation for which the bank would accept a Burgess & Noble note. Recalling that they were able to meet the payment demand within a few days, he attributed his newly-strengthened financial capacity to the fact that "Providence had covered my $20 gift," to his mother.

These sentences in the *Memoirs* hint at something inherent in the writer's motivation. Certainly, an autobiographical account of a life will present it in the best form consistent with the facts as perceived by the author. RN's was an aggressive, driven personality, augmented with considerable natural talent, intelligence, and interpersonal skills. His frequent references to his own charitable instincts, perhaps often at odds with the perception of his business associates, suggests his desire to paint an alter ego with somewhat softer characteristics.

In a vignette interesting for its description of the contemporary justice system, RN described his role in extricating Hattie from a difficult and potentially expensive legal problem. On coming west with her mother and sons in the mid-1890s, Hattie had cosigned a note for another brother not fully understanding the implications of such a co-signature. The brother was trying to obtain financing for a candy store in Buffalo, New York, and the lender required a co-signature. After convincing Hattie to co-sign, the brother defaulted and the lender filed suit against Hattie. The case came to court in Concord before Judge Burke.

On learning that his regular attorney, W.S. Tinning, Sr., was unavailable do to prior commitments, RN decided to represent Hattie himself. With counsel and instructions provided by Tinning, he appeared in court, sitting through the prosecution's case against his aunt. Shortly thereafter, when the judge gaveled a recess, RN went to a nearby bar favored by the Judge, ordered a double bourbon for him, and had it waiting when he arrived. Judge Burke inquired as to Hattie's circumstances and her predicament and RN related her story. The two then returned to the courtroom, via separate routes, and when the Judge called for the defense, RN presented her case, explaining her misunderstanding about the co-signature, her situation as a single mother supporting three children, and moved for dismissal. Judge Burke promptly agreed to this, dismissing the case, adjourning the court, and relieving Hattie of all associated costs. RN's characterization of the events was that "Judge Burke was a character, always chewing tobacco...but he took care of his flock as he saw it, and his law procedure was with dignity. I often wondered what book gave him his guidance."

In these words, RN was describing a late 19th century judge in almost biblical terms. Beyond the irregular judicial process, involving a decision made over drinks in a bar during court recess, he invokes the Christian image of the judge as shepherd, the people as flock, and his power coming directly from God. Other, similar allusions flow throughout the *Memoirs*, doubtless the hidden influence of Father Joshua Burgess.

After Christmas, early in 1897, RN informed K.G. Raaf of CBS&R that he would accept the job of ranch manager of the Hookston Ranch, offered with terms that must have seemed good to an eighteen-year old. He would move to the Henry Hook ranch house, which he described as "a very nice place." His salary was $300 per month, net of all his expenses including room and board. It was expected that he would hire an Assistant Manager, whatever additional staff he would need to run the operation, and be given time to wind up affairs at Burgess & Noble. He now had a place to live, a real home, and substantially expanded responsibilities. The oversight of ten thousand acres of land, hundreds of laborers, and their bosses and foremen, all devoted to the planting, cultivation, and harvesting of sugar beets under contract with one of the largest growing and refining operations in the area was a significant promotion for a man of his relative youth and experience. In a period of less than two years, he had developed a reputation and the experience required to gain the trust and confidence of a major agricultural operator and to be put in a position of significant responsibility. He was not yet nineteen years of age.

CHAPTER 5

Hookston

RN's introduction to business was in farming and his arrival in 1884 coincided with an evolving agricultural scene in California. The state possessed enormous natural resources for agriculture including rich coastal soils and a climate which would ultimately prove suitable for over two hundred varieties of fruits and vegetables. The vast Central Valley, only beginning to be employed to its potential in the early 1880s, the coastal ports, and the extensive inland waterways all facilitated the shipping of products, both domestically and internationally.

The transition over the half century between the discovery of gold and the year 1900 was dramatic, involving a complete change in land use. California had begun in pre-Gold Rush times with cattle grazing over vast tracts of underused acreage; the grazing of sheep followed and, with the discovery of gold, mining assumed the leadership of California's nascent economy. Hundreds of thousands of miners spreading out throughout the Sierra foothills needed to be fed and the soil of the delta between the Sacramento and San Joaquin rivers proved to be what was needed to accomplish this task and to provide the stimulus for continued agricultural development in the state.

Historian Kevin Starr suggests that large-scale wheat production provided the link between the mid-century mining and later agricultural economies of the new state. Wheat, in which vast acreage was planted in the decades of the 1860s through 80s, required no irrigation, did not have the spoilage problems of produce, and was accordingly shipped from California ports throughout the world. Wheat growing, scaled up to thousands of acres, employed productivity-enhancing technology. The steam-powered combine which could cut, thresh, and sack up to a hundred acres each day so impressed young RN that he recalled his train in 1884 stopping just west of Sacramento so the passengers might see this agricultural wonder of the day at work. It must have been a meaningful display to RN. Just prior to departing Nova Scotia, the family had visited his uncle's farm where they had seen a new mower, capable of cutting ten acres a day, and a mule-powered threshing machine, only just then replacing hand held threshers and scythes. Seeing the twenty- horse team pulling the combined harvester, capable of an order of magnitude improvement in productivity, must have opened his eyes to the possibilities inherent in his new home.

Large scale wheat operations in the late 19th century were a mixed blessing for California. Global exports through Port Costa, California, made a handful of men wealthy, but, at the scale necessary to support such exports and with the investment in technology required, deep pockets were needed, thus necessitating corporate farming and large-scale land ownership, which reduced opportunity for small farmers. The social consequences and attendant farm labor unrest would become a signature element in California's history.

Growing wheat in sufficient quantities for world-wide export in the 1870s and 1880s was a land-wasting enterprise and it exhausted the soil. Wheat, in this sense was rapacious in the same way that large-scale mining extraction was. Both enterprises utilized technological advances to increase yield, employed unskilled labor in short lived opportunities, and made very little in the way of permanent investment in the land. The fruit and vegetable farming which replaced both activities contrasted in that it required a large commitment of time and investment before results were realized. It required patience, a commitment to the land, and cooperation with neighbors. Thus, it was a socializing activity in ways that led to the development of more permanent institutions than those resulting from wheat farming and gold extraction.[1]

Kevin Starr, *Inventing the Dream, California Through the Progressive Era* (New York: Oxford University Press, 1985), 128-139.

In the late 1880s one of the large grain exporters, Abraham Bubois Starr, desiring to increase his already substantial grain exporting business, began work on a large flour milling plant on the waterfront at Crockett. At the end of a seven-year construction period, however, the grain exporting business had begun to wane as prices, weakened by the depression of 1893, no longer supported an earlier volume of production. By 1895, wheat was no longer the product farmers wanted to plant. As planned, the Starr flour mill was designed to process six thousand barrels of grain a day, to be loaded on as many as eight ocean-going grain transporting ships at a time. By the time the plant was completed in the early 90s, declining demand for wheat resulted in production of barely seven hundred barrels a day. Starr was in serious financial straits and would die shortly thereafter. [2]

It was in this context that RN became involved in the sugar beet business, his second serious commercial undertaking. Most of the world's sugar is processed from cane sugar, a product of tropical climates like the Hawaiian Islands and the Caribbean region. Around the middle of the 18th Century a German Chemist, Andreas Marggraff, developed a method for extracting the sucrose from beet root which proved an economically attractive alternative to cane processing. The world's first beet sugar refinery was built soon thereafter in Germany. The Napoleonic Wars of the early 19th Century provided the impetus for additional acreage devoted to sugar beets in France. Finding it difficult to import sugar from the West Indies because of the ongoing conflict with Britain, Napoleon directed that 80,000 acres be devoted to sugar beets in in France in 1812 and also prohibited the import of any sugar from the West Indies in 1813. In consequence, by the end of the first third of the 19th Century, France had 542 beet factories operating with production of 35,000 tons of sugar, compared with 1,400 tons in Germany. [3]

---

[2] Nelda Rego, Days Gone By, Contra Costa County Historical Society, 3 volumes, (Martinez, California, 1992-2001).

[3] Keith Olsen, The Saga of Crockett and Sugar Beets, July ,2012, The Saga of Becoming Sugar Town, September, 2013, A Gathering of Celebrities, Sugar Comes to the Carquinez, September, 2013. The

In the United States, after several unsuccessful attempts at growing sugar beets in the early 19th Century in the east, and after the U.S. Department of Agriculture had identified several promising areas for cultivation, a fifty ton per day capacity mill was established in Alvarado, California in 1869. This undertaking ultimately prospered and has been described as the first successful American sugar beet factory. Nineteen years later, Claus Spreckels built the second successful American mill in Watsonville, California. By the last decade of the century, with additional mills operational in Grand Island and Norfolk, Nebraska, and in Chino, California, the American Beet Sugar Manufacturers Association was formed, and what seemed to be a very promising business opportunity in America was underway.[4]

Described by United States Senator Leland Stanford as "...the hope of American agriculture," the sugar beet industry was seen by many as an economic opportunity second only to the earlier Gold Rush. San Francisco pioneer, George McNear, Sr., understood the Crockett plant's potential for processing sugar and bought the facility in 1895 with the intention of converting its operations to sugar and cane beet refining, with both locally grown sugar beets as well as cane sugar from the Hawaiian Islands. RN's opportunity to manage Hookston came from the same San Francisco men he had represented earlier trying to persuade local farmers to put more land in beets. These farmers now saw a better opportunity leasing their land to CSB&R instead of planting and cultivating it themselves. The widespread devotion of so much land to the beets, however, spelled the end of the business. RN was ahead of his time in recognizing that soil consistently worked for decades without rotation would result in declining crop yields, and recommended to his principals that they plant alternative cover crops such as clover, vetch, and cow peas, ploughing them under to promote bacterial breakdown and aeration. These recommendations were not implemented, however, and ultimately declining crop yields spelled the decline of the business in Contra Costa County.

Crockett Signal.

Ibid.

The work of sugar beet farming was highly labor intensive and much of the labor utilized in raising sugar beets on a commercial basis was done by Japanese immigrants. Japanese immigration to America began modestly in the mid-19th century, increased somewhat during the 1880s, and then climbed sharply at the turn of the century. The year 1900 saw the commencement of a large wave of Japanese arrivals with more than 100,000 coming within the early years of the new century. These were still small numbers as a proportion of the existing population, but opposition soon grew within the laboring classes because of the threat associated with very low wages and within the native population in general because of increased Japanese ownership of the land itself.

Emblematic of native opposition to Japanese and other Asian immigration were the comments made in a 1905 interview of San Francisco Mayor Eugene Schmitz. "I would sooner see the bars of civilization let down on this western borderland to the heathen Chinese and meet all the grave dangers incidental to their coming, than to witness an unrestricted Japanese immigration ... and the many great evils that would at once beset our industrial welfare if the brown toilers of the mikado's realm (*sic*) were permitted to swarm through our gates uninhibited ...The Japanese are far more dangerous to us than the Chinese ... they are to be feared more than the Chinese primarily because of the cheapness of their labor ... Where a Chinese will work upon the farm at starvation wages, a Japanese has the ability to acquire the property itself. The Chinese are dangerous enough, but the Japanese would drive all competition out of business." [5]

These attitudes coalesced into legislation and a 1908 agreement between the U.S. and Japan in which the Japanese agreed to limit emigration to America in return for America's allowing wives, children, and other relatives of existing immigrants to come in. By 1913 the California Legislature had passed the Alien Land Act barring all aliens ineligible for citizenship (i.e., all Asian immigrants) from

[5] E.C. Leffingwell, "San Francisco's Mayor Wants Exclusion Act to Bar the Japs," April 1, 1905, Newspaper Enterprise Association. Library of Congress, American Memory.

owning land in California. In the *Memoirs* RN reveals himself as a person of his times, using the pejorative "Japs" when referring to his labor force and their bosses, and relating several episodes which portray the large gap between the cultures so prevalent at the time.

***

RN's was manager of the Hookston Ranch for almost seven years, from early 1897, the time of his nineteenth birthday, until late 1903. The ranch consisted of between five and ten thousand acres (the actual size is not clarified and probably varied throughout the period), leased from local farmers by RN on behalf of the California Beet Sugar & Refining Company. As manager, he was responsible to two men, The General Superintendent, Mr. Larsen, and to the General Manager of Ranches for the firm, K.G. Raaf, who in turn reported to the President, R.P. Rithet. His earlier successes convincing reluctant farmers to plant their acreage in sugar beets together with his growing reputation as a young man who could get things done so impressed senior management of the company that he was given the job. His duties in this new role far surpassed his responsibilities at Burgess & Noble. In that situation, as a middle man in the chain of production between the farmer and the consumer, he had to contract with local growers for the purchase of their crop, manage a crew of fruit handlers and packers in their efforts to get the product dried and packed, and deliver it to the rail line by a deadline. No simple task, certainly, but also not comparable to being the managing farmer at the head of an integrated chain of activities, directing the planting of thousands of acres in sugar beets, overseeing a large immigrant labor force in the process of cultivation and ultimate harvesting of the crop, and getting it loaded on beet wagons for transport to the rail head for shipment to the refinery.

To assist with this work, he hired a foreman, Mr. Jones, and began the considerable work of expanding the existing improvements on the Hook ranch to accommodate the staff, livestock, and equipment necessary for a large beet-growing operation. The existing headquarters facility had a ranch house for residential use and a barn. A mess hall for twenty laborers was among the first buildings completed. It was soon followed by another barn, a tool shed, a bunkhouse, a foreman's room, drafting office, and dispensary for animal medicine. The planning, supervision, and completion of all this work fell to RN as ranch manger, a significant set of responsibilities for a young man.

In addition to the headquarters improvements, bunking and mess facilities were required at five other locations on the leased acreage to house and feed the Japanese labor force which consisted of fifteen or so bosses and large numbers of Japanese laborers. At various times, there were as many as six hundred laborers working under the supervision of the bosses. The cultural and labor relations challenge this arrangement must have presented to RN could not have been trivial and the creativity and determination he brought to the job were soon tested during a frustrating and time-sensitive work stoppage.

The arrangements with the Japanese labor bosses were such that contracts would be signed with two or three bosses for one camp covering between 1,000 and 1,500 acres. This meant seven to ten groups of eighty or ninety Japanese laborers, each run by a team of two or three Japanese bosses, who in turn reported to Caucasian foremen, who reported to RN. All were under contract for a season of planting, cultivating, and harvesting of sugar beets. The workers and bosses were paid on an interim basis for their work thinning the beet plants during the cultivation cycle and on a final basis calculated on tonnage harvested. The payday procedure was that payment was in cash only, gold or silver coin, with the coolies seeking to be paid directly at mealtime, trust in the bosses being low. Work slowed noticeably for a day or so after each payday as gambling took precedence over cultivating. RN opined that "most of the cash reached the pockets of the bosses in the end."

Trust among the bosses themselves was also apparently in short supply because at harvest time they came to RN and asked that they *also* all be paid at the same time as insurance against cheating among themselves. After securing his agreement to their request, each partner was to pay him $20 twice each year, a side deal apparently approved by the company in view of the extra work involved for him.

Because so much depended on the reliability and effort of the Japanese labor force, special consideration was given to their needs. In each of the labor camps built to house the laborers a special hot tub was required facilitating a daily bath, perhaps unusual to the hired supervisors but essential to the culture of their laborers. Each tub would consist of a 4'x4' water-tight box with a sheet iron bottom which would be set on bricks allowing a fire underneath. Each day, after all the workers had used the tub, the water would be drained and replaced.

At Hookston, RN's biggest challenges were with weather and with labor relations. In RN's accounting, 1898 was part of a cycle of dry years with serious implications for agriculture. In anticipation of continued dry years and potential water shortage, the CBS&R Company sought to make alternative arrangements, buying water rights from the town of Walnut Creek, thus capturing water from there north to Suisun Bay. A dam was designed and built by The People's Water Company, creating a series of levees and a catch basin behind a dam which diverted water to irrigation ditches when the water level reached the top. The ditch network then carried the water throughout the cultivated beet fields. Only marginally successful because of the uneven nature of the terrain, this dam and its associated water transport network were to cause serious difficulties for RN.

When the rains finally came in February of 1899, they put the San Ramon Valley Creek and all other water courses in the Diablo Valley, each of which drain north into Suisun Bay, into flood conditions. The Hookston property lowlands were directly in the path of the flood waters and were not spared; completely under water, all the flood control mechanisms so recently built were destroyed. Several unfortunate consequences attended this disaster including idle labor, a partially destroyed crop, and conflict between RN and his seniors at CBS&R.

To satisfy the need for large numbers of horses needed in the sugar beet operation, RN contracted with local liveryman for the rental or purchase of stock and teamsters to handle the animals. When idle for a month, as they were after the flood, significant labor problems developed with the teamsters which it became RN's job to solve. As he reported it, with nothing to do but tend to their horses and play cards all day, a "climate favorable to dissent" was soon created. Indeed, a refusal to continue work without a pay increase was soon forthcoming and RN and Foreman Jones had their first labor challenge. They were able to identify the leaders of the insurrection, teamsters from a liveryman in Pleasanton, a Mr. Fong, and RN soon corresponded with him seeking advice. Fong's counsel was to pay off and fire the teamsters, replacing them with others of RN's choice, but under no circumstances allow them to keep the horses.

A confrontation soon followed in which the teamsters refused to begin work without a pay increase from $1 per day to $1.25. With all the teamsters, including the ringleaders, and horses arrayed in the yard, RN faced them down. To their threat to quit unless given the increase, he responded "Well, under those conditions you have already quit, so crawl down off your horse and get your blankets and hit the road. You are paid to date and have had a month's free board." When the leader suggested they would take their horses with them, RN displayed a letter from Fong denying that permission.

RN then confronted one of those remaining, a man to whom he had extended personal financial assistance some months earlier, and suggested that if he wished to remain on the job he should "get started-you are now fifteen minutes late." As that man returned to work, RN explained to the remainder that "I know you work hard and I will have something to say about increasing your pay later."

He subsequently offered an increase subject to conditions, all consistent with his now urgent objective of getting his beet plants into the ground quickly because of the delays occasioned by the flood. He told them that all who remained until July 1st, helping with the planting and cultivating, would be paid an extra $.25 per day, effective immediately and continuing thereafter. Further, anyone who quit during that period and later returned seeking re-employment would need to work for a year at the lower wage before being eligible for the higher level.

There was no further trouble with the teamsters and in this way, he got his beets planted, cultivated, and harvested in a year which, because of its delayed start, might have turned out quite differently. RN's ability to sense that the teamster's demand needed to be taken seriously, to rid the operation of the leaders of an insurrection, and to accomplish his business objectives, all speak to a natural inclination to leadership and native managerial competence. Such a multi-dimensional problem was obviously not in the curriculum in his Danville grammar school; a combination of his limited experience (he was just twenty-one), his brains and his courageous style resulted in a successful solution.

The same flood of 1899 caused additional labor conflict, this time with the Japanese bosses but, before encountering that challenge, RN needed to face a direct threat to his own employment. The floods had destroyed almost all of the flood control efforts of the prior year, leaving flattened levees, a destroyed dam, and a financial loss occasioned by the time, labor, and materials committed to the work. Some senior management at CBS&R were understandably unhappy, perhaps looking for a scapegoat, and, as manager of the operation, RN was at risk. In particular, George McNear, a Director of the company, suggested to the Board that RN be removed from his job and replaced with Vincent Hook, one of the land owners from whom RN had leased acreage for the beet operation. On direction from President Rithet, the Corporate Secretary, Mr. Huntington, prepared a letter carrying out the instruction to fire RN. Thereafter, Rithet had a change of heart and instructed Huntington not to mail the letter. On learning it had already been sent, he told Huntington to go to the mail box and retrieve it, feeling that he owed RN a chance to explain his side of the story.

In a meeting with Rithet, RN said that if they wanted to change managers that was their decision and he could live with it. Before they took that step, however, he suggested they look into the circumstances of the original leases with Hook, a man about whose character RN had serious questions. There were three five-year leases with Hook, two of which were signed at inception and delivered. The third, for his mother's land, covering property that served as headquarters, and on which the company had invested in substantial improvements, was never signed or delivered. When asked, Hook suggested his mother was ill and continued to insist that she was too sick to be troubled by such matters. Finally, at a time when Hook appeared seeking his rent check, RN advised him that no rent would be paid without a signed lease on all of the parcels.

At that point, Hook, suggesting to RN that he needed compensation for his trouble in gathering the lease signatures and collecting all the documents, demanded a payment of $300 before he would provide the last signed lease. Characterizing Hook's actions as "little short of blackmail," and, in light of the importance of that particular parcel to the overall operation, RN acceded to the demand and wrote Hook a check for the $300. As this unfolded, it became clear that Hook had been in possession of the final signed lease all along. RN explained to his boss that he had previously included a full explanation of these facts in a letter accompanying check vouchers submitted earlier.

Rithet then requested that Secretary Huntington bring in the vouchers so RN's could be located and his story verified. The voucher was located but the accompanying letter was not signed by RN, causing Rithet to suggest that he could not present an unsigned letter to his board as evidence in support of a motion to suspend the termination order. Secretary Huntington then asked to see the letter, indicating that because of RN's habit of using the word "perhaps," and mispronouncing and misspelling it, as "praps," he could vouch for RN to the board, since the word appeared in the letter. Rithet closed the meeting by telling RN that he should "go back to the ranch and attend to your duties. I will take care of this matter."

At a distance of so many years, it is difficult to fully understand what actually happened in this situation. One wonders why, if the levee work had all been done at company expense and presumably with company approval, RN would later be blamed for damage caused by an unpredictable and unpreventable flood. Might it have been a pretense for getting rid of a very competent, but sometimes prickly and difficult employee? Possibly, but later commendations from President Rithet, at the end of RN's service, would appear to belie this construction. One does get the impression, however, that RN's associates, particularly those in positions senior to him, were not often eager to support his cause.

The floods of 1899 not only caused labor troubles for RN among his teamsters; the same idleness that afflicted the teamsters also had an effect on the Japanese labor bosses who soon set up a committee to approach RN, demanding a 15% increase in their contract price. Initially, he was not involved because CBS&R management had determined it would handle the matter at headquarters in San Francisco. But as farm manager, RN would bear responsibility for a lost crop and, as the negotiations dragged on and his planted beets grew to two inches in height, he became impatient. If the beets were allowed to continue to grow without being thinned (a labor-intensive process requiring the reduction of each plant to a single seedling), the crop might well be lost. He went to San Francisco for a visit with President Rithet, explaining the importance of getting the labor problem settled in time to save the crop. Rithet, apparently exasperated with RN, suggested that if he thought he could do better than the company's expert labor negotiators he was welcome to try, so long as he coordinated his efforts with General Counsel Donald Y. Campbell.

This episode is instructive in gleaning insight into RN's character because it required of him a cultural sensitivity and approach which must have been unusual at that time for a man his age. He conceived a plan to bring in the fifteen or so Japanese bosses to two separate meetings, each in the best meeting suite available in the Occidental Hotel in San Francisco. Coordinating with the hotel manager, he arranged the meeting room so that the chairs were set up in circular fashion at eleven in the morning on two successive days. When his guests arrived for the first session, RN greeted them at the door with two waiters nearby to take drink orders. Aware that the guests would take the same seats the following day, RN memorized their faces, their seating order, and their drink orders. He then commenced a short session in which he proposed a toast to "A happy settlement to your request for increased pay - the beets will soon be ruined if not thinned." He then suggested they go home and "think about how we can best reach a settlement," instructing them to return at the same time on the following day.

On the next day, in the same circle of chairs, he asked if each wanted the same drink he had had the day before. When they indicated they did, he impressed them with his memory, not only of each of their names, but of their drink order as well. He then presented his offer of settlement, acceding to the 15% increase, but conditioning it on their willingness to escrow the funds in a bank of their choice until such time as the principle reached a value of $500,000. He also insisted on each contractor accepting joint and severable liability for his portion of the contracted work, insuring thereby that each would stay on the job and complete the work. The contractors selected the Yokohama Specie Bank which was acceptable to the company and RN described the agreement to General Counsel Campbell and Superintendent of Ranch Operations Larsen, both of whom handled the drafting and execution. Within several days the agreement was executed and the teams were all back at work.

It is of course unknowable just how much of all this RN did on his own and if the settlement idea was his alone or reflected the thinking of the General Counsel and other participants from management. What does ring true, however, is the creativity in his approach to the negotiation, his care in memorizing names, places, and drink preferences displayed in the first meeting. There are a number of instances in the *Memoirs* where creativity and sensitivity to a negotiating counter-party are displayed, suggesting that, at the least, his role in the set-up of the meetings was his alone. For a man barely twenty-one years of age, this suggests a mature awareness and high level of interpersonal skills.

A contemporary reader may be forgiven if he sees only the working side of RN's personality as his writing did seem to exhibit all the attributes describing today's workaholic. But in an interesting diversion, he offered insights into his social life during the Hookston period, providing a view into a different side of his personality. He relates that he normally took two weeks or so of vacation, staying in the vicinity of Hookston and reachable if necessary. His location of choice during one of these years was in Diablo Canyon in the foothills of Mt Diablo.

These interludes sound like a good deal more than merely camping out, as he had a full staff of cooks and roustabouts to attend to the cooking and clean-up work involved. His description of his guest list includes names prominent in the social milieu of the late nineteenth century Bay Area. "Our regular party consisted of Mrs. Scammel (his aunt) and her sons Noble and Teddie, Miss Ruth Sutton, sister of the recorder of the University of California at Berkeley, and a friend of hers, Miss Ethyl Bates, sister of Charles Bates (Charles Married Lacressia Burnham of Oakland) and myself…" RN's propensity to drop names signals a hunger to belong, to be considered a member of an elite strata of society; the *Memoirs* are full of these references to socially prominent people of his time and he made it his conscious practice to develop relationships within these groups.

His regular party was frequently augmented by visits of other guests, apparently almost every day. He goes on, "One Sunday Mr. Huntington, secretary of the company, and his daughter (with some guests) came out and I know they enjoyed it very much." Other guests included individuals prominent in the Hawaiian cane-sugar business, "I remember Mr. Wallace Alexander came out with his sister from Piedmont, and Mr. Alexander and Mr. Baldwin of Alexander & Baldwin of Honolulu." RN was still a bachelor and, with Aunt Hattie as an informal hostess acting as a chaperone and arranging the flowers and tables, he must have been quite the entertainer as he built relationships with a number of senior Bay Area business men.

The first several years of the new century found RN busy with the responsibilities of managing the Hookston with a workload as varied as it must have been arduous. He described the necessity of shooting three horses during an epidemic of glanders, a contagious disease potentially communicable to humans, under orders from the County Health Offices as part of a general quarantine of all his horses. He characterized the annual job of shoeing between 160 and 250 horses as a hot, hard, and dangerous job, and one which on one occasion necessitated experimentation with sedatives.

Horseshoeing was typically a month-long job, usually beginning on the first of July. One such morning, he was told that there were two dead horses at the shoeing crib and, upon inspection, determined that the horses had been killed, perhaps with ball-peen hammers. By way of background, he pointed out that the horses he employed for the beet operation were man-killers because he bought the meanest animals; these horses were the cheapest, but also had the greatest stamina and could handle the work well. Such horses were obviously not easy to handle and the difficult job of shoeing often brought out anger and frustration on the part of the men.

In a remark indicative of a tendency to impulsiveness and a short temper, RN suggested that "Fortunately, the blacksmiths had left for the day, because had they been there we would probably have clashed, and I would have fired them. That would have been disastrous because we were just starting harvest." Having heard that gypsies often drugged their horses to shoe them, RN set out to visit some gypsy camps and obtain some of whatever they used. When this proved unsuccessful, he called on the veterinarian in Concord seeking morphine and a syringe. Obtaining the doctor's cooperation when he understood the medicine was to be used only on horses, RN promised to record each instance of use and results for the veterinarian's benefit.

This proved to be a successful solution to a difficult problem; the first horse, a 1400 pounder, became quite docile under a 12-grain shot, even cooperating by holding his foot in the air when the blacksmith returned to his forge to fashion the new shoe. The treatment worked on the other horses at Hookston as well and the problem never reoccurred.

In February of 1901, RN was just 23, managing the Hookston Ranch, and continuing to find time to engage in an array of social activities. Within two weeks of his birthday, he hosted a small party in the Opera House in San Francisco, attending a performance of the Italian operatic tenor Enrico Caruso. Again, his guest list sounds like a social register of the time with three girls, all unaccompanied by other young men. Included were "Miss Huntington, daughter of W. H. Huntington of San Francisco, and Miss Spaulding and Miss Irwin of the Hawaiian Islands." The young ladies were expecting to greet friends arriving on a steamer at its expected docking the following day. As the group walked toward Market Street to fetch a taxi, they came across a large group of excited people clustered around a news blackboard. The ship in question, the *Rio de Janeiro,* had just run aground outside the Bay with the loss of all 128 passengers (Later reports were that 85 of 220 passengers and crew survived).

By the harvest of 1902, the sugar beet business was declining, a victim of the over cropping, declining yields, and lack of interest on the part of local farmers. In one of his final challenges managing Hookston, RN was again confronted by management at CBS&R for his handling of an instance of drunkenness among his foremen. On finding three of them drunk one afternoon, he told them that failing to stay sober would cost them their jobs. When two of the three were passed out from too much drinking again the following morning, he had notes attached to them and sent them, with their personal effects, to the Rogers Hotel in Walnut Creek. With pinned notes saying, "Keep your handiwork, I don't want them back," they were deposited on the front porch of the Hotel. Why he chose the Rogers Hotel, the business of his Christmas night benefactor back in 1896, is not clarified.

Apparently, the termination of two key men during harvest season was unacceptable to Mr. Larsen, the General Superintendent of Ranch Operations, and he protested to RN, indicating that by his actions he had thrown a monkey wrench into the operation at a critical time. RN, quoting his own response, displayed more of the independent combativeness which so often seems to have characterized his approach when working in a hierarchical, corporate situation. "Larsen, I put this organization together and it would be a very nasty situation if the teamsters follow the foremen's example and get liquored too. Our operation is going on just as smoothly as ever, and if you doubt it I will take you around so you can see for yourself. This afternoon we shipped a string of cars as large as ever. One thing is certain, Jones and Smith will not set foot on this ranch again while I am here." RN suggested that Larsen's response to this speech sounded like a threat, though he never heard more of the matter and was confident that President Rithet and Secretary Huntington would side with him on the matter of drunkenness on the job.

By the end of 1903, RN's sugar beet-farming days were coming to an end. A year earlier, in the fall of 1902, after the completion of the harvest, CBS&R President Rithet informed him of a planned visit by several stockholders to the Hookston Ranch, asking if he would show the group around the acreage. Driving a coach with four horses, he met them at the train station in Martinez and conducted the tour as directed. He returned the group to the station and while awaiting the arrival of the train was informed by Rithet that the firm was planning to get out of the sugar beet growing business and concentrate on refining cane-sugar from Hawaii. Rithet further suggested that if RN could find someone willing to pay $5,000 and assume all the local leases on sugar beet acreage they would sell out. RN related that he responded, asking if Rithet's remarks constituted a binding offer, to which the President indicated they did. RN's response: "Then you have found a buyer. I accept your offer." After initially appearing to backtrack on his offer, Rithet directed RN to work out an agreement with Corporate Attorney Donald Campbell and to prepare and submit his final closing reports on ranch operations. Substitution agreements eliminated a potential problem of liability for future lease payments (the firm did not want to be liable in the event RN failed to make the required $60,000 lease payments after the deal was signed) and he was on his own, with, as he put it, "a world of responsibility and no cash. I had asked for it."

The decision of CBSR&C to exit the business of sugar beet farming initiated a process that set RN up as a twenty-five-year-old entrepreneur and land developer in Contra Costa County. On a final visit to San Francisco headquarters, he declined a personal reference letter from Rithet who, RN reported, indicated that, "...you managed one of our large ranches for five years, (*sic*) and lost us less money, and gave us less trouble and kept your operation free from litigation. That is more than I can say for any of the other managers." The discrepancy in dates is curious; in RN's telling, he was running Hookston for CBS&R for seven years, 1897 through 1903. His rationale for declining a letter of commendation testifying to this record is never mentioned, though from his actions it seems clear he didn't contemplate another similar employment in a corporate setting.

While preparing for his final meeting with Rithet and auditing his books, RN noticed a significant error. One of the lessors to the Hookston Ranch, The London and San Francisco Bank, owners of the 240-acre San Miguel Ranch in what is today's Walnut Creek, had failed to collect their December 1902 rent check. After his visit with Rithet, he went to the Bank to advise them of the error, calling on Mr. Mackintosh, the branch manager. Mackintosh, incredulous that the Bank's books could be in error, challenged RN who then, with the intercession of Mr. Black, the Cashier, proved that indeed the bank had not received their December rent check for $500.

After arranging for Black to get the $500 owed to him at the nearby offices of CBSR&C, discussions with Mackintosh soon uncovered another opportunity for RN. Mackintosh suggested that RN buy the San Miguel Ranch property from the Bank because they were selling their assets to The Bank of California who did not want any land in the deal. The Bank of California would take the Ranch if it were a receivable on London and San Francisco's books, but not otherwise. Mackintosh therefore proposed to RN that he buy the parcel, thereby converting it to a receivable, at book value, telling him that it was on the Bank's books at a value of

$8,500, half of its market value. Further, Mackintosh would extend credit of $8,000 for three years at 6%, requiring only $500 down. To RN's response that he didn't have the $500, Mackintosh asked what he did with all his money. RN's response reveals some of his personal financial arrangements and obligations. "I told him I had a father and mother that required help at times, two sisters at Mills College who needed some assistance, two brothers going to the University of California in the same fix, and my Aunt Hattie and her three minor boys lived with me, the oldest eleven years old. There is never any money left over." RN's comment contains more than a little hyperbole. Having begun classes at the University of California in the early 1890s, it is doubtful that both brothers were still in attendance by 1903 when this meeting occurred.

Nonetheless, on hearing of RN's financial situation, Mackintosh suggested that he close the small account he had with the London and San Francisco Bank and go to the Bank of California with Mackintosh's personal recommendation. At Bank of California, he would open a new account and seek a loan of $500 for one year. The Bank of California Manager agreed to this proposal and RN was able to acquire 240 acres of excellent land for only his personal note. He reported that two years later he refinanced and paid off both the mortgage and the note.

These land acquisitions, the leases on the former sugar beet acreage and the new 240-acre San Miguel Ranch, put RN in a position in which he controlled land and could begin to think about additional acquisitions of sub-dividable property throughout the Diablo Valley. In the space of eight years he had started and successfully run a fruit packing business, managed one of the largest sugar beet ranching operations of the California Beet Sugar Refining Company, and acquired the rights to enough good land to begin the next phase of his professional development. He was on his way.

CHAPTER 6
San Miguel Ranch

The combination of the end of his relationship with CBS&R and the opportunity of a favorable purchase of the San Miguel Ranch in Walnut Creek put RN on a new life track and provided him with the means for large scale land development. For the first time in the *Memoirs*, he advised his readers that he planned to acquire and subdivide a number of significant parcels of land throughout Contra Costa County and that he was spending considerable time at his new San Miguel location researching and plotting on parcel maps the acreage he would like to acquire.

The San Miguel Ranch consisted of 240 acres, a combination of lowlands and hills just east of downtown Walnut Creek. In today's terms, it covered the San Miguel neighborhood and lower and upper Lakewood. When RN moved in, in November of 1903, the ranch gave him a real home, though it took some time for the property to be fully built out as such. Initially, he allowed his foreman, Mr. White, to occupy the existing ranch house with his wife and three children, while bunking himself in the barn in a room over the cow and horse stalls. He planned to build a cabin on a nearby hill from which he could survey the ranch, Lafayette, and the Berkeley hills to the west. Somewhat poetically, he described that it was "... here in the rarified air of my castle in the sky that I studied the county maps and marked off the large holdings as possibilities for future real estate syndicating, with the idea of cutting up and marketing them as ranches."

RN's economic prospects in late 1903 were driven by his ability to farm the acreage he had assembled and to manage his expenses so as to earn a profit on ranching while he began to implement his land acquisition strategy. His landholdings included 20 acres of hay land adjacent to Bonny Vista in Danville (the same parcel he bought with the assistance of his teacher, A. J. Young, in 1893), the 240 acres of San Miguel Ranch, subject to the purchase money mortgage with the Bank of California of $8,500, and the leases on approximately 5,000 acres formerly leased to CBS&R for sugar beet operations.

He also controlled, through those leases, the former headquarters of the Hookston Ranch and the earlier improvements built there. He left his Aunt Hattie in charge of the ranch house at Hookston when he relocated to Walnut Creek. She lived there with two of her sons, serving as RN's eyes and ears on the property and in charge of the only telephone available to him, as San Miguel did not yet have one. He brought along Mr. Stark from Hookston as a foreman at San Miguel to work with Mr. White, the existing foreman, at the property. Conveniently, they each had work horses, eight and four respectively, which, when combined with RN's team of four, gave them sixteen horses with which to begin farming operations. Given his plan to plant the acreage in hay, wheat, or oats, he needed equipment and the funds to make these expenditures. To finance plows, harrows, seeders, and seed, he sold some of the leases from the Hookston property and borrowed $2,500 from his Aunt Hattie and an additional $5,000 from the Bank of Martinez, mortgaging the crop as security on the loan. His payroll for labor and horses came to about $40 per month. His annual debt service on the Bank of California loan at 6% per annum was $480.

A characteristic of his *Memoirs* is that RN remembered and included extensive detail about his real estate and other transactions over the years. Preparing such exposition could not have been easy for a writer with an eighth-grade education, nor is interpreting them in the way he might have intended always possible. Inspection of his numbers, however, leads to the conclusion that with his cash flow as he described it, he was in financial red ink in the beginning of 1904. In any event, he was saved from such deficit financing by the arrival, early in that year, of two wine merchants from New York.

The Samuel brothers owned a large winery and extensive vineyard acreage in Clayton. Diseased vines necessitated pulling out all of the plants and replanting in more resistant stock. This proved problematic as the terrain was uneven and hilly and thus difficult to lay out in symmetrical rows. In anticipation of a visit from their lender, an important visit because the brothers hoped he would finance improvements on the land, they needed professional surveying help and hired RN. Using the knowledge and equipment he had acquired from Surveyor W. F. Boardman in 1898 when constructing the water course, dam and catch basin for CBS&R, he proceeded to lay out beautifully aligned rows of vines over an extensive, six-ridge area for the Samuel Brothers. The result was a successful loan negotiation and a winery business.

Once again revealing himself both as a man of his time and as a firm negotiator, RN related how he reacted when the Samuel Brothers tried to renegotiate his fee during the middle of the job. He reported that, "They were very pleased with the way the stakes lined up, but they were of the Jewish persuasion and said the county engineer only charged $10 per day and I was charging $15." Upon hearing this, RN began packing up his equipment in preparation to leave the job, and, when they asked what he was doing, responded that he was "getting ready to leave, I am not your man." The Brothers backed down and a lasting business relationship was formed, resulting in several more years of his surveying service on their behalf.

From comments in the *Memoirs*, by spring of 1904 his monthly cash flow, before considering his loan payments and income from plantings in the ground, was about $60, and he had a rich crop of hay and grain ready for harvest. To harvest the 2,000 acres of crop, he utilized four teams of horses pulling mowers, sometimes at night during periods of exceptionally hot weather. He worried about being able to sell his crop, 5,000 tons of coarse hay, but he found a buyer from Hawaii willing to take the entire crop at a price that left him a profit. As a result of the successful grain and hay growing season of 1904, almost all the owners of the leased acreage (obtained in his buyout from CBS&R), observing his success, decided they wanted to buy back their leases. Indeed, his plan all along had been to sell these leases back to the owners; the timing was perfect and he was able to sell for about $1.00 per acre, with the headquarters lease going for an even higher premium.

By mid-1904, the hay crop was harvested and domestic issues changed his living arrangements when Aunt Hattie relocated to San Miguel from Hookston with two of her sons, Noble and Marious. At this point, both foremen were ready to move on, and space opened up in the San Miguel Ranch house for RN. Aunt Hattie's boys were available to help around the ranch and they did chores and other useful work in a life where, as he put it, "everyone worked." RN's relationship with these boys must have given him his first taste of parenting since Hattie's husband was not in the picture. His description of each boy, and his judgment on the child's prospects in life, reveal his own character and life outlook.

Noble, he felt, would make something of himself and, accordingly, RN later helped him get started by financing a down payment on a ranch in Yreka. His description of Noble is telling: "He made a home for his mother, brothers and a couple of uncles. He became the Noble family mainstay." Marious, a reader, seems not to have impressed RN, who characterized him as "a day and night dreamer throughout his life." In describing the youngest brother, Teddy, RN damned him with faint praise saying that "Teddy did nothing startling. He was a willing comfortable fellow without much drive. He went to work selling insurance." RN's descriptions, for the most part unflattering comparisons of his cousins to himself, reflect a marked lack of patience for young men who lacked his drive and ambition.

He described an incident where he spanked Noble with a board which had, unknown to RN, a two-inch wire nail protruding, making a bloody mess of his bottom, much to the boy's mother's anger. This punishment was for a repeated transgression which might have been dangerous and expensive had it not been nipped in the bud. Noble played with fire and gunpowder, in spite of warnings from both RN and his mother, and, on the occasion in question, RN found him striking matches among 300 tons of bailed alfalfa hay. RN said that Noble never played with matches again.

Throughout 1904 and into 1905, RN continued to improve the San Miguel property, building a dairy operation on the flatlands in front of the ranch house, erecting a 90-foot windmill, and installing a 50,000-gallon water tank on a nearby hill for increased and convenient water access. The scope of his work and his expertise in preparing this dairy operation is impressive, given his age and experience to that point. With only, "a couple of handy men," he prepared ground and planted alfalfa, converted an existing structure into a dairy barn with 30 milking stations with feed troughs, installed milking machines, an underground ice house covered by a milk-and-wash room, an ice making machine, a milk separator, cooler, aerator, and steam boiler. The *Memoirs* contain no mention of where the capital came from to support this investment, but, by this time, RN had become increasingly comfortable with borrowing money and his credit was good based on his accomplishments to date.

During the fall harvest of 1904, an incident occurred that presaged a major land acquisition several years later and involved a relationship with the family of Tom Rice, a Southern California farmer and large landowner. When the wheat on the San Miguel Ranch was ready to be harvested and threshed that fall, it was necessary to hire a horse-drawn threshing machine to separate the grain from the stalks and husks. Representing large capital investments, these threshing units were typically shared by groups of ranchers, an arrangement which became problematic for RN.

Access to his San Miguel Ranch wheat fields from the county road was gained only by surmounting a very steep hill, which proved difficult for the threshing equipment. A nearby flat 20-acre parcel belonging to the Rice family was available, however, affording much easier access for removal of the grain. Seeking to facilitate easier access to his own crop, and improve access to the highway and railroad, RN authorized the removal of a portion of the Rice fence and instructed the foreman of the threshing operation to thresh the Rice grain as well as his own. He did this without asking for the owner's permission, but felt he would have no trouble securing approval inasmuch as it was work that the owner would require anyway.

The owner of the 20-acre parcel was Xarissa Hill, one of the Rice heirs, each of whom had inherited a seventh of the entire property. The Rice Ranch consisted of 1,750 acres, part of the larger San Miguel tract in Walnut Creek. She proved a difficult and unpleasant adversary for RN, denying him access to her land. Describing her as "a widow, noted for her size and for her devotion to the Methodist Church," he related how she admonished him, "No, young man, you will have to learn to load your wagon according to the hill," and shut the door in his face. Several years later, their paths crossed again when RN, this time working through her brother Tom, would not only buy her parcel, but the entire 1,750 acres himself.

By mid-1905, the San Miguel Ranch was a successful ongoing operation with acreage in wheat, grain, and alfalfa. The alfalfa supported the dairy operation, with important customers in San Francisco, including the Occidental, the Fairmont, and the St Francis Hotels, all of whom contracted for his dairy products. Having accomplished his initial objectives, he turned to the business of land acquisition and development. Two years earlier, at the time of his initial move to the San Miguel ranch, RN had identified several large parcels of land in which he was interested for purposes of future subdivision and development. These included the Los Medanos parcel, a 13,000-acre tract west of Antioch, a 40,000-acre parcel in Brentwood, owned by English investors (clients of Balfour Guthrie), and the Moraga Grant, 12,000-acres between Lafayette and Oakland owned by Mr. Carpentier of New York, and managed by the Corn Exchange Bank. The last opportunity ultimately did take place, but not for a decade and a half. In 1904, these larger parcels were out of his reach, but after San Miguel was up and running successfully, he had the time to explore and close on several nearby smaller plots. He began with 40 acres of the Larkey Ranch, contiguous land to his San Miguel piece. To the south of that he purchased the 20-acre Thadeus Johnson orchard and a small right of way parcel which gave him access to the county highway on level ground. These relatively small land acquisitions were the earliest assemblages of what would later become substantial holdings.

The land purchases utilized all his excess capital from ranch operations, and 1905 marked the final year of his note on the San Miguel property with The Bank of California. Its due date was approaching and RN lacked the capital to pay it off. A fortuitous meeting served to provide a solution to this refinancing problem. On a hot summer day an automobile load of strangers arrived at San Miguel seeking something cool to drink and some relief from the heat. Mr. H. C. Morris of Oakland had been in the country visiting his cousins, the Pennimans, in today's Ygnacio Valley. The Pennimans, former prune customers of RN's, had directed the party toward San Miguel in their quest for a cool and restful place in which to picnic before returning to Oakland. After introductions, RN produced a cool pail of fresh milk from his ice house for the picnickers, and, in the ensuing conversation, explained his farming and dairying operations to Morris.

Whatever RN said that afternoon must have impressed the older man, because he offered financial assistance, including a loan if needed. Explaining that he did indeed have an approaching refinancing requirement, RN described his need. Morris responded that he would fund the new loan whenever RN was ready to move forward. In this way the purchase money mortgage with The Bank of California was closed out prior to its actual due date and a profitable and long-lasting business relationship began with H.C. Morris.

In the fall of 1905, another encounter occurred that had important consequences for RN's land acquisition goals. While digging post holes for a holding corral, he noticed a visitor approaching. Tom Rice himself, Xarissa's brother from Oxnard, California, was in the area checking on his family's holdings. In conversation, Rice explained that his visit was in the way of an apology for his sister's behavior, particularly in the face of RN's thoughtfulness in directing his thresher to thresh her grain for her as he sought easier access (denied by her) to his own fields. In conversation Rice allowed that the land in question was detached from the primary family acreage and "really should belong to you." In a now familiar pattern, RN responded, asking if Rice had a price for the parcel. He did, and RN thought it reasonable, but soon learned that Xarissa was not inclined to sell her portion, thus precluding the whole sale. After more discussion, Tom agreed to intercede with his sister in an attempt to obtain her agreement. This conversation would bear fruit, but not until after a series of portentous events which would change RN's life.

As 1905 drew to a close, ranch operations were progressing well with acreage planted, a new dairy operation up and running, and new, more commodious quarters completed in the ranch house. The first part of the following year continued as such, and, by April of 1906, this twenty-eight-year-old rancher and would-be land syndicator was quite successful. The event that would change his life occurred on the morning of April 18, 1906 at 5:12. He wrote that as he got out of bed, he was confused by swinging French doors and a swaying windmill tower. That earthquake and the related San Francisco fire sent his young life along a new tangent with building opportunities and demands for housing beyond his wildest imagination.

CHAPTER 7

Game Changer

In 1906 no Richter scale existed to measure the magnitude of earthquakes. But the quake that greeted RN as he arose around 5 o'clock on that April morning has been estimated at between 7 and 8 on that scale. He was at home in the ranch house at San Miguel and noticed his French doors swaying dramatically as he tried to get to his feet from the bed. He had been out the evening prior and his initial thought was that he had over-imbibed and was feeling the effects of a massive hangover. He was starting his day just as a major seismic event occurred across the Bay, an event unprecedented in the short history of California as a populated state. There had, of course, been earthquakes before, but at times when San Francisco was either unpopulated or sparsely occupied. In 1906 San Francisco, with a population of 410,000 living in mostly wooden or brick buildings not designed with seismic safety in mind, was particularly at risk that morning as pressures on the San Andreas fault were relieved and the earth began to shake.

When the dust settled and the ensuing fire was extinguished, the city lay in ruins. In the context of today's seismic terminology, the quake of 1906 is rated with a Mercalli intensity of X1, extreme, and the wreckage and resulting fire reflected that highest of all scales.[1] Some three thousand people died, a record of lives lost in a disaster that still stands in California history. Almost eighty percent of the city was destroyed, 90% of that not by the shaking, but by the following fire. Out of the population of 410,000, between 250,000 and 300,000 were left without dwellings and with only the personal possessions they could remove from their homes in baby

---

[1] Mercalli intensity measures the observed effects of an earthquake as opposed to the energy released as in the Richter Scale.

carriages or similarly convenient means of drayage under such an emergency. The ultimate destination for up to half of these refugees was the East Bay, primarily Oakland, or Berkeley.

***

RN's Aunt Margery was a visitor at San Miguel Ranch that week in April 1906 and the sound that first greeted RN as he struggled to get dressed in the confusion was Marjory's shriek as she ran to the balcony with the intention of jumping to the ground below and the safety she thought lay there. RN stopped her, assuring her that she was safest, given the construction of the house, if she placed herself in a doorway and away from any nearby chimney. Looking out the window, he spotted Mike, the Dairy Foreman, who, apparently unaware of the earthquake, assured RN that he had completed his milking routine and that his cream supplies would soon be ready to go to the train station in Walnut Creek for its daily trip to their customers in the San Francisco. Mike, a skeptical Irishman, did not believe RN when he told him of the quake and, in RN's colorful telling, responded in dialect, "Aw, go 'long which youse foolin."

The San Francisco train left Walnut Creek at 7:00 am; it was cousin Noble's job to get the dairy products to the train for delivery to the hotel customers in the city. Noble returned from the railroad station to report "excitement and confusion" in Walnut Creek. No trains or mail were moving and the telephone service was inoperable. Rumor had it that Oakland was on fire, and RN, on the roof repairing the destroyed chimney of the ranch house, could indeed see a plume of white smoke rising to the west, as if in in confirmation of Noble's report. By late that afternoon, RN had rebuilt the chimney facilitating a fire for cooking in the kitchen below. Dinner was announced at 6 o'clock. At the table with Noble and three additional hired hands, RN announced that he had long been thinking about going into business in Oakland, and that this event could well be just the opportunity he was seeking. He planned to explore the situation and gave orders to hitch up his buggy and favorite horse, Lady. He promised the crew that upon his arrival in Oakland he would find a bank in which to cash a check and send funds home to meet the coming ranch payday.

With his suitcase packed and his goodbyes behind him, he was climbing into his buggy when one of the crew approached him informing him that the hands had taken up a collection. They could live without their pay for several weeks, if necessary, and they wanted him to have $140 in the event he was unable to find a bank open under these circumstances. RN's reaction to this display of generosity is characteristic, "Loyalty gives one a wonderful feeling and builds courage." With that, he was off to the west, and what must have seemed a smoky and uncertain, nonetheless exciting, future.

One imagines this wagon journey in the late dusk of an emerging April night over the county road through Lafayette and Orinda, up to the Inter-County tunnel, in the context of a young man's dreams as he approached what he thought might be a significant opportunity. He was a builder, and a natural catastrophe had presented him with an almost unbelievable chance to build homes, many homes, for innumerable displaced people, all fleeing the smoke he could see in the night sky as he headed west. Ever the opportunistic entrepreneur he was headed, alone in his wagon, to the opportunity of his lifetime.

Except that the opportunity was not the result of Oakland burning. As he exited the tunnel, it became apparent that the fire was in San Francisco, not Oakland. Descending the hill toward Oakland, he could see clearly the Call Building at Third and Market with smoke and flames pouring out of its windows, signaling the seriousness of what was happening across the Bay.

Finding a livery for Lady and his wagon, he headed to the Oakland City Hall and encountered Mayor Frank Mott. The Mayor's response to his request for a ride into the burning City was incredulous, "Bob, what in hell do you want to go to San Francisco for? We are making every effort to evacuate people from the City." What RN imagined he might actually accomplish by going into the scene of an unfolding disaster is not clear. Some combination of youthful exuberance, curiosity, and a desire to make himself useful under circumstances in which competent, energetic young men might be needed, urged him on in this pursuit. His determination to take advantage of the conditions which would result from this horror is clear to a modern reader. His brash decision to jump, unprepared, into the physical and human disaster six miles to the west is less so.

Ignoring Mott's incredulity and concern for his safety and demonstrating again a talent for quick thinking under pressure, RN came up with a credible rationale, convincing Mott and securing a seat for himself on a police boat departing shortly. He told Mott that he was on an assigned mission to locate his Uncle, Dr. John Albert Noble, House Physician of the Palace Hotel. Once again revealing his flair for the dramatic, he suggested to Mott that, "Anyway, Frank, if the city is to burn Nero is to have nothing on me."

RN estimated his arrival time at the Ferry Building in San Francisco at around 1:30 or 2:00 am on April 19, a little less than twenty-four hours after the earthquake. Looking west on Market Street, the gravity of the situation became clear. While the Ferry Building itself was not destroyed, clear evidence of serious damage lay on Market Street in the form of street-buckling, fallen cornices, and looming crevices. Moreover, fire that would ultimately destroy most of the city was already in evidence south of Market Street along Mission between the waterfront, and Third and Fourth Streets.

The fire burning the Call Building that he had seen from Oakland had begun about noon on the first day. By the afternoon of that day, St Mary's Hospital at First and Bryant Streets had been abandoned and some 750 people had already been hospitalized throughout the city. The dynamiting of buildings at Fifth and Mission as a fire break had commenced, and, around 3:00 p.m., Mayor Eugene Schmitz had just selected The Committee of Fifty. This was the group of citizens in whose hands the governance of the city would rest during the crisis. The Mayor's announcement included the information that three people had already been shot for looting and that police and Army troops were prepared to do more of the same to any "who seek to take advantage of the city's awful misfortune."

At about the time of RN's arrival, the St. Francis Hotel, on Powell Street began to burn and the city, state, and nation were beginning to react to the disaster. Governor Pardee from Sacramento arrived just as the United States Secretary of War, William Howard Taft, had wired orders to the Army in Vancouver to send 200,000 rations to the City along with every available tent in the United States Army. As he headed up Market Street toward the Palace Hotel, three San Francisco newspapers, the Call, The Chronicle, and the Examiner, had all collaborated on a combined edition printed in Oakland.

On reaching the Palace at Market and Montgomery, and observing it from his street-level vantage point, RN initially believed that the damage had been limited. Built of brick, but with reinforcing steel cables wrapping its walls, the hotel appeared as if it might have avoided any significant damage. Inside inspection, however, proved otherwise. Designed with six upper stories around an atrium, its guest rooms looked down upon a beautiful courtyard accessible to horses and carriages entering and unloading under a massive glass dome on top. The steel-wrapped construction protected the walls; the glass dome was another matter. The shaking brought the entire dome down, a rainstorm of glass shards descending upon its balconies, subjecting the guests to serious injury when their fear and curiosity brought them outside in their bedclothes to see what had transpired.

Attending to these numerous casualties had been Uncle John Albert Noble's first order of business as House Physician and he spent most of the first day treating guest-patients with severe lacerations. By RN's arrival, at the beginning of the second day after the quake, the hotel had been evacuated and he encountered only three men, one of whom was the bartender who reported that Dr. Noble had finally left the premises, exhausted from his work, carrying two suitcases to his office a few blocks away in the Shreve Building on the corner of Post and Grant Streets. The Shreve Building was relatively new at the time and was reported to have been built to the latest standards of fireproofing. In the suitcases, the Doctor had packed personal effects of both himself and his wife which he wanted to get away from the Palace premises and to the protection afforded by his own office.

Trying to place RN's movements throughout the ravaged and smoky, fire-enshrouded City, and the times of his activities at various places, is not easy as his chronology is primarily event-driven and anecdotal in nature. But if he arrived at the Ferry Building in San Francisco at 2:00 in the morning, as he suggests in the Memoirs, he would have been at the Palace Hotel in the darkness of night or by very early dawn. Following the bartender's suggestion, he headed over to the Shreve Building, a distance of only a few blocks, in pursuit of Dr. John Albert, arriving there at approximately 8:00 am. At the Shreve Building he found two open elevator doors in the lobby, one of which contained the Doctor's two suitcases, but not the Doctor. RN concluded that Dr. Noble had decided against carrying the luggage up six stories to his offices and left his suitcases to be picked up on a return trip. RN began to backtrack to the Palace, thinking that his uncle would have returned for the rest of his belongings. On the return trip, he was accosted by an Army soldier (early on the first day of the crisis, Mayor Eugene Schmitz had called in Federal troops to assist in civil affairs management and refugee control) who told him that the Army was planning to dynamite the area through which RN was walking and that he was not allowed to proceed.

Describing John Albert, RN asked the officer if he had seen anyone answering the description. The officer confirmed that he had indeed seen such a man resting on a bed in a nearby house which had recently been evacuated. He said the man was unconscious and accordingly given to the crew of a military van for transport to one of the hospitals in Golden Gate Park. RN decided to head in that direction.

A twenty-eight-year-old man wandering through such a scene of devastation and destruction would have been shocked by what he was seeing. Throngs of displaced, panicked, and frightened people, drifting about, aimlessly, and with no seeming purpose other than to move away from the growing conflagration south of Market Street threatening to engulf them all. He was surprised to learn that under such circumstances, most people are normally kind and generous with each other, each trying to help, share food or water, or comfort under the difficult conditions. He remarked upon the numerous means employed in the transport of personal effects, bed frames on rolling casters, baby carriages, and assorted other wheeled vehicles, noting that the evacuation of Chinatown was particularly colorful, with terrified ladies in evening dresses pouring out of night clubs, ladies whom he somewhat prudishly suggested, "by some rights should have been at home."

As is common in conditions of such chaos, rumors were the currency of frightened and bewildered people. "Los Angeles was wiped out - Chicago was swamped by enormous waves from the lake. To many it seemed the end of the world." Describing himself as not easily excited, RN reported that, under such conditions, the frightened crowd and the ever-present and growing fire threat, affected him. "It just seems to have seeped into my blood, and I took on some of their high blood pressure."

About mid-morning on day-two, April 19th, RN decided that the safest place lay in the direction of Telegraph Hill and he headed that way. Proceeding generally north, he reached the eastern slopes of Nob Hill, a vantage-point from which he could see the Fairmont Hotel and the Crocker home and art gallery. He watched as the art was removed from the latter. Climbing Nob Hill, he noticed the destruction below to the south and east as well as the growing threat associated with an expanding fire. These views contrasted with the relatively undamaged properties higher on the hill, all of which the spreading fire threatened to change. As the fire started up Nob Hill, it was propelled house by house by explosions, sending burning pieces of wood into the sky. The pieces, borne by the growing wind, flew further and further west up the slope. He reported that these developments undermined his confidence in staying ahead of the fire and he determined that the best course now lay in a westerly direction, toward Van Ness Avenue.

At this point, he headed to the hospital operated by Dr. McNutt, the Burgess family physician during their San Francisco years. The McNutt Hospital, then in the vicinity of Sutter and Polk Streets not far east of Van Ness Avenue, became his destination because he felt there was some possibility that Dr. Noble might be there. In this he was disappointed, as the staff reported that they had not seen the Doctor. What he did find at the McNutt hospital was considerable confusion and, typically, he jumped into the middle of it. Finding the facility full of still-wrapped bandages, towels, and gauze, all materials that would prove useful in the current crisis, he challenged Dr. McNutt, asking him if he was going to leave "all this valuable property for the fire?" Not only were there expensive and much needed medical supplies, but the McNutt art collection and personal library were also lying about in various stages of evacuation. On hearing that the Doctor felt that the fire would never reach the hospital, RN responded, "Doctor, the fire has already jumped Polk Street and is only three or four houses away. Will you let me move this property out to your house if I can get help?"

Dr. McNutt, after conferring with his Hospital Manager, finally agreed to his urgings and RN began issuing instructions to the staff to assemble all the materials to be moved down to the lower hallway for loading on to some means of transport, which he then set out to arrange. Heading for Van Ness Avenue, he encountered a brand-new drayage wagon with two draft horses, apparently ready for hire. The drayman was surrounded by 10 or 15 would-be customers, all arguing with him about his rate. RN stepped up on the wagon wheel and asked if the dray was for hire. The drayman responded that it was, provided he could get his price, saying that he was "tired of draying for $20 an hour. Probably one more load will be the last, and I want $300 an hour." RN's response: "Taken" and he jumped into the passenger's seat and began giving the driver instructions to his destination. At RN's instructions, the driver headed north on Van Ness Avenue and east at Sutter towards the McNutt Hospital. Upon making their right turn onto Sutter Street, Army guards stopped them and informed them they could not pass as the east side of Van Ness was being prepared for dynamiting in an attempt to create a fire break. On impulse, RN yelled "Relief for the McNutt Hospital - Gang way, gang way," and was surprised when they were allowed through.

Arriving at the hospital, RN instructed the Hospital Manager, Miss Cronan, who had earlier helped him convince Dr. McNutt to allow him to help, to organize her staff in a line of bundle-passers to facilitate quick loading of the wagon. Anticipating that the process would be slowed down by the drayman, he went out to the street to lend a hand there and they soon had the wagon loaded. He then warned Miss Cronin to get her nurses and staff out of the hospital and over to Van Ness Avenue as quickly as possible, advising her that the area was about to be blown up and a backfire set. As RN was giving directions to the McNutt home to the driver, the drayman asked about his pay, eliciting a typical RN response: "You haven't delivered the goods yet. Hurry up, that powder is due to go off any minute." After this comment the driver was underway immediately.

As they were pulling away, Dr. McNutt came out and was pleasantly surprised to see that all the materials were loaded and accounted for. He asked what the rescue of the goods was going to cost and RN responded with the drayman's price. On the Doctor's response that he couldn't possibly pay such an amount, RN replied in a way that invoked his childhood background. "God doesn't intend you to. You must hurry out of here before they start blasting, and you hurry home and try to get there before the drayman and receive the goods. If he asks you for the pay tell him to see me." RN never saw the driver again. His view of the circumstances, and of the driver's motivation, was that "The thought reached him of all that effort to help the sick and the injured, and my guess is that he wished to extend a helping hand too (*sic*)." RN's charitable thoughts as to the man's motivations may or may not have been accurate, but the record demonstrates that looting and all other manner of price gouging and opportunistic activities occurred during the initial hours of the crisis. It would be surprising had it not. Until the Army announced that looters would be shot on sight, all types of unbecoming human behavior took place in those first hours.

By late afternoon or early evening of the second day RN crossed Van Ness Avenue to the western side and witnessed the futile efforts of fire fighters to contain the blaze by creating a backfire. As they dynamited homes along the east side, new fuel for the on-rushing fire was created and, as the fire reached it, new fires erupted. When the two blazes came together they did so with a roar, and an accompanying hot easterly wind, which carried burning bundles of wood across the 200-foot-wide avenue to the west side of Van Ness, igniting additional roof fires. Residents fought these new fires by hand on their roofs, spreading blankets, clothes, and wet sand in an attempt to control the flames. RN's description of a rain of burning embers from the dynamited houses provides an idea of the terrifying scene in which he was immersed. The miraculous arrival of trucks from a local winery offered temporary respite as wine was used to soak blankets and help smother newly erupting roof fires. RN became apprehensive about his ability to escape the fire and leave the City and therefore decided to head west toward Golden Gate Park to stay ahead of the flames.

At that point a wind shift occurred that helped ease the worst of the fires. He described an onshore wind, one which would have accompanied the cooler air of a forming marine layer and provided a buffer to the fire-caused easterly wind. Although fires continued to burn throughout the next couple of days, the worst of the blaze was under control by the evening of this second day.

Heading for Golden Gate Park, he encountered a bread wagon, part of a relief effort originating on the Peninsula. It was mobbed and, seeing no chance of getting close enough to obtain food, he stationed himself on the sidewalk, accosting the first person carrying a loaf who came along. "A half loaf or fight," RN challenged the man as he tapped him on the shoulder. "He eyed me, and I guess my grim face and four-day beard turned the trick, for he gave me half his loaf." This exchange seems another example of RN's attraction to hyperbole because he had, by this time late in day two of the crisis, been in the City for only a day. Needing water, he began to explore the basements of abandoned houses, finding in frustration that others had beaten him to the punch with the same idea. Persevering, he found a faucet from which he was able to extract several cups with which to enjoy his "bread and water feast."

In his *Memoirs*, RN repeatedly wrote of how impressed he was with the readiness of people to help each other under very trying circumstances. Sometime on his way west he stopped at a small grocery store in search of food. He asked the grocer, who was busy moving his shelved groceries to his counter top, if he might purchase some food. The merchant replied that he was not selling his food, he was giving it away and by piling it on his counter he hoped to encourage visitors to help themselves. He planned to leave the premises and wanted it clear that his intention was that the food was available and free. Reluctant to take more than an appropriate share, RN was slow to respond and the grocer selected a bag and filled it for him. After an apology from the proprietor for his lack of bread, RN left the store with hard tack, two cans of tomatoes, a can of chipped beef, and a can opener, for all of which the owner refused to take any money.

Continuing west he came to a small park, perhaps today's Lafayette Park or Laurel Hill Playground or another then-undeveloped piece of ground upon which he could pass the night and get some much-needed rest. Covered with refugees and a posted sign saying "No Vacancies," the site was not welcoming. A man approached him, however, asking if he sought a place to rest. On RN's nod, he suggested that, "You look done in and had better join us." With three in his party, including his wife and daughter, he appeared to not have much space to share but volunteered half of his daughter's pillow. RN, exceedingly weary at this point, accepted the invitation and lay down to sleep. He described the daughter as a girl of sixteen or seventeen with luxuriant chestnut hair and he felt an awkwardness when he awoke at dawn, so stole away so as to "save my host's embarrassment too". He never learned the source of this generosity.

At dawn of his second day in the city, he had been there just over twenty-four hours and was continuing his exploration when he encountered a small group of men. Approaching them, he inquired as to any news they had heard and learned more fantastic rumors, among which was that Los Angeles had been wiped out with a tidal wave, similar to Chicago. Impressed by the very human tendency to trade rumors in times of such confusion and distress, he mused that "a town-crier to cheer the people and get them thinking right would have been a blessing." One useful bit of information, however, was that boats were loading refugees bound for Oakland down at the foot of Van Ness Avenue. He set out in that direction, soon arriving and locating a "vessel loading human freight." He paid the $1.00 fare and was soon under way to Oakland.

On his return, his first priority was to get some money which he did after locating his recent benefactor Henry Morris and borrowing enough to last a week. Morris also promised to lend him considerably more, $1,500.00, as soon as the Central Bank opened its vaults in a week or so. After a phone call reassured RN that Dr. Noble and his wife Margery were safe and reunited in Walnut Creek, he sought out another acquaintance in Oakland, Arthur Breed, Sr., an Oakland real estate operator and partner in the firm of Breed and Bancroft Real Estate. Breed had earlier tried to convince RN to try his hand in real estate and the timing now seemed propitious.

Dr. Albert Noble needed quarters to replace his destroyed San Francisco offices, so RN's first assignment was to locate a place for the Doctor; he did so, at No 1 Telegraph Avenue in Oakland. Breed provided an office for RN to begin his real estate career and he joined the firm which was swamped with the demands of refugees from San Francisco for housing in the East Bay. On Sunday, April 22nd, RN returned to San Francisco, this time with his new associate, Arthur Breed, to examine the ruins from the earthquake.

On arrival, they went to the Shreve Building in an attempt to retrieve Dr. Noble's belongings in the lobby elevator and to inspect his offices on the sixth floor. RN described the new fire-proof Shreve Building as "a skeleton with the frames of floors and room walls which were fire-proof all in one place." The doors, door-stops, typewriter tables, and other office accoutrements, however, were all reduced to small piles of ashes. The structure had maintained its integrity but all contents were destroyed beyond recognition. Downstairs in the lobby, the two suitcases no longer sat in the elevator where Dr. Noble had left them on the morning of the quake. Vandals had relocated them to a spot in the rear of the lobby, slashed them open, and left the contents strewn about the floor. RN gathered Dr. Noble's belongings, which included six new shirtwaist dresses made by Margery, all in perfect condition save for a tiny burn mark on one. He theorized that the vandals had taken the suitcases to the rear of the lobby with the intent of stealing the contents. After throwing them about the floor area, they must have left. Shortly thereafter, the fire arrived and created such a strong up-draft through the elevator shafts that the adjacent rear lobby area was completely protected from the heat and nothing was damaged.

After leaving the Shreve Building, RN and Breed went to the home of Archibald Baldwin, President of the residential real estate firm, Baldwin and Howell. A friend of Breed's, Baldwin was so strapped for funds in the crisis that he borrowed $20.00 from him. From Baldwin's home they went to the Civic Center where RN marveled at the survival of the US Mint, the Post Office, and the Federal Court Building, all "boldly proclaiming their worth, intact but scarred."

To the west of Franklin, beyond the outer boundary of the fire, RN again noted the impressive generosity of victims. Residents prepared their meals on the street in improvised brick stoves. Denied access to their homes until electrical and chimney inspections were completed, residents were forced to live outdoors and RN and Breed were offered food and coffee by some who were willing to share their meager provisions.

RN's initial midnight visit to the wrecked and burning San Francisco lasted a day and a half. He toured the aftermath of the earthquake, helped where he could, and participated in one of the signal natural disasters of his lifetime. Within a week, he returned a second time with his new real estate associate to further explore the damage. He had at first been drawn to what he thought was a fire in Oakland and the prospects it might imply for his professional ambitions. He found a much larger catastrophe, encountering humanity under circumstances unlike any other he had experienced; he doubtless emerged a changed man after exposure to so many thousands of homeless, distraught and frightened people, all uncertain about what their futures held in store. For RN, such mass destruction and misfortune became a gateway to a new future as a financier, builder and developer.

The Palace Hotel burning just hours after RN's departure for the Shreve Building and points west. Courtesy OpenSFHistory.org

A view east down California Street showing lingering smoke. This is close to the view RN would have had climbing Nob Hill as the fire was beginning to spread. Courtesy OpenSFHistory.org

RIGHT 1906, PILLSBURY PICTURE CO,   PALACE HOTEL.

The Shreve Building looking northeast after the fire.
The damage that RN described can be seen clearly.
Courtesy OpenSFHistory.org

*Refugees curbside cooking on outdoor stoves,
managing the crisis as RN described.
Courtesy OpenSFHistory.org*

CHAPTER 8

A New Builder and a Real Estate Boom

History reports that the men who can manage men manage the men who can manage only things, and the men who can manage money manage all.
Will Durant—The Lessons of History

A great tragedy, loss of life, and thousands of disrupted lives were the preamble to RN's greatest professional accomplishments. From immediately after the San Francisco Earthquake and Fire of April 18, 1906, and for the next eight years, he prospered as a young, aggressive, smart, and shrewd builder throughout the Bay Area. In that very productive period of his life, between the ages of 29 and 37, he built hundreds of homes, commercial buildings, and hospitals and acquired thousands of acres of land throughout Contra Costa County. In accomplishing these things, he used borrowed money almost exclusively. He was not risk averse; nothing in his short life to that point would have developed that temperament in him. Everything he had touched, at least on his telling, had been successful. He always found sources of financing, usually older men impressed with his youthful enthusiasm, his track record and optimism, his vision of the future, and exceptional insight into what he felt were important real estate trends in the Bay Area.

Within a year and a month of the San Francisco Earthquake, in May of 1907, a national economic slowdown began. Prior to the 1913 legislation that created the Federal Reserve system, the United States had been without such a central monetary controlling agency for 77 years, a fact that contributed to many economic contractions and associated bank runs and failures. Today, as was the case then, our banking system runs on trust, the confidence in the mind of the depositor that his bank has sufficient funds to return his deposits if he wants them. If too many depositors want their money simultaneously, however, the typical bank cannot handle the demand and a run results.

In the basically agrarian economy of early 20th century America, a cycle of liquidity occurred each year in the large urban banks, in particular in New York. In the fall of each year, as harvests were sold, money flowed out of New York city banks to finance the sale of agricultural products, lowering the supply of funds in that city. In an effort to attract replacement funds, interest rates were increased and foreign funds poured in in response. This fluctuating supply of available money had serious implications for the health of the economy. This pattern in 1906 was exacerbated in the western part of the country by the San Francisco earthquake and fire in April which produced a greater than normal demand for money.

In 1906, the stock market, responding to an economic slowdown, began to correct early in the year and continued its downward course through mid-year. By July, the Dow Jones Industrial Average was down 18%, but then recovered almost half its losses by September. Additional vulnerability followed in the railroad sector when Congress passed legislation giving the Interstate Commerce Commission (ICC) power to set maximum rail rates, causing a decline in the railroad stock sector which contributed to a further 8% decline in the market. In March of the next year, an additional 10% decline in stocks occurred and by October, the month of the Panic of 1907, the market had declined by 24%.

The bank runs that became known collectively as the Panic of 1907 began in New York with an attempt to corner the market in the stock of the United Copper Company. The corner was an attempt by certain investors to acquire sufficient shares of the company's stock that they could manipulate the price. The scheme failed, but in collapsing it produced a number of runs on banks that had lent funds to the would-be manipulators. New York's third largest Trust Bank, The Knickerbocker Trust, went bankrupt and the resulting contagion swept up numerous other banks, trust banks, brokerages and financial intermediaries in the city and across the country. Disaster was averted by the leadership of J.P. Morgan and the intervention of the United States Treasury. Morgan, in his role as the city's most visible and famous banker, became personally involved, managing the crisis, and persuading other financial leaders to invest their money to keep the system afloat.

The resulting depression lasted for 13 months, from May of 1907 until June of 1908, a 33-month long contraction in business activity. According to the indexes in use for measurement at the time, the period saw a drop of 29% in economic activity. The failure in New York of the Knickerbocker and the spreading panic and loss of confidence all contributed to a decline in industrial production unprecedented in the history of bank runs. In 1907, the United States recorded the second highest level of bankruptcies in its history, production declined 11%, imports declined 26%, and unemployment increased to 8% from an earlier low of 3%.

Largely as a result of this contraction, a National Monetary Commission was formed in May of 1908, the purpose of which was to study the panic, the conditions underlying it, and to make recommendations for legislation to reduce the likelihood of recurrence. The Commission issued its report in early 1911, but it was not until December 31, 1913 that Congress finally passed the final enacting legislation, the Federal Reserve Act, ushering in the era of central banking that continues to this day.

***

As spring turned into summer in 1906, RN found himself heavily involved in his new profession. The offices of Breed and Bancroft in Oakland were awash with refugees from the earthquake, all seeking either to buy or rent housing in Oakland and Berkeley. As a new man in the firm, RN soon realized the disadvantage of not being familiar with the geography of his new territory as he competed with men experienced in the local market, and felt he might make better headway building speculative houses. To this end he asked Arthur Breed if he had any good lots for sale and was shown 40 lots on the east side of Telegraph Avenue between 44th and 45th Streets with an asking price of $20,000, $500 per lot.

RN offered to buy them all, subject to his ability to obtain financing for the project, which he described as a $500 down payment and additional weekly payments of $500 at which time the lots would each be released to him. Breed responded that such an offer was "impossible," to which response RN inquired if Breed was the owner or an agent. On learning that Breed was in fact only the owner's agent, RN suggested, "Then make my offer to the owner and tell him it figures he will be paid in full, in cash, in forty weeks..."

Shortly thereafter, Breed reported to RN that his offer was acceptable. Because all utilities (water, sewer, gas, electricity, and telephone service) were already installed, RN was able to begin construction immediately. All he lacked was capital. He had signed his note for $19,500, needed $500 more for his down payment, and additional funds for the construction financing of his 40 houses. He also had a need for cash to make his payrolls in Contra Costa County at the San Miguel Ranch. From his *Memoirs*, it appears that he had committed himself to the lot purchase without getting any of this financing in place and his first stop was Mr. H.C. Morris.

Giving his personal note to Morris, he secured $1,500 to handle the San Miguel payroll and the down payment on the Oakland lots. Securing office space in the McDonough Building in Oakland, on Broadway at 14th Street, he ordered business cards, stationary, a drafting table and tools. A local builder provided five suitable house plans at a price acceptable to RN and he contracted for the first five houses with everything lined up except the money to build the homes.

A contemporary reader will marvel at RN's boldness in making these commitments without any provision for construction financing, particularly given his relative lack of experience or track record in his new market. One hundred ten years later, the process would be just the reverse, if it occurred at all. But RN was nothing if not brash, and he was certainly confident of his ability to get things accomplished in his own way. So far, nothing had stopped him.

To arrange capital for building the homes contracted for, he headed to his home territory and presumably to investors who knew of him and his reputation. In Lafayette, he stopped his horse and buggy at the home of Mr. Peter Thompson, the local blacksmith. Thompson said he'd lend RN $10,000 on his personal note and would accept payment in land contracts. Today, land contracts, more commonly known as installment sales contracts, are not used as much as they were when RN began in real estate. They have been replaced in California and many other states by mortgages and deeds of trust in which a third-party lender retains legal title to a sold property until such time as the conditions of the sale have been completely met. In his day, RN would have made an installment sales contract with a buyer of one of his new houses and would retain legal title while the buyer would have equitable title and use of the home until all the terms were satisfied, usually after a ten-year period. Essentially, IOU's, committing to a series of payments, at a specified interest rate, and at named frequencies, these notes were negotiable instruments and could be sold to investors seeking an income stream. Thompson was agreeing to getting his loan back in the form of such sales agreements. They would be a critical component of RN's future capital raising strategies.

Having arranged for some of his construction financing, RN returned to his new office in Oakland and took out an advertisement in the Oakland Tribune promoting new homes for sale in the Telegraph Avenue neighborhood. He offered terms to prospective buyers of 10% down and monthly payments of 1% of the unpaid balance, including interest at 6%.

His relationship with H.C. Morris soon proved helpful again when Morris suggested they combine offices and cover for each other. Morris proposed that he would move into RN's new offices, provide furniture, pay half the office expenses, and cover for RN in his absence and RN would reciprocate. Shortly thereafter, Morris expanded his offer of collaboration in a significant way. He suggested that he would buy all RN's land contracts, as each house was sold, and would thereafter cover his construction financing, in return for 40% of the profits. Such a proposal was exactly what

RN needed to allow him to spend all his time on construction and sales, confident of his financing arrangements. The resulting partnership agreement created a company, R.N. Burgess & Co., which began business in early 1907, and specialized in speculative home building. The success of this venture soon manifested itself in a need for larger office space. New quarters in No. 1 Telegraph Avenue followed as did acquisition of a stenographer-bookkeeper and a building superintendent, the latter eliminating the need for outside builders. They were a completely self-contained shop, in a market with no shortage of demand, thanks to the earthquake and fire across the Bay.

RN's investment in the 40-lot subdivision on Telegraph Avenue was a good one. He reported that each house sold as soon as he completed its frame. Expanding his operation in the East Bay, he purchased lots in the Adams Point District, in Linda Vista, and in Piedmont. In addition, his land holdings in Contra Costa County at this time included 1,458 acres in Walnut Creek, and 20 acres each of hay land and orchard in Danville.

The dairying operation, however, was about to come to an end. After suffering the loss of his three largest hotel customers in the earthquake and fire, other customers in the East Bay provided some business but sales were down and RN must have felt he needed help in expanding the operation. His cousin, John E. Burgess of Kentville, Nova Scotia, had come west intending to get into dairying and RN arranged to build a facility in Oakland to support a new milk route. RN reported that the route initially prospered but that competition and labor problems plagued his cousin's efforts from the start.

Early one morning in the Linda Vista neighborhood, while John Burgess was in the rear of a customer's house making a delivery, his wagon and horse were attacked and his wagon was set afire. The horse panicked and ran down the street connected to a blazing dairy wagon. When John caught up to the wagon, it was destroyed and the horse in agony from burns. A policeman soon arrived and put the horse out of its misery, suggesting that this was the work of either a competitor or a union person who had poured coal oil over the wagon while John was in the rear of the customer's house.

The following morning, RN got a phone call from his attorney, Fred Wood, who asked him to come to his office as soon as possible. Wood, a former neighbor in Danville, had read of the incident through an account in the daily paper and wanted to know what RN planned to do about the matter, saying that "I have known you for some years and know about your gun-packing days." RN responded that he planned to purchase a replacement wagon and horse so John could resume his deliveries, except that from now on RN would be behind John on a motorcycle, "with my .44 caliber six-shooter along for our mutual protection." Attorney Wood responded that he was afraid of exactly that outcome and had asked RN to come in to try to persuade him to get out of the dairy business altogether. Suggesting to RN that, "You are surrounded by two of the toughest gangs in the Bay Area. Your lands are good and growing in value, and you are doing well in R.N. Burgess & Co. Ever since the earthquake and fire destroyed your San Francisco outlets you have had nothing but trouble, and there are a lot of others in the same business that are hunting for an outlet for their dairies (sic). Bob, just get rid of all that trouble and concentrate on your successful businesses." Apparently, RN was impressed with the advice because he sold the Oakland dairy within a week and began the process of selling his herd.

RNs chance meeting with Henry C. Morris in the summer of 1905 was an important encounter for him, producing as it did a relationship with a member of a prominent Oakland family and a source of financing for several years in the future. Morris, born in 1858, was 20 years RN's senior. The son of an Oakland lawyer and judge, Henry S. Morris, the younger Morris was impressed with RN's intelligence, drive, and track record and was willing to extend him credit. This confidence seemed only to grow with time and proximity and Morris was similar to many other older men at this stage of RN's life whose trust resulted in financing, opportunity, and additional relationships.

Henry C. Morris was appointed cashier of Central Bank in Oakland in July of 1901 at 43 years of age. Both he and his father were stockholders and directors of the Bank. The Oakland Tribune reported at the time of his appointment that he was "well and favorably known in financial circles." The Tribune's records reveal extensive mention of the Morris name, in particular in connection with social events, suggesting a prominent family in the community at the time. Such a relationship for RN produced more than financial credit however. It also led to relationships within that milieu which would have consequences throughout his life. [1]

The Morris's had family in Contra Costa County. Hiram Penniman of Walnut Creek was a cousin. Penniman had been an early customer of Burgess & Noble from whom RN bought numerous carloads of prunes and other farm products in the late 1890s. Another cousin of Morris's was Albert Mussey Johnson of Chicago. Johnson, the son of a successful Ohio businessman who later became wealthy in his own right, married Hiram Penniman's youngest daughter, Bessilyn. Johnson met Walter Edward Scott, Death Valley Scotty, when he and a business partner were approached by an intermediary with an offer, from Scott, to invest in a gold mine in Death Valley. The story of Scott's history as something of a swindler who for years tried to sell interests in this and other non-existent mines, as well as Johnson's apparently endless patience with him, has been well told. RN met Scott, apparently through Johnson, but reported in his *Memoirs* that he never visited the famous Scotty's Castle. The Morris, Johnson, and Death Valley Scotty connection is given space in the *Memoirs* for reasons that are not entirely clear; RN was not a business associate of the eccentric Chicago millionaire, nor of Scott's. And his account of Scott's life and that of Johnson is flawed in several aspects, including the death of Bessilyn in a train accident in 1899, possibly due to the passage of so much time between the early Morris relationship and the date of writing the *Memoirs.*

RN made references to Walter Johnson as being "Scotty's gold mine," and suggested that Morris served the same role for Johnson. Johnson, a seemingly tireless investor in Scotty's schemes,

[1] Central Bank's New Cashier Henry C. Morris Will Take the place of the Late Charles Yates," Oakland Tribune, 29 July 1901.

supported him, and his son and wife, for most of their lives but never realized any profit from his investments. How Johnson was in this role with Henry Morris of Oakland is not made clear in RN's recollections.

RN's association with Morris, however, is very clear from his writing. Morris provided financing and contacts to a young man in whom he had confidence and apparently boundless trust. On one occasion, shortly after the start of their collaboration, Morris planned a trip east with his wife. Indicating that "There are between two and three hundred thousand in negotiable securities there that I use when needed to borrow at the bank. If you see something that you wish to buy and need additional money you may use these securities as collateral," Morris handed RN the key to his safe. This episode reveals a remarkable level of trust in RN on the part of a man who had known him only a few years. The ability, in his early years, to inspire such confidence was one of his most valuable characteristics.

That the Morris relationship was also social is indicated by an anecdote about a birthday dinner given Morris by his family at their home. Probably his 50th, it was an elaborate affair in which the main course was duck. RN, displaying characteristic eagerness to be seen as socially adept, related that he was able to provide the ducks because of his membership in the Volante Duck Club of Suisun Bay. As a member and as a young man about town, a "Club Man," he was accustomed to going with his club mates to the San Francisco French Restaurant Marchants with their partially dressed ducks, which would then be dressed for consumption by the restaurant. During these visits, he was exposed to the correct techniques for carving ducks, so it was with some pride that he agreed to that task at the Morris birthday when asked. His lengthy description of his process of correctly carving eight ducks, without spilling a drop on the white table cloth speaks volumes about his identification and appreciation for the finer things in life among the smart set of early 20th century San Francisco.

As 1907 drew to a close the effects of the recession of 1907-08 were being felt throughout the nation. In the Bay Area, money was scarce and increasingly difficult to obtain, particularly in the business of speculative home building. RN reported that his lots and homes were almost all sold off in Oakland and that it seemed to be the wise thing to do to slow down a bit. He described the derision he received from one of his competitors, John McGregor, who laughed when RN told him he was slowing down. McGregor, who had gone out of business in an earlier building boom, told him that "It takes courage to be a speculative builder." RN seemed to take some pleasure in reporting shortly thereafter that McGregor also went under, for a second time.

The banking panics of the pre-Federal Reserve days were frightening affairs. Street rumors might be stimulated by nothing more than unusually long lines at a particular bank. The rumors fed the fear which in turn produced more rumors, sometimes becoming self-fulfilling prophesies. In 1907 the R.N. Burgess & Co. borrowed $50,000 from the Union National Bank of Oakland. Morris became suspicious about the bank on seeing long lines at the teller window on a routine visit. With an outstanding loan, their firm was at risk of losing the use of that money in the event the bank got into trouble and was forced to suspend operations. Under the rules of a suspension, a borrower could not use any funds in its checking account and the bank would be able to demand immediate payment of their loan. Even if a payment demand was not received, funds in a frozen checking account could be tied up for years pending the liquidation of the assets of the bank.

Morris' experience and awareness of these conditions led him to suggest to RN that he go immediately to the bank and repay the recent loan. Using language that conveys the urgency of the situation in his mind, he said, "Burgess, I wish you would take a check for $50,000 and go to the bank and look carefully at the cashier's face and others, and if you feel as I do, that they are under a considerable strain, go to the note teller's window and tell him we wish to pay our note." On arrival at the bank, RN saw lengthening lines and, sensing that all was not well, proceeded to repay the loan. Henry Morris, by virtue of his earlier banking experience at Central Bank in Oakland, thus brought invaluable experience and knowledge to their partnership, in this instance saving them $50,000.

Morris was about to leave the partnership, however, having decided to get back into the banking industry. An opportunity to buy a controlling interest in the Central Bank was the catalyst behind this change and Morris suggested to RN that he could have a job as bank cashier under Morris's presidency. RN declined the offer, not attracted to the life and perhaps growing weary of the Morris relationship. "He was inclined to be possessive. He would take me to the cafeteria for lunch every day and occasionally to San Francisco to dinner. He would offer me a cocktail. He did not drink. He would order cigars for me. He did not smoke. I was having my fling under safe supervision." The evidence suggests that RN was souring on an early mentor and benefactor, perhaps not surprising given his independent streak and desire to control his own destiny.

With Morris headed in a different direction, RN was shortly to be on his own, without the experience and background of an experienced former banker in his shop. He was also in debt, owing $50,000 to several banks, but most to a bank headed by Phillip E. Bowles. Bowles was President of at least three banks (The American National Bank of San Francisco, The First National Bank of Oakland, and the First Trust and Savings Bank of Oakland) and it is not clear to which of the Bowles banks RN's debt was owed at the time, but Phillip Bowles figures in RN's life on several occasions, both as a lender and as a competitor in land acquisitions in later years. He was the son of a California pioneer family and was born in Arcata, Humboldt County. His father and mother had arrived in San Francisco by schooner in 1850 and settled on the north coast from where Joseph Bowles operated a business supplying mining camps and Indian settlements. After his death during P.E. Bowles' infancy, the family relocated to San Francisco where young Bowles spent his youth. He graduated from U.C. Berkeley in 1882, a member of the largest graduating class in the history of the University to that time. His marriage in 1883 to Mary McNear was fortuitous in that it promised access to the family and associates of his new father-in-law, George McNear. Known as the

"Grain King," McNear was the largest shipper of grain on the west coast and a former adversary to RN as we saw during his Hookston Ranch days.

RN's characterization of Bowles as a "likable but ruthless fellow," who, "if you beat him at his own game he would laugh... on the other hand, if he put anything over on you he would laugh twice," hints at a strong desire not to be beholden to him. Searching for a mechanism to get out of his debt, RN embarked on a new strategy in which he solicited people with whom he had long-standing relationships and tried to persuade them to trade their savings passbooks for his loans. With the Panic of 1907 recent and bank safety a major concern, his pitch to convert savings accounts to loan paper might be persuasive. He drove in a new automobile, his first, purchased at year-end 1907, out to Contra Costa County calling first on Peter Thompson. Thompson owned a passbook saving account with $7,000 in it and was willing to exchange it for one of RN's loans with a face value of $7,600, giving his personal note for the $600 difference.

His next prospect was John Baldwin who had $10,000 in the Oakland Bank of Savings and was also willing to make the exchange. Next, he called on Mrs. Numa Boone (her husband figured prominently in RN's later sheep ranching venture in New Mexico) who had a $40,000 savings account and committed to thinking about his proposition. After she had done so she also committed to taking $36,000 of his notes in return for her passbook. Apparently in her case, the rate on the mortgages was sufficiently high (RN reported that 8% was a typical rate) that she could do better even though the face value of the mortgages was $4,000 lower than what she had in the bank because RN reported that "no notes were required."

These actions on RN's part present an interesting window on both the times and on his personality. He was in effect selling his notes by suggesting that the risk of bank failures was greater than the risk of default on his mortgages. He was taking advantage of the economic uncertainty which must have been on his prospect's minds after recurring bank failures, and during a serious economic recession. Such creativity would be tightly controlled today, but in the early 20th Century few of today's regulations concerning mortgages were in effect and his entrepreneurial instincts were unimpeded by such rules.

RN's next step was to go to the banks involved and tender the passbooks in payment of his firm's debts and he recorded some interesting dialogue with several of the officers of these banks. At Oakland Bank of Savings, he presented John Baldwin's passbook representing $10,000 of savings and reported that the bank president, William W. Garthwaite, was "highly indignant." Garthwaite's inference was that RN's conduct in seeking these trades was unethical. Typically, rising to the banker's challenge, RN responded that "it was more ethical than a bank president agreeing to take mortgages when the notices of completion were filed, then to back out when a panic came along." Garthwaite ultimately accepted the Baldwin passbook in settlement of RN's $10,000 obligation and he closed his account at that bank.

Notwithstanding RN's characterization of Bowles, the banker's response was much friendlier than that of Garthwaite. Apparently not sharing the reservations of the president of the Oakland Bank of Savings, Bowles asked if RN had any more such passbooks, offering to buy them all out at face value. To RN's concerns that the others were not all written against his bank, Bowles said it didn't matter provided they were issued by a good bank. With his sights on opening an office in San Francisco, RN was pleased at Bowles' response. As president of the American National Bank there, Bowles would be well positioned to help him. The exchange was made and the R.N. Burgess Co was in what RN described as a comfortable position, having disposed of most if not all of its debt.

As 1908 began RN was developing a track record, with business and banking relationships in both San Francisco and Oakland. His business was profitable, he had cash reserves earning interest income at 8%, and he was looking to expand further. To do so he began calling on architects, one of whom was Julia Morgan. By 1907-08, Julia Morgan had been practicing architecture in the Bay Area four years. As the first woman licensed in her profession in

California in 1904 and as a graduate of both U.C. Berkeley and the Ecole des Beaux-Arts in Paris, Morgan was becoming well-known for her distinctive style, integration of site and landscape, use of native materials, and her employment of local artists and craftsmen in the work. When the earthquake and fire occurred, the lack of damage to her Mills College Tower, El Campanil, reflected advanced knowledge of the use of reinforced concrete and added to her reputation, producing many commissions for her and ultimately great wealth.

The *Memoirs* are unclear as to exactly when RN began to build houses for Morgan. The evidence suggests it was probably in 1908 as business activity began to pick up after the recession of 1907-8. In any event, he reported building five of her homes and commented upon his experience working with her in a complimentary manner, saying that when she said " 'tear it out and do it right,' there was no arguing with her." In the not too distant future, they would share an important client, William Randolph Hearst. Morgan had begun working with Hearst after an introduction by his Mother, Phoebe Apperson Hearst. She had worked closely with Mrs. Hearst during their collaboration on the University of California Master Plan.

RN's success in selling or trading his purchase money mortgages drew him into the mortgage sale business more actively and it became a mechanism for turning his receivables into ready cash to finance continued building. A result of this activity was the establishment of a new customer for his loans, Mrs. Lafayette I. Fish. Mrs. Fish, the widow of a prominent early Contra Costa County pioneer, Lafayette Fish, who had passed away in 1900, was a regular buyer of loans from RN. He reported showing her other property, the loans on which were available for purchase, including a large commercial building, the Lyon Van and Storage Company, on which she purchased a $40,000 note. She bought this note from him and, in passing, mentioned that she had plans ready for bid on a new home at a lot at 2325 Piedmont Avenue in Berkeley. On his request to prepare a bid, she said she would direct her architect to send him a set of plans at the appropriate time. On his receipt of the plans he submitted his bid and won the job. The home he built still stands today as the home of the Pi Phi sorority at the University of California, Berkeley. His work on that job brought him into a closer relationship with Frances Webster Fish, her daughter Anne Holcomb Webster Fish, and her son Irving Webster Fish. The home would be his first home with his new wife, Anne Webster Fish.

***

RN's experiences in selling his receivables as a means of obtaining consistent and regular capital for his growing building business led him to contemplate both his future in Oakland and a more formal corporate structure than what he had been using. In his late twenties, unmarried, living in Oakland at the Athenian Nile club, he was troubled by both the East Bay location of his prime business interests and the structure of that business as a capital-raising entity. Real estate and land development activities are inherently capital dependent. A builder, and RN was not exceptional in this regard, borrowed cash to acquire land and to buy the materials and labor required to build the property. A business so dependent on borrowed funds was at serious risk when such funds were no longer available. The Panic of 1907 had exposed him to such conditions when savings banks, building and loan associations, and insurance companies restricted their lending, necessitating his going to friends and acquaintances seeking to exchange their saving passbooks for his receivables. Such financing strategies, exchanging passbooks for loans and selling loans to a few local investors, were not sustainable and could not be scaled up in a way consistent with his ambitions. A more formal structure was needed which would systematize his capital recycling objectives.

He also had a sense that, for his primary building activity, he was on the wrong side of the Bay. He had clearly experienced success in the years following the earthquake and fire, but the financing worries troubled him as did a nagging feeling that his future lay in San Francisco. With the earthquake and fire damage providing an almost endless source of demand, subject only to the availability of financing, he could build in that city for a long time. He also began dreaming about the future of his home county. He felt that if demand for housing in Oakland could be partially redirected to central Contra Costa County, and if some of the workers in the new industrial facilities being built along the county's north shore could be persuaded to commute from Walnut Creek, a significant market would exist for building on the land he was assembling in that area.

His land ownership in Contra Costa County expanded substantially during the years of 1908-1910 as RN made two large acquisitions. These included the 3,700-acre Foskett and Elworthy ranch in two parcels in Concord, between the Sacramento River and Mt Diablo, and the 1,750-acre Rice property in Walnut Creek. He purchased the Rice ranch in the spring of 1908 from Xarissa Rice and the Foskett and Elworthy property in October of 1910. [2]

His purchase of the Rice property is worthy of examination because of his approach to the transaction. In the spring of 1908, when he encountered Tom Rice on the San Miguel ranch, RN was still not on good terms with Xarissa Rice. Her denial of his request to allow his threshing unit to cross her land in 1905 had created a riff that still existed. Rice told RN that he was one of four heirs who owned the property. He had two sisters, one of whom was Xarissa, and one brother. Tom Rice controlled 57% of the property, another brother and sister controlled 29%, and Xarissa had 14% of the ownership of the 1,750-acre ranch. Tom explained that all the siblings, except Xarissa, wanted to sell the ranch, but hadn't been able to come up with a plan to convince their sister. Everyone except Xarissa had agreed that a sale for $75,000, with $25,000 down and balance payable in three years at 6% interest would be acceptable.

RN advised Tom that "I will purchase the place on those terms if you can make delivery soon." Rice demurred, saying he didn't know how he might handle his sister Xarissa's objections. In RN's

---

[2] Edna May Andrews and Janet Settle, Arlis Harmon, and Takako Endo, *History of Concord, Its Progress and Promise,* Concord Historical Society, Concord, California, 1986.

account, he explained to Tom what was obvious to him, that Xarissa's problem was that she was frightened and uncertain about her future. Her Walnut Creek home was the only one she had known and a sale implied more uncertainty and stress than she could manage. If the family had a reunion, hosted by Tom in his Southern California home, and also presented a credible plan to Xarissa for her future she might be persuaded to sell. Further, RN explained, Xarissa resented the fact that Tom had never invited his sister to his home in Oxnard, and a reunion there might help the siblings reach an agreement. He continued, advising Tom on how this might work, "Make it a jolly occasion, and after dinner consider the sale, but not until you have worked out an inviting future for your sister. Remember, her vision is limited to the boundary of Walnut Creek."

On Tom Rice's acceptance of his idea, RN further suggested a mechanism through which the sale could be effectuated. After a reunion dinner and after assuring Xarissa of a future, Tom was to write out a wire to RN, detailing all the terms of the Rice family's offer of sale. RN requested that the wire be written with all the deal terms they had discussed, signed by each of the siblings with their signature as it would appear on a deed. Under these conditions, RN said that he would "guarantee the sale of your ranch."

The wire arrived, but it was unsigned. On being advised by a notary that he couldn't notarize an unexecuted document, RN returned to Western Union and sought the agent's signature to dispel the notion that he (RN) had typed out the agreement on a blank telegraph form. The Western Union agent finally signed the document and the notary vouched for it. The head of the title company, attorney George Rogers, soon thereafter advised RN that the unsigned document would, at minimum, cloud the title until such time as an agreement between the parties might be reached.

With this in mind, RN then proceeded to the Bank of Martinez, the president of which, W.S. Tinning, was also his attorney, advising Tinning that he was going to give a draft (an order for the bank to pay on his account) for $25,000 to the bank cashier. He then asked that Tinning instruct the cashier to put $25,000 in gold coins in a tray, and be prepared to display it to attorney Jim Stow, Xarissa's lawyer, when he came to the bank the following week. RN wanted the cashier to demonstrate to Stow that the funds were available for the down payment on the ranch under the terms of the deal as agreed.

On the appointed day, RN was at the bank when attorney Stow arrived with his client Xarissa Rice, and indicated that she was unwilling to go through with the deal. As arranged, the cashier arrived and, as instructed, announced that he had RN's $25,000 ready and would make the down payment. Just as RN indicated that he was ready to execute the agreement, another man, unknown to the others in the room, interrupted the proceedings, calling out, "Mr. Burgess, my clients have notified me to go ahead and purchase the 1,750 acres for $125,000." After dismissing the "stranger," RN announced to attorney Stow, "Jim, there seems nothing left for me but to sue you and Xarissa for $50,000 damages." Stow's reply was his capitulation, "No Bob, you win. Get the papers ready and we will put them in escrow."

This series of events, commencing with RN's suggesting to Tom Rice how he might gain the acceptance of his sister to a sale that she had no interest in undertaking, and ending with RN's arranging for a man, posing as a buyer, unknown to the parties in the meeting at the bank, suggests an approach to business both bold and somewhat devious under the circumstances. It is tempting to judge historical characters in the light of contemporary standards, but such assessments should be cautiously made. RN was a man of his times, and his times, in early 20th century California were unabashedly aggressive in the business practices being pursued. One is, however, struck by his brashness, as a 30-year old, in advising an older Tom Rice as to the best way to solve an obviously internal family matter. And the use of a "shill" in a charade suggesting that RN had an offer on the property, for $50,000 more than he was about to pay, seems even more aggressive on his part. His apparent pride in this transaction, however, belies any sense of his behavior being outside normal practices, and rather emphasizes the creativity and chutzpah he brought to the situation.

***

With the Rice and Foskett properties and his acreage at San Miguel, a little in Danville, and a few leases remaining at Hookston, RN reported that he had assembled 7,000 acres on which to pursue his land development and subdivision plans in Contra Costa County. More land would be purchased within a few years but more pressing needs, involving the availability of financing, drew his attention to his business in Oakland and San Francisco.

A growing inventory of land in Contra Costa County, aggressive building plans for post-earthquake San Francisco, and his continuing financing challenges coalesced into a plan that promised to eliminate his periodic capital-starvation problem. He reasoned that if he could determine a way to continually recycle his receivables, he would never run out of cash. But to do this he needed to create a more formal structure, one that would be acceptable to investors. His solution was to create two companies, one a building company, and the other a mortgage company. As properties were developed and sold, the loans for each would be sold to the mortgage company, providing a ready and consistent supply of cash. The mortgage company, in turn, would deposit the loans in a trust company and create certificates of participation against 90% of the value of each loan. The trust company would certify the 90% proportion, thereby rendering the certificates marketable to investors.

After discussions with his attorneys and with possible trust banks, RN proceeded to incorporate the R. N. Burgess Company. His capital structure, the securities he sold to obtain operating funds, included $1,000,000 of participating preferred stock and $1,000,000 of common stock and he put into this company all his assets. These included his ranch property, all buildings, and the assets of his insurance business. Selling the common and preferred shares provided cash for the operations of the business. The key to his plan was the regular and consistent sale of his loans, and to that end he incorporated the R.N. Burgess Mortgage Company, capitalizing it at $1,000,000. This company would purchase the loans, deposit them with a trust bank, and issue the participation certificates for up to 90% of their face value. The last step was the creation of a sales force to actively sell the certificates to investors.

Before that, however, he needed to establish his banking relationships, secure a credit line, and identify a trust bank. His relationships helped him get started on these tasks and his first thought was Phillip E. Bowles at American National Bank in San Francisco. He held off on contacting Bowles, though, feeling that he ought to do more due diligence on competing banks before he finalized a commitment. The Mercantile National Bank was highly recommended and they had a sister trust bank, a separate corporate entity, which would facilitate the implementation of his idea with a single financial institution. In particular, John McKee, Vice President, was recommended to RN and he met with McKee who seemed impressed with his plans and offered him a $75,000 credit line, conditioned on his relocating to San Francisco and committing to work on the restoration of the destroyed areas of the City.

After securing McKee's approval, he called on Mercantile's trust officer who also approved of his idea and agreed to prepare a draft trust agreement and the participation certificates for RN's legal review. He also engaged office space in San Francisco, in the First National Bank building at the intersection of Market, Montgomery, and Post Streets. His new office would be on the third floor and improvements were begun with occupancy scheduled for ten days later. His plan to relocate to San Francisco was now committed and he moved into the new offices in November 1908.

One of his first clients in the City was none other than Dr. John McNutt for whom RN had been so helpful on April 18th, 1906 in the face of all the terror and destruction of the earthquake and fire. Dr. McNutt had a lot on Jones Street and wanted RN's help in building a new hospital. He had in mind a 90-bed, reinforced concrete hospital for which he also needed financing.

***

An earlier look at RN's social life, in particular during his Hookston Ranch period, revealed a young bachelor, working hard, but also enjoying an active social life. It's as if he was making up for the years as a poor farm boy on the homestead in Danville, when farm work, daily school and weekly Sunday School both under the direction of A.J. Anderson, consumed all of his hours, leaving very little in the way of social activity and the interpersonal relations to which by nature he was attracted. His descriptions of his activities entertaining prominent local business men at his camp-outs in the foothills of Mt. Diablo, learning to carve duck at upscale French restaurants in San Francisco, or entertaining young ladies at Enrico Caruso opera performances, portray an interest in the finer things in life, so absent during his childhood period.

Early in 1908, RN, a bachelor almost thirty years of age, lived in the Athenian Club in Oakland. At the intersection of 14th Street and Franklin, the Athenian Club was the address of choice of young and upwardly mobile professional men. Patterned after San Francisco's Bohemian Club, it was Oakland's most prestigious gentlemen's club, counting among its membership many of Oakland's elites. It was the kind of gathering place that an ambitious young man would seek to be associated with, providing access, otherwise denied to an outsider, to prominent men in the east bay's social and economic setting.

RN's description of his life at the Club reveals his place in a world long gone and perhaps something of his pride in his situation. He described his butler in the Club as his "mentor," who, when messages were left for RN, would offer comments and suggestions as to appropriate social connections for the young man. "There is an invitation for youse to go to dinner, but they are not the right people, so I said I would tell you but thought youse had a previous engagement." RN's reaction to this provides insight into his agenda at the time. "At first I resented his management, but soon found out he had many years in such service and knew the social strata of Oakland much better than I." On one occasion, upon receipt of an invitation to tea, the instruction was, "Those are the right people, so I laid out your clothes and put the links in your cuffs. Youse shower and dress, and I will be back a little later and look youse over."

RN's recollections of this club experience are humorous, and reveal a self-assessment elevating him comfortably into the social setting he aspired to associate with. "Well, girls, my advice to you is not to marry a club man – they are almost sure to be spoiled. I was invited to join the Oakland Cotillion that winter and did, and met many nice people, including the Chickerings, Olivers, Walshes, Burnhams, Barrys, and many others." Precisely who "the girls" to whom these remarks were directed is never made clear, though his daughters seem the likely audience, but the contacts and associations made were important to a young man on his way up in a world in which he was not native.

RN's Memoirs are almost totally silent about his relationship with women during his youth and young manhood. His descriptions of his social life, however, suggest that this was an important part of his life and it is not unreasonable to think that his Presbyterian reserve was responsible for this silence. The few exceptions to this are interesting, though.

Recalling his brief encounter with Mrs. Flournoy and her gift of the $5 gold piece on the morning of his departure from Bonny Vista on his birthday in 1895, reveals a wider network of family, friends, and acquaintances which might have been a catalyst for his early relationships with women. Mrs. Flournoy and her husband had three daughters, Laura, Dora, and their oldest who is unnamed by RN. This unnamed older daughter married Tom Rice, RN's frequently-described business associate. Apparently, Rice, who was from Oxnard in Southern California, came into the Danville community through this marriage and ultimately acquired a large block of local land as we have seen. This was the Rice ranch, the purchase of which has been described.

In the *Memoirs*, RN mentioned his Mother's opinion of the girls he was seeing in his youth, indicating the importance to her of both religion and his choice of women. He recalled "I had once escorted a girl home when Mother did not approve, so at a Wednesday Prayer Meeting she headed me off and said, 'I wish you to escort your Sunday-School teacher home, Laura Flournoy.' " Laura Flournoy was a generation ahead of RN, but he apparently thought highly of her, indicating that, "I was glad to be her escort on every available occasion until I left home in 1895."

A little more than four years later, in June of 1899, he was escorting Blanche Rice when a humorous incident occurred at Mills College. The College, founded in Benicia in 1852, had been relocated to Oakland some 18 years earlier by its owners Susan Tolman Mills and her husband Cyrus Mills. Susan T. Mills must have been an impressive woman, serving as the school's Principal for 20 years, and then becoming President of the College, a position she held for 19 more years.

On the June afternoon in 1899 when RN arrived at the campus, he was calling on Blanche Rice. Tom Rice's daughter was then an undergraduate student at Mills and would have been an eligible prospect for RN. As he drove his wagon up to the hitching rail in the front of the College, he was accosted by none other than Mrs. Mills herself, by then in her ninth year as the President of the school. In his account of the episode, she immediately began to challenge him on his arrangement of the tack on his horse's head. Saying, "Young man, how dare you drive in here with your horses' heads checked up so tightly," she immediately began to adjust the check reigns so as to loosen them. RN, knowing he was driving a team of mean and dangerous horses, tried to stop her. But Mrs. Mills was adamant, asking him if he didn't know that "a horse won't hurt you if you are kind to him." This scene is striking. RN was a 21-year-old man, who had grown up on a farm and knew horses and their temperament well through years of exposure and trial, was being accosted by an academic woman, who, in his estimation was all of five feet four inches tall, weighing about 110 pounds. Mrs. Mills impressed him, however, "What she lacked in size she made up in courage," and they soon got down to the purpose of his visit.

She asked him what he wanted on the campus, to which he replied that he had "driven about forty miles that day for the purpose of calling on Blanche Rice." Giving him direction as to how to proceed, she then suggested that if he intended to take Blanche for a drive, he should take care to return her and exit the College gate before 5pm, as it was locked on the inside at that time, precluding his departure. And then, with "the suggestion of a smile," she advised him that if he was indeed late, and locked in, that he should "take a good look at the gate." In fact, he was late in returning Blanche and found it necessary to inspect the gate as instructed by Mrs. Mills. Finding a flaw in the mechanism, he let himself and his team out and was on his way.

These anecdotes suggest a man who reflected the Victorian ethic of his parents, but who also, because of his intense focus on pulling himself up in the world, was at least as interested in his work as he was in women. This would change in 1908-09 after his introduction to Mrs. Lafayette Fish and her daughter Anne. While a resident of the Athenian Club, a growing part of his social scene were Sunday night dinners at the Fish home in Berkeley. He described these dinners as involving several regulars, including Anne and her mother, a professor of Theology from U.C. Berkeley named Dr. Bodie, a jeweler from San Francisco described as a pleasant gentleman, and RN. Initially, he mistakenly thought that Anne was engaged to the professor from Berkeley or at least felt her mother would be pleased with such a union. He described spending Saturday afternoons with Anne when she would meet him, driving her Stanhope (buggy) and spirited blacks down Piedmont Ave to their appointed meeting place. He characterized Anne as a "striking and able horsewoman" with a "tall, straight figure." His description of her dress sounds very much like the early 20th century wear seen in photos of that era. "She would often have on a leghorne (plaited straw) hat with a wide brim, and a yard of ostrich feathers." Also, "she could handle that team...I believe she delighted in taking the corners on two wheels, to her mother's horror."

Almost 31years old in January of 1909, RN's writing conveys a sense of needing something else in his life. As he described it, Mrs. Fish had taken ill in the spring of 1908 and her Daughter Anne was monitoring the finishing work on the Piedmont Avenue home. This put him into a working relationship with Anne, which, in combination with the Saturday buggy drives around Oakland, must have ignited a spark of something more than just business in his mind.

Perhaps it was love, or some minor ailment, but when he began feeling unwell, RN took the night train south to Los Angeles for a consultation with Dr. Visher, a German specialist on stomach disorders. He described his condition on the train going south as troubled and out of sorts, not only physically, but also emotionally. He slept very little, apparently troubled by something, but something not immediately apparent to him. On further reflection, he decided that his problem was that he was lonely and that the life of a bachelor was growing stale. His recent hours with Anne Fish were having an impact and he realized he was falling in love with her. "Anne's bright, cheerful and intelligent outlook on life left me longing for her companionship. I soon realized I was in love with her - a love I have held fast to all these years."

On arrival in Los Angeles, he went immediately to the best jeweler he could find. Ordering a gold breast-pin with figures of two dancing horses embedded, he mailed it home to her with a brief note. In his account of his actions on that day, he said he had at first been hesitant about the best way to proceed in light of his feelings, finally deciding, as he put it, that "'Faint Heart Never Won Fair Lady,' and I would boldly court the lady I loved." He sent her a second note expressing again his deep feelings for her and indicating that on arrival home he would advise her so in person and propose marriage.

Prior to his departure from the Bay Area, Anne had requested that he make time in his visit south to meet with her cousin Leila Webster and he made arrangements for this call after his correspondence with Anne. He called Cousin Leila and asked if she'd like to take an afternoon drive with him. Calling at their home, he met Leila and her Mother Aunt Nettie, both for the first time. He described his choice of conversation topics as very limited as he had only one subject on his mind at that point, her cousin Anne. He didn't tell Leila why he was so focused on Anne, but described himself as talking on endlessly about her and in the process created a lifelong friendship with the cousin.

After returning to Oakland, he called on Anne but before he could get his proposal out she interrupted, advising him that he ought not to try to see her, or to call her for two weeks, indicating rather enigmatically that "When I am ready for you to call, I will let you know." Long before the expiration of two weeks, however, she contacted him, but with an emergency, not what he was expecting. Anne had only one sibling, a younger brother, Irving Fish. Anne's early call to RN had been prompted by Irving's getting into trouble with one of his cousins, a "gay blade," as RN described him. Just what the trouble was is not mentioned, but it was serious enough that he was placed in the county jail in Martinez for his offense. Anne, quite upset, was seeking RN's help and advice under the circumstances.

In writing his recollections of this event years later, RN admitted to some imaginative reconstruction as to her motivations in reaching out to him. He ruminated about her calling one or more of the Sunday night dinner guests at the Fish home prior to placing a call to him. He speculated that if she had spoken to Dr. Bodie from the University first he might have counseled her to see the Chief of Police of Berkeley. The other gentleman, the man from San Francisco, would have offered similar advice. But if he felt he might have been third or fourth on her list, he was not unsure of the course of action he would counsel. "I will be off in my auto in ten minutes. I am going to Martinez and bring Irving home with me. I know Sheriff Veale. I controlled the deciding vote for his first nomination, and I am a deputy sheriff at large. Sheriff Veale will release Irving in my custody. If you wish to go along put on a warm coat and soft hat, and I will stop for you in twenty minutes."

Sheriff R.R. Veale was an institution in Contra Costa County. Its longest serving sheriff, he was elected for the first time in 1894 and continued to serve for four decades. RN's relationship with the Sheriff dated to the 1890's when Veale appointed him a sheriff's deputy in 1894 and continued until well into the 1930s as evidenced by correspondence from RN to the sheriff in August of 1934. In this hand-written letter, RN asked for the sheriff's intervention in a minor matter involving road frontage along his and a neighbor's street. In the note, RN reminds Veale that his was the deciding vote in Veale's first election back in 1894, in what was apparently a tie-breaker situation. [3]

The trip was a success. Irving was released, restitution for his offense was arranged, and no charge was filed against him. RN's sense of drama is on display in this episode once more. His rumination, daydreams about Anne's priority of individuals she would call on for help, are one of the very few times in his *Memoirs* he provides an interior view of himself. His love for Anne, his intentions for her, and his typical sense of the dramatic all coalesce in this anecdote about the rescue of Irving from the Martinez jail. His propensity to move, to swift forceful action in a situation where others might have counseled a more modest approach, are revealing, as is his evident pride at being able to tell Anne that he knew the sheriff personally, had done him a favor, years earlier and that he could be counted on to provide a quick and successful outcome to Anne's problem. The relationship with Anne thus moved to a new level; RN, in positioning himself as a heroic, well-connected man of action and effecting the release of Irving, doubtless showed Anne a part of him that she liked. He reported numerous Sunday evening visits to her and her mother over the course of the next several weeks in January and early February 1909 and finally, after securing her mother's permission, they became engaged at the end of February, 1909.

The wedding, scheduled for July 20 of that year, is memorialized in a photograph taken on the front lawn of the new Piedmont Avenue home. The photo, situated so as to reflect a late July afternoon with the subjects facing west towards the Bay, reveals thirteen guests dressed in their formal best in the style of early 20th century America. Anne and RN are positioned in the center of a line of eleven other guests, mostly couples, all the siblings and spouses of Ann's mother, Frances Webster Fish. Later in the day, before the new couple had left the party, they were startled by

---

[3] Letter to Sheriff R.R. Veale from R.N. Burgess, 25 August 1934. Collection of Contra Costa County Historical Society, Martinez, California.

raucous laughter emanating from the front lawn and a summons to come out quickly. They were surprised to find on the lawn a large bail of oat hay and a deliveryman awaiting his payment for a COD delivery. As RN stepped up to pay the driver, he noticed the hay-bail had been addressed and that it was directed to Anne. The accompanying sign indicated that the bail contained, "All of Bob's wild oats."

A curious aspect of the wedding is that there is no mention of RN's mother and father in attendance, nor are any in evidence in the admittedly rather meager photographic record. RN's father lived until 1935; though he does not mention it in the *Memoirs*, his mother passed away in 1920, eleven years after his marriage to Anne. Both still living, presumably they would have been in attendance as might some of his siblings, but the *Memoirs* and the photos contain no mention of them on this important day in RN's life.

The *Memoirs* describes the honeymoon they took and includes anecdotes which again reveal much about RN's approach to problem solving, this time on a personal basis. Their honeymoon took them to the Pacific Northwest, to the 1909 World's Fair in Seattle, to Vancouver, and on to Lake Crescent in the Olympic Mountains on the Olympic peninsula. On their first day in Portland, in the Portland Hotel breakfast room, Anne set a rule of married life that RN claimed he never afterward violated. Arriving at breakfast with a newspaper, he was greeted by Anne's comment, "Robb, if you wish to read at the table, always bring two papers." And RN, speaking again in the *Memoirs* to the "girls" he addressed in his recollections of the Athenian Club experience, commented, "Girls - that is one of the bad habits club men have."

At their destination, a lodge in the Olympic Mountains, a location reached only after a long, arduous journey by steamer, stagecoach, and motorboat, Anne was tired and not pleased with the somewhat primitive accommodations. Anne Fish, in RN's description, was a beautiful woman, though not possessed of stamina or robust health. These characteristics are the subject of numerous comments in the *Memoirs*. In the mountain lodge, their rooms were decorated in a rough finish and were on the second floor, with very little in the way of insulation between the floors. After a day of fishing with an Indian guide, RN returned to find Anne quite upset. The cause of her concern was her apprehension that some of the other guests, in particular a group of four women older than she, had been talking about them behind their backs. Apparently, Anne perceived that their new clothing, suitcases, and manner were telegraphing an unflattering picture to the other guests.

Being disinclined to give up his five days of fishing, contracted and paid for, and in the face of Anne's suggestion that, if he didn't do something they would have to leave, he agreed to approach the four ladies she had identified as the worst offenders. He introduced himself to the ladies and one asked if they were a new bride and groom. His response, a glib and creative lie, was "Well...if you can apply the term after four years of marriage, yes." The woman challenged his account by asking about all the new clothing and suitcases, to which he responded, "We were burned out, and the doctor felt the shock was so hard on my wife that he thought I should take her to the mountains for a change." Then, feeling a need for a stronger story, or more emphasis, he added, "He also thought the change would help Mrs. Burgess realize her heart's desire. She longed for a baby without results, so now you ladies can help. My wife is very sensitive and unhappy, and if you wish to be helpful...just try to get her mind on other things." Following the next day's fishing, RN reported that Anne was back in good spirits and asked him what he had said to the women, all of whom had approached her in a warm and friendly fashion that morning. RN never shared with her the approach he took to warming up the older ladies.

RN's marriage to Anne Webster Fish portended a significant change in his prospects and broadened considerably his circle of acquaintances, both personal and professional. Anne also brought a measure of wealth into his young life. Although at the time of their marriage she had as yet no inheritance, after her mother passed in 1923 Anne did inherit considerable wealth, but RN takes pains in the *Memoirs* to explain that he kept their finances separated so as not to subject their family to the risks inherent in his chosen profession. Anne's family is the subject of the next chapter and their history will reveal important associations and relationships that RN enjoyed for the rest of his life. She was the daughter of a true Contra Costa County pioneer. An immigrant to California during its gold rush days, Lafayette Irving Fish became a successful farmer, rancher, financier, and pillar of his community. There is no evidence that RN ever knew Fish because he passed away in 1900 prior to the time that RN met his widow. It seems reasonable to conclude, however, that RN became the beneficiary of Lafayette Fish's extensive relationships throughout Contra Costa County and perhaps even broader venues as he pursued his own career objectives.

The Homestead house that RB bought from Tom Rice in 1908.
Courtesy Contra Costa County Historical Society.

A view north on Montgomery Street, from Market and Post, of the building that housed RN's first San Francisco office in 1908. His suite was on the third floor. Courtesy OpenSFHistory.org

2325 Piedmont Avenue, Berkeley, CA.
The home RN built for Ann and her Mother in 1908.
Courtesy Burgess Family collection.

Wedding party at the Berkeley home of Frances Webster Fish, July 20, 1909. Left to right: Jeanette and Eugene Webster, Jessie Whiting, Ernest Webster, Anna Pettit, Jessie Pettit, Anne Webster Fish, R.N. Burgess, Frances Webster Fish, Leila Webster Sundin, Howard Webster, Alice Pettit and Millard Webster. Courtesy Burgess Family collection.

RN and Anne on their wedding day with RN's bail of 'wild oats.'
Courtesy Burgess Family collection.

Anne Holcomb Webster fish before her marriage to RN.
Courtesy Burgess Family collection.

CHAPTER 9

A Propitious Union

The family of RN's father-in-law, Lafayette Irving Fish, was from upstate New York. Lafayette's father Libeus Fish, was the son of Revolutionary War officer Josiah Fish and his wife Elizabeth Hazelton Fish. Libeus married Polly Holcomb on January 1, 1805 and they became the parents of eleven children, nine of whom grew to adulthood. In addition to Lafayette, the surviving children were Josiah, Charles, John, Eli, Caroline, Minerva, Mary, and Cornelia. Following the death of Polly Holcomb Fish, Libeus married Rebecca Carter Vaughn and two additional children were produced in that marriage, Albert and Julia.

Lafayette's birthplace in Batavia in October of 1824 lies in what is today known as the Genesee Country of western New York state. Formed in 1802 by Joseph Ellicott, the town was part of a large land purchase in 1792. In that year founding father and colonial banker Robert Morris sold 3.25 million acres in western New York to the Holland Land Company, a consortium of Dutch bankers. This massive land purchase was later sold off in a series of transactions between 1802 and 1846 and formed the basis of the settlement and development of western upstate New York.

Libeus Fish is noteworthy for his early involvement in political activity and for being among the group of men who started what today is the Republican Party. He was a participant when a group of anti-slavery advocates met to consider ways to counter the Kansas-Nebraska Act of 1854, legislation that extended popular sovereignty into the newly opened territories of Kansas and Nebraska. Under the new legislation, the population of almost exclusively white male voters would be allowed to vote on the question of the extension of slavery into those areas. In a meeting held in

Jackson, Michigan, Libeus' home at the time, on July 6, 1854, these men protested the Act and nominated a slate of statewide candidates, constituting the first meeting of self-designated Republicans, the forerunners of the party which nominated Abraham Lincoln for the presidency six years later.

The Fish brothers received their primary and secondary education in Batavia and later in Jackson, Michigan, to which the family moved when Lafayette completed grammar school. Following high school, Charles moved to Monticello, Mississippi, where he engaged in clerking for a retail establishment. Lafayette assumed the same profession in Jackson for a year or so before leaving to join his older brother in Mississippi. After a period in Monticello, he returned to Jackson and resumed his former situation.

The lives of both Charles and Lafayette, as well as that of the oldest brother, Josiah, would change dramatically after James Marshall discovered gold in Coloma, California, in January of 1848. In the following ten years, Josiah, Lafayette, Charles, Cornelia, Caroline, and finally Julia would all emigrate to California. The men, after various early business and mining ventures, would settle in Martinez and encourage the women to follow them. Ultimately, the six would comprise a pioneer Martinez family making significant social, economic, and educational contributions to that city.

The Bancroft Library in Berkeley has microfilm of 45 documents from the papers of the family, many of which are hand-written letters between the siblings and their father Libeus. [1] These letters, written between the 1830s and 90s, paint a fascinating picture of life in California in the second half of the 19th century. They include descriptions of life in early Yerba Buena (San Francisco's initial name) when it was a tent city at the dawn of the Gold Rush. Activity in the mining areas of the gold fields on the Feather River are included, as is life in Martinez as it grew, along with its neighbor Port Costa, into one of the largest grain exporting locations in the United States.

---

[1] Family letters among the Fish siblings and their father Libeus written between the 1830s and 1890s. Collection of Fish Family Papers, Bancroft Library, University of California, Berkeley, CA.

Josiah, arriving first, lived in his tent in a cluster of similar dwellings on the shores of Yerba Buena Cove. Though not destined for the success in California enjoyed by his two younger brothers, his eagerness and optimism are clear in a July 29, 1849 letter to Charles, still in Monticello, Mississippi. "Close up your business at Monticello as soon as you can and come here. You can now get here for your services as a clerk for a year as much as your stock of goods is worth. If you can bring capital so much the better. At present money is the best thing to bring. Tell Fayette (a shortened version of his full name) to come on at once. He can earn more here in one month than he can in Michigan in a year."[2]

Lafayette soon followed on January 8, 1850, taking the same Isthmus of Panama route, his brother Josiah had taken the previous year. Optimism must have been high as Lafayette, in a letter to his sister Mary Fish Randal dated April 1, 1849, anticipated returning "with a tremendous quantity of gold." The reality expressed in most of the Fish letters was anything but that. They all struggled on arrival to get established in a hostile frontier environment.

Lafayette's physical strength and personal character are described by multiple sources, all in terms of admiration. In a letter written to her father in the fall of 1858, a few months after her own arrival in California, his sister Caroline described her brother in glowing terms. "It seems to me that Fayette has grown too since he was home he is so tall and broad across his shoulders. I often think the hardships and exposure he has been through, have made him tough and healthy. I have often compared him to the oaks that are only toughened by the blasts of winter." [3]

In a book written for family publication only, Liela Webster Sundin, Anne's first cousin, wrote of the respect in which he was held by his customers and fellow miners while in the gold mines north of Marysville in 1850-51. "Lafayette so commanded the respect of those with whom he came in contact that during this period of lawlessness and crime and theft, after a day or more of mining he would often return to his cabin to find that miners

[2] Fish Family Papers.
[3] Fish Family Papers.

wishing to buy from his goods would often help themselves, write on slips of papers their names and purchases, then weigh the slips with gold dust and leave them upon the table which frequently held such payments."[4]

That his peers in Contra Costa County saw him as a leader and man of strength is suggested by numerous positions Lafayette held in his community throughout his life. At the end of his first decade in California, the County Agricultural Society in its first meeting in Walnut Creek on January 15, 1859 elected Lafayette president. From the names of the other participants, it is apparent that the purpose of the society was to organize and promote the activities of area farmers.[5]

RN's future father-in-law was more than modestly adept in business. He was a natural leader and a gifted trader with an eye for value and a keen sense of how to take advantage of the myriad circumstances presenting opportunity for profit in a new country, characterized by shortages of all manner.

His business acumen was displayed early in what must have been one of his first transactions in a lifetime of deal-making. Before leaving New Orleans, anticipating a shortage of butter in California, he invested in a quantity of it packaged in small wooded tubs or firkins. Thinking he would sell it for a good price in California, he was surprised when, in Panama crossing the Isthmus, he received a good offer. Insisting on a sample, his buyer asked Lafayette to bore a small hole in the firkin to facilitate the inspection. On making the opening, he found the butter in a liquid state (not surprising in the climate of the Isthmus), stopped up the hole and declined the sale. In San Francisco, he sold it all successfully for $1.05 a pound.

Within a month of his arrival, Lafayette was at the mines in Marysville, California, joining with several other men, including Josiah, in forming a company to pursue their mining objectives. Equipped with a team of oxen and other provisions, they left for a

[4] Liela Webster Sundin, *The Circle of Our Years*, Unpublished Manuscript, c 1949-1950.

[5] Fish Family History, Ancestry.com

claim on Slate Creek only to learn that the claim had been abandoned in favor of another one on the Feather River. Ultimately, they established claims on Nelson Creek, a tributary of the Middle Fork of the Feather River. Mining was far from the only activity the group engaged in, later opening a retail store which also served as a hotel for visiting miners. Later, Lafayette and another associate, Mr. Lathrop, bought out the original partners and subsequently expanded further by acquiring the mercantile business of William and Jerry Ford of Marysville.

After almost two years in the gold fields and the accumulation of a measure of wealth, Lafayette and his partner left the mines and headed south to Contra Costa County. Contra Costa had become one of California's original twenty-seven counties at the time of statehood in 1850 and was an exceptionally productive agricultural area. Lafayette was interested in agriculture and in the prospects of large scale farming in the area and it was a natural location in which to begin his post-mining business interests.

In March of 1853, Lafayette's older brother, Charles, arrived in San Francisco after a perilous journey via the Isthmus and up the west coast. Charles had been living in Monticello, Mississippi, pursuing the clerking that had been his profession throughout his adult life. He had also been providing financial assistance to both Josiah, his older brother, and to Lafayette as they attempted to make a go of it in the mines of California. Accordingly, Charles was broke and eager to have his own chance at a fortune in the west. He wrote to his father in December of 1852 that he was impatient to get started on the trip to Marysville (near the site of the other Fish brothers' mining claim on the Feather River). His hands had been tied the last few years helping his brothers, precluding the advancement of his own career, and he was confident that he and Lafayette would be successful in California because "we both understand business." [6]

Charles' trip to California, however, was to be anything but encouraging. After passing the Isthmus his vessel, the Independence, was shipwrecked near Magdalena Bay off lower California, leaving

[6] Fish Family Papers.

himself and numerous other passengers marooned on San Juanita Island for a period of weeks until a San Francisco-bound whaler, the Meteor, spotted them and picked them up. Much of whatever wealth Charles had managed to amass was on his person and he lost everything in this disaster. In consequence, his first few years in California were anything but comfortable. After a year, he lost his clerking employment in San Francisco and was very nearly destitute until he and Lafayette were able to begin their formal business partnership.[7] The brother's initial plan was that Charles would join Lafayette in a venture devoted to large-scale farming and other businesses.

Before that, however, another opportunity beckoned. Shortly after arriving in Contra Costa County, Lafayette had recognized that an excellent financial return might be realized by bringing scarce livestock to California. The potential for profit from such a venture was made clear in a letter Charles sent to his sister Mary on December 28, 1853. "The price of sheep still keep up here (*sic*) and no doubt will for many years to come. American sheep are worth from $10 to $14 and Mexican from $8 to $10 but they are not as large. If Fayette gets through with 8,000 head his share of the profits would be $10,000 or $12,000."[8]

With these prospects in mind, Lafayette planned and executed an ambitious undertaking to purchase and herd sheep and cattle across the plains for resale. He put together a company and traveled east to buy sheep. They planned to winter the stock in Missouri, and then assemble a company of wagons and herders for transporting them back to California. On May 2,1854, the group started west with five thousand sheep, eight ox teams, a cattle herd, saddle horses, and mules. Arriving, in late October 1854 in the northern Sacramento Valley, they had three thousand sheep, one hundred forty-one head of cattle, and twelve horses and mules. In spite of the forty percent attrition of sheep, their profits were still quite good, reflecting the cost of $1.50 per sheep in the east,

---

[7] *History of Contra Costa County California with Biographical Sketches*, Historic Record Company, Los Angeles, California, 1926.

[8] Fish Family Papers.

saleable in California for between $10.00 and $14.00 each. This margin would have produced a profit for the partners, on the sheep alone, in 1854 of $22,500, equivalent to just over $6,000,000 in 2017 dollars. Lafayette's share is unknown, but inasmuch as he led the group, and was one of the principals, it would have been sufficient capital to finance the purchase of considerable farming acreage in California.

Once reunited on Lafayette's return, the Fish brothers wasted little time in establishing themselves as ambitious and talented farmers and business men interested in profiting from their own efforts and investments but also eager to advance the commercial and cultural interests of their new home. In the 1850s Contra Costa County was almost entirely farmland and the leaders in the County, seeing its potential, were eager to begin collaborations and investments which would bring that potential to fruition.

During these years beginning in the mid-1850s, Lafayette and Charles Fish began acquiring large land parcels, sometimes jointly and sometimes with other partners, with the intent to engage in large-scale farming activities. One such purchase by Lafayette alone was a portion of the Welch Rancho. William Welch, a native of Scotland had acquired his property pursuant to a petition to the Mexican government in 1832 for a land grant. The Welch Rancho, or Welch Valley as it was called in a letter (which included a hand-drawn map) from Charles Fish to his sister Cornelia in August of 1856, was part of the much larger 1834 grant known as Rancho de la Nueces y Bolbones.[9]

The Rancho de la Nueces y Bolbones was an 1834 Mexican Land Grant to Dona Juana Sanchez de Pacheco. It consisted of 17,734 acres of land between a point just south of today's intersection of Rudgear Road and San Ramon Valley Boulevard, north along the east side of Walnut Creek to Concord, east to present-day Clayton, and back to Walnut Creek. The grant was made in consideration of Dona Juana's deceased husband Miguel's service to the Mexican

---

[9] Isabelle Spencer Brubaker, *1850-1950 100 Years of Growth, A History of Walnut Creek, Contra Costa County, California,* Copyright 1975, Isabelle Spencer Brubaker.

Government as a corporal in the Mexican Army in its revolution against Spain. The Mexican grants had conditions attached: A map had to be drawn; the grantee needed to reside on the land; a permanent residence had to be built within one year; and livestock had to be placed on the land. These conditions were often ignored leading to the presence of squatters on many of the grants, particularly after the discovery of gold in 1848 and the consequent increase in the local population. Dona Juana renamed her land the San Miguel Ranch in honor of her husband Miguel, drew her map, and placed stock on her acreage, which was operated by her sons and grandchildren while she remained in the family hacienda in San Jose. In 1853 she sold that portion of her holdings which RN would later acquire to her grandson Ygnacio Sibrian for $4,000.

This tract, of about 4.5 square miles, was approximately what RN bought fifty years later from the Bank of California. Essentially the southwest corner of the original 1834 grant, it extended from today's Walnut Creek Alamo border north along the creek to the Ygnacio Valley Road Walnut Avenue intersection, and then southeast along Shell Ridge, including present day Lakewood, Walnut Heights, Walnut Knolls, Indian Valley, Rudgear Estates, and the present Walnut Creek open space.

Ygnacio Sibrian and his wife Antonia Moreno de Sibrian built their home on a small creek which fed into the larger Walnut Creek, on the site which RN would later expand into his Homestead. His expansion would have to await the intervening ownership of the Rice Family, however, who purchased the Sibrian homestead, plus additional acreage, in October of 1860 for $15,000. RN's acquisition, in 1908, of the Rice acreage has been described in the preceding chapter; his improvements to the property were considerable and included a substantial expansion of the main house as well as damming the small creek and creating Lakewood Lake. [10]

The property that Lafayette Fish purchased on the Welch Rancho was on the west side of Walnut Creek, part of a larger parcel

---

[10] Turalu Reed Brady, *Lakewood, A History of Walnut Creek's Unique Neighborhood, 2nd Printing,* Copyright 2004 Turalu Reed Brady.

that extended north up the Diablo Valley to Martinez. After Welch's death, his widow subdivided much of the land into 25-acre parcels and sold it off to farmers during the 1850s at prices of between $3 and $4 per acre. It seems probable that Lafayette bought one of these as did his partner Lathrop. [11]

Adept at farming, particularly at growing wheat, Lafayette became one of the largest growers in the San Joaquin Valley in addition to his extensive acreage in Contra Costa County. Like his future son-in-law, he was ahead of his time in understanding the necessity of fallowing his land and thus ensuring greater yields in subsequent seasons. He joined his brother Charles in a partnership to farm, to conduct warehouse operations, and to buy and sell grain. Having the foresight to understand and appreciate productivity advantages in farming, he sent east for state-of-the art farming equipment. Employing these advantages, he was reputed to have made the first grain shipment from the San Francisco Bay region to New York.

Some sources suggest that the Fish brothers, Lafayette and his older brother Charles, were the first millionaires in Contra Costa County. If this was true, it was likely the result of their decision to enter into extensive wheat farming. Early on, the two jointly purchased a large tract of land between Martinez and Pacheco and commenced farming activities. Early success apparently begat the acquisition of additional acreage and their holdings grew to 18,000 acres under cultivation. It is also reported that the brothers were among the first to incorporate mechanized farming methodologies into their practice, purchasing and shipping west a steam-powered plough built in 1862. Whatever their results in terms of individual wealth, the wheat business, particularly the export of it, in the 1880s was the place to be. In her 1963 paper, *Port Costa a California Wheat Center*, Margery S. Hellman reported that California was one of the world's leading grain processing and exporting areas. Large wheat harvests from California's interior were loaded for export in San Francisco bay and shipped via sailing vessel, mostly to

---

[11] George Emanuels, *Walnut Creek, Arroyo de Las Nueces*, (Sonoma, California: Diablo Books, 1984), 4.

Britain around Cape Horn. For various reasons Port Costa became the location of choice for grain shippers and, particularly in the 1880s, profits were high, stimulating more acreage devoted to wheat. In five of the twelve years between 1872 and 1884, California was the nation's leading wheat producer, including a record 39 million bushels shipped to Europe in 1881-82. By the year 1884, California had more than three million acres under cultivation in wheat.[12]

The physical plant constructed to support this operation was impressive extending four miles along the bay reaching from Crockett to a point just east of Port Costa. Wharves were giant edifices, up to two-thirds of a mile in length, each supporting a warehouse of up to 1,000 feet in length. Total storage capacity exceeded several hundred thousand tons. When the English grain traders of the day commented on the origins of their shipments from California, they spoke of Port Costa, not San Francisco.

It was this economic environment that Lafayette Fish entered the export business in the summer of 1882 with his brother Charles, Gabriel Blum, Jasper Jones, and Barry Baldwin. The Record Union of Sacramento, California, reported in its July 8, 1882, issue that Fish and others had incorporated the new Carquinez Wharf Co. with $10,000 of initial capital for purposes of building, operating, and maintaining wharves, warehouses and other buildings. Prospective operations also included the right to take tolls, rents or dues, and to buy and sell real estate. This investment, in time to take advantage of what would become California's largest grain exporting decade, must have further cemented the Fish Brothers' reputation and financial results.

Lafayette's commercial activities and successes produced another opportunity in 1873 when he saw the need for a bank and, working with several associates, chartered the Bank of Martinez on October 6, 1873. Serving on his board of directors were W.W. Cameron, Simon Blum (also a partner in a later grain exporting operation), Henry M. Hale, and William M. Hale. One of the first

---

[12] Margery Saunders Hellman, *Port Costa a California Wheat Center*, The California Geographer Vol 4, (1963).

banks in Contra Costa County, it prospered and Lafayette served as its President until his retirement from active business in 1890. A number of sources on the history of Contra Costa County indicate that Lafayette made two crossings to California. The first, through the isthmus of Panama, was in 1850, when he arrived in San Francisco on January 8th. The second in 1854 when he and others brought the livestock across the plains. An account of a third crossing is in the archives of the Bancroft Library at Berkeley. Entitled *Across the Plains in 1860, A Diary Kept by Lafayette Fish,* this account contains detailed descriptions of daily progress, roads used, stream-fords made, type and suitability of vegetation encountered, water sources found, encounters with Pony Express riders, and all of the other experiences faced by immigrants coming via covered wagon. No account of a third trip by Lafayette is contained in the extensive histories of Contra Costa County, although its mention of encounters with Pony Express riders correctly places it in 1860.

In an interesting parallel to RN's life, and his cultural and charitable instincts, Lafayette's half-sister, Julia Fish, has been called the Mother of the Martinez Library. Coming to Martinez in 1875 from her native New York, she lived with her brothers until they married and then remained in Martinez, living alone, until her death in 1927 at 92 years of age. Early in her life in the community, unhappy with the meager opportunities for reading available, she proposed a reading club for the young men of the city. With weekly sessions on Wednesday evenings, the activity soon became so popular that she proposed a new public library. Writing and producing a musical production and charging an entrance fee of one book, the book club acquired over 100 books, the core of the new collection. Later, Dr. Strentzel donated an old building, a former saloon, and Julia Fish led a work party in cleaning, painting and improving the facility which became the new Martinez Library. Several decades later, RN would donate a parcel of his land in Walnut Creek which would become that city's first formal library in 1915.

***

In the late 1870s or the early 1880s, Lafayette began courting Frances Lillian Webster, whom he eventually married. She was living in San Jose at the time, a teacher in the San Jose Normal School, the forerunner of today's San Jose State University. Born in 1853 in Stockholm Center, St. Lawrence County, New York, by the early 1880s she had five or six years of teaching experience. In 1875-76 she taught reading and geography in Leavenworth, Kansas. Relocating to Cedar Falls, Iowa, she taught at the State Normal School in Cedar Falls before coming west in 1878 to assume her position in San Jose. Her education, extensive for a woman during her time, qualified her for teaching above the high school level and her sense of culture and appreciation of the finer things in life suggests a highly competent and aware professional woman. Liela Webster Sundin suggests in her family publication that Frances was one of the participants in the development of the initial curriculum at the State Normal School in San Jose. [13]

That Lafayette must have been smitten by Frances is clear from a letter quoted by Sundin. Lafayette writes, "I had heard of her before I saw her and was almost ready to worship her, but when I saw her my heart sank and hope almost died, she looked and appeared so superior and more than worthy of a man much better than myself." Lafayette, born in 1824, was twenty-nine years her senior, a member of a previous generation. The couple had two children, Anne Holcomb Webster Fish and Irving Fish.[14]

The community of Frances' birth, Stockholm Center, is in northern upstate New York, just under 80 miles southwest of Montreal, Canada. The town was organized in 1806 and lies on land suitable for farming and other agricultural pursuits. The Webster brothers, Warren and Samuel had arrived in Stockholm Center a year prior to its formation, immigrating from Orwell, Vermont, where Samuel had been a Baptist minister. Samuel founded the first church in Stockholm Center and the stone house he built still stands in the community. As a founding father, Warren Webster, was named the

---

[13] Liela Webster Sundin, *The Circle of Our Years*, Unpublished Manuscript, c 1949-1950.

[14] Fish Family Papers.

town's first "constable and collector." Among the children from his marriage to Anna Phelps was Samuel Warren Webster. Samuel's marriage, in October of 1843, to Mary Ann Nichols of Massachusetts produced eleven children, eight of whom lived into adulthood. Frances Webster Fish was the fourth.[15]

Frances' siblings are pictured in a photograph of her wedding to RN Burgess on July 20, 1909 in what would be her family's last reunion. Pictured are Celestia E. Webster, Alice Webster Petit, Ernest Webster, Ann Caroline Webster, Eugene C. Webster, Howard Webster, and Willard Webster.

Frances' forebears were woven into the fabric of American history beginning with the landing at Plymouth in 1620 where one of the leaders of the Puritan group was Isaac Allerton a direct antecedent. Isaac Allerton's name follows that of John Carver, William Bradford, Edward Winslow, and Elder Brewster on the signature page of the Mayflower Compact. Once ashore at Plymouth, Allerton's history with the pilgrims was not without controversy. His business and trading interests, expanded through numerous Atlantic crossings in subsequent years, later involved him in disputes and conflict within the original group and he was censured accordingly.

Other connections, rich in colonial history were present in the Webster family. Sundin reports that Frances had prepared a family genealogy that was in the possession of RN and Anne. This work, mentioned by RN in his will, has been lost, but it demonstrated a direct line back to Rebecca Towne Nurse, a resident of Salem, Massachusetts, in the late 17th century. Rebecca, accused of practicing witchcraft, was the first person to be hung, at the age of seventy-one, during the period of religious fanaticism in 1692. According to Frances' genealogical records, the Webster's could trace themselves directly back eleven generations to Rebecca's second child, Rebecca Nurse Preston.

Frances' father was a Civil War veteran. Samuel Warren

---

[15] *History of Stockholm, New York From our County and its People a Memorial Record of St Lawrence County, New York,* Ed. Gates Curtis, The Boston History Company, 1894.

Webster was initially a private with H company of the 16th New York Regiment. Promoted to Second Lieutenant in June of 1861, he resigned at that rank early in 1862. Later in the war, he rejoined as a commissioned officer of engineers and served for the duration in that capacity. Liela Sundin's manuscript contains an entertaining account, in a letter written by him to his grandchild, Frances, in 1899, of his service at the (first) Battle of Bull Run in July of 1861. He recounts confusion in the ranks because of a misunderstanding in which the infantrymen of his unit thought erroneously that the Union Army had been victorious. [16]

Samuel Webster's account is fascinating. He describes his unit getting orders on Tuesday, July 16th at their bivouac near Alexandria, Virginia, to move southwest to Fairfax Court House on the Warrenton Turnpike, in the direction of Bull Run with "three day's rations and 70 rounds each." While marching, they encountered a unit of the 5th Alabama Infantry and undertook a bayonet charge only to find that the rebels had departed in a hurry and left their rucksacks and gear. Pursuing the retreating rebels Webster's unit found their command post and abandoned supplies and rations all burning from a recently set fire.

The defining day of the battle was Sunday, July 21, 1861 and Webster's New York Infantry had been bivouacked on Centerville Heights northeast of the battlefield until six that morning when they were ordered to Blackman's (now Blackburn's) Ford four miles downstream where they were placed in a defensive position in support of an artillery battery. During the early afternoon of July 21st some of the fiercest fighting occurred but Samuel Webster's unit could only hear it and see the dust of moving rebel troops in the distance. In the middle of the confusion one of General Irvin McDowell's aide's rode up and advised Webster's commander, Colonel Davies, that his troops should "Take care of your guns the Enemy is in full retreat." This encouraged his unit as they took up full defensive positions against a rebel charge. Union artillery stopped the charge with devastating results and Webster's New

---

[16] Liela Webster Sundin, *The Circle of Our Years,* Unpublished Manuscript, c 1949-1950.

York regiment was soon ordered to withdraw towards Centerville their departure point earlier in the day. On reaching Centerville, they realized that McDowell's aide had been mistaken, it was *their* army that had been defeated. The message had actually read "Take care of your guns the Army is in full retreat." Thus, Samuel Warren Webster, RN's wife's grandfather had participated in one of the first major battles of the Civil War, a significant defeat for the green Union troops involved.

Frances was married to Lafayette in Los Angeles on March 31, 1881, and thereafter lived in Martinez, raising her family in that city until she relocated to Berkeley following the death of her husband in 1900. She was a remarkable person. A professional, with two teaching assignments at the college level to her credit when she came to San Jose, her marriage to Lafayette seems to have relieved her of the necessity of working for a living. She was not, however, an idle woman. Her obituary in the September 1923 Contra Costa Gazette describes an individual actively involved in charitable activities in her original married home in Martinez as well as in Berkeley. "Through all the years Mrs. Fish was an active worker in the Congregational church and was very active in a quiet way in philanthropic work both here in Martinez and in Berkeley. Mrs. Fish was a woman of unusual insight and understanding of human nature and her generous sympathy made her beloved by a large circle of friends." [17]

In 1906, at the age of fifty-three, Frances applied for a passport to go abroad with her children for a world tour. The passport application indicates that she initially planned to take only her daughter, Anne, but apparently changed her mind as Irving also made the trip. Her account of this eleven-month sojourn is a 200-page detailed description of an extensive grand tour typical for members of her class in the 19th century. Her education and refinement come through clearly in these pages, as do contemporary attitudes of Americans of her status in life, toward those they perceived as below them. Her knowledge of history, the classics,

---

[17] "Mrs. Lafayette I Fish Who Passed Away Saturday Was Well Known Here," *Contra Costa Gazette,* 1 September 1923.

and the art displayed in the countless museums they visited throughout Europe, the Middle East, India, and the Far East, was extensive, reflecting a thorough background in these subjects acquired during her school years.

Thus, on July 20, 1909, RN, with just an eighth-grade education but with considerable business success achieved by age thirty-one, was united in marriage to a young woman with an impressive lineage and social position. Also, Anne had the prospect of attaining considerable wealth in her own right, thanks to the successes enjoyed by her father. This wealth and the secure social status that attended it could only have enhanced RN's personal ascendancy at a time when a nascent business career was showing signs of promise. The next ten years would see business successes piled on top of one another until the level of achievement may well have exceeded even his own ambitious dreams. These achievements are the focus of the next part of his story.

RN's mother-in-law, Frances Webster Fish, as a young woman.
Courtesy Burgess Family collection.

Lafayette Irving Fish; RN never knew his father-in-law.
Fish passed away in 1900.
Courtesy Burgess Family collection.

Home of Lafayette Irving Fish in Martinez, CA.
Courtesy Contra Costa County Historical Society.

Anne Fish Burgess grandfather, Samuel Warren
Webster, a veteran of the Battle of Bull Run.
Courtesy Burgess Family collection.

CHAPTER 10

A Gainful Period

When RN and Anne returned from their honeymoon in the fall of 1909, they agreed to live in Anne's mother's new home as she was planning a trip to Europe and wanted the house occupied during her absence. Her trip was delayed by Anne's pregnancy and a new baby was delivered in May of 1910. Robert Noble Burgess, Jr. was the couple's first child. After his arrival Frances Fish departed on her planned one-year tour of Europe.

The successes RN enjoyed during the period beginning with his marriage in 1909 and up to 1915, including construction in San Francisco and the East Bay and land acquisition in the far East Bay, seemed destined to put him on a track of singular success for the rest of his life. His ingenuity, his creativity in the arena of finance, and his pure ability to get things done on time and under budget, attracted others, eager to invest with him. His reputation was spreading and older men who lacked his energy and youth, but recognized his talent, wanted to be part of his success story. He was approaching the apex of his financial life and prosperity during this period.

In Contra Costa County between 1909 and 1913 RN developed fifteen different tracts in Walnut Creek, Lafayette, Concord, and Clayton Valley. He also subdivided portions of Moraga, Richmond, Port Chicago, Clyde, Berkeley, and Diablo. His purchase of the Rice Ranch in 1908 in combination with other land already owned gave him in excess of 7,000 acres on which to pursue his subdivision and development plans. The first major development was the 3,000-acre San Miguel Ranch which he named Walnut Heights. The parcel extended from Ygnacio Valley Road on the

north, south to Mountain View Boulevard, and from the railroad
tracks in Walnut Creek east to Shell Ridge. The property consisted
of fifty-five lots plus the 532-acre "Lot A," which he reserved for
his family home. Lot A was the site of the old Ygnacio Sibrian
home described in Chapter 9. In an effort to protect Anne and his
future children from the risks inherent in his profession, he deeded
this parcel to his wife in 1909.[1]

RN's land acquisition and development work in Contra Costa
County was aided immeasurably by the extension of the electric
railway. As described by the Oakland Tribune in an August, 1910
article, the new Oakland and Antioch Electric Railroad was to run
from the Oakland train ferry terminal (the Key system) up Claremont Avenue to the base of the Oakland hills and thence through
the intercounty tunnel out to Lafayette, Walnut Creek, Concord,
through Bay Point to a terminus in Antioch. A branch line was to
be completed between Concord and Martinez with ferry service
available to Benicia. At the time of the Oakland Tribune piece, sufficient funds had been raised to build the road between Bay Point
and Lafayette, leaving the nine miles between Lafayette and Oakland as well as the easternmost track beds unfunded. Money for
the remaining work was to be raised through the sale of bonds,
$1,000,000 of which were available from the Bond Department of
the R.N. Burgess company. These were 5% thirty-year gold bonds
according to the article, available in blocks of $10,000, $20,000, and
$30,000. A favorable engineering report as well as aggressive mar-
keting were being employed to complete the sale of these bonds to
investors who, it was alleged, could "find no better investment
today, from both a monetary and public commercial standpoint
than the Oakland and Antioch Railway bonds...The R.N. Burgess
company has completed a beautiful booklet, coveting views of the
right of way and giving in a concise form data in regard to the financial backing of this road, and anyone interested may receive one
of these booklets on application to the R.N. Burgess Company."[2]

---

[1] Brady, *Lakewood*, 20-23.

[2] "OAKLAND AND ANTIOCH ELECTRIC RAILROAD, New Electric Road to Connect Alameda and Contra Costa Counties Means Much

RN's marketing of land on his Walnut Creek acreage to prospects in Oakland, Berkeley, and San Francisco reflects his intuitive understanding of marketing decades before that discipline was named in the curricula of business schools. He advertised land as income property, reflecting the notion that a buyer, seeking a summer cottage or permanent home in Walnut Creek could buy acreage planted in walnut trees and perhaps alfalfa, use the income from annual crop sales to service any debt incurred with the purchase, and ultimately own the property after payoff. His pitch, in an Oakland Tribune article of August 22, 1910 was typical; he was quoted in the article suggesting that, "The Walnut Creek Development Company is in position to start you off with income paying property that will be worth more money and have greater fame than the orange groves of southern California or, the apple and pear orchards of the Rogue River Valley…Twenty acres of walnuts started now will be worth at least $20,000 ten years from now. In the meantime, while the trees are growing, a substantial income can be realized from the ground. At the end of ten years the walnuts will have paid for your investment and you will have an assured income, increasing as the years go by, for the walnut trees improve with age. Twenty acres of walnuts from ten years old and up will yield you a steady income of $2,500 to $4,000 per year. Can you endow your family with a better income for the same investment? Think it over."

In 1910 he had several major jobs under construction in San Francisco as well. For Dr. McNutt, his old childhood doctor whom he helped during the earthquake, he was building a new hospital. The San Francisco Call reported on May 28, 1910 that he was building a "substantial reinforced hospital with accommodations for 77 patients and 35 nurses. The operating department will be equipped with all the latest and most sanitary devices and has in conjunction an X ray room, laboratory, surgeons' wardrobe, bath and lavatories, linen rooms and complete sterilizing rooms…the total cost of the building, which is being erected by the R.N. Burgess company, is $85,000." The Call also reported in November of that year that

to Oakland," *Oakland Tribune*, 22 August 1910.

among numerous construction projects in the area destroyed by fire in 1906 was a new hotel being built by the R.N. Burgess company on the south side of Bush Street just west of Powell. Described as of the French Renaissance style, every room was planned to have an outside exposure with "a dressing room, a private bathroom, private hall off the main hotel halls, a large closet and an especially designed high disappearing bed so that the room may be used as a living as well as bed room. There are 78 of these suites in the building...A gymnasium, completely equipped and ventilated, will be established in the basement, and in connection with it will be plunge and shower baths, lockers and dressing rooms. A glass enclosed roof garden solarium, the first in this city, will be built on the roof."

In addition to these projects, RN's San Francisco business also included a ten-story, 90-unit apartment building and the Chinese Free Mason Temple. To manage these operations, he was commuting from Berkeley via train and ferry-boat daily to his offices on Market Street. He continued his earlier financing arrangements, using his receivables from sales or construction projects as collateral after selling them to his mortgage company which deposited them in the trust bank which then generated new capital by selling them to banks and investors as mortgage participation certificates at 90% of their face value. He set up a sales force to sell these certificates to outside investors and used the cash generated to fund additional building.

RN's financial creativity is again on display as he describes these new projects in San Francisco and his subdivision activity in Contra Cost County. As he stated it, other alternative financing methods all had problems implicit in their design. He might, for example, have sold stock in a land company, bringing in equity investors to supplement some measure of debt in capitalizing his land development in Contra Costa. However, "It was not only difficult to finance the sale of a subdivision by the sale of land company stock; if you succeeded you would soon lose control of your operation. But if you sold participating certificates against your receivables you could expand as long as you had receivables, or cash to back the certificates, without diluting your capital stock." RN's deep-rooted desire for independence, consistently displayed since childhood, made these arrangements perfect for him.

He described how his approach attracted others dealing with the same needs. The automobile industry, for example, had trouble financing the sale of its autos as it transitioned into a mass-production operation in the early decades of the 20th century. Banks, understandably, perceived the potential sale of cars subject to financing as a threat to their franchises and were slow in cooperating with the auto manufacturers. One morning in 1910, RN was visited by Russell Clifford Durant in his San Francisco offices. Durant was the son of William Crapo Durant an early builder and marketer of automobiles who was then engaged in the business of buying automobile manufacturing firms and was frustrated at his inability to arrange financing for the sale of his cars. According to RN, "He had heard of how I pledged trust deeds and receivables in connection with financing buildings, and the sale of land in trust and issued certificates against them and asked me if I was willing to explain the procedure to him." RN was more than willing and provided Durant with a detailed explanation of the procedure as well as with copies of the forms and other documents he used. In what might be another example of the hyperbole to which he was inclined, RN related that these ideas ultimately resulted in the formation of the General Motors Acceptance Corporation, the financing arm of General Motors Corporation.

At the same time as the construction projects in San Francisco were being completed, he was developing land already acquired in Contra Costa County. He had subdivided portions of the San Miguel Ranch, the Larkey acreage, and the Rice Ranch in Walnut Creek and was preparing to build on them. He had a sales force charged with the responsibility of disposition of the lots and it would create marketing events to promote these sales.

In the fall of 1910, he closed on the 3,700-acre Foskett and Elworthy parcel which extended from the shore of the Sacramento River as far south as Clayton and up the northern slopes of Mt. Diablo. The following March, on opening day of a large lot sale in

Concord, he ran into trouble with the President of the Bank of Concord in a dispute that displayed his combative tendencies. In this instance, plans had been laid to bring customers and sales people on a special Southern Pacific train from Oakland up the coastal route to Concord, transfer the party on to the new Oakland and Antioch electric-train spur running from Bay Point to Concord, and deliver them to the site of the land sale in Concord. Expecting a large crowd, RN had prepared for this event thoroughly, setting up a free barbecue and employing Concord's Silver Band. RN wrote that the President of the Bank of Concord, Melvin Lyon, was angry because the Burgess companies would not give him their banking business and he set out to ruin the celebration.

Lyon instructed a group of his salesmen to board the special train at Port Costa and to inform RN's prospects that they had lots across the street from the Burgess property for sale at cheaper prices and to distribute sale information accordingly. Lyon also had erected a sixty-foot banner at the train station with the same message. A member of the Burgess sales team cut down the banner, but RN wrote that the day was ruined and he vowed to retaliate.

RN conceded that, "I guess I was very combative. If so, he and others like him made me that way. I set my sights to really get Mr. Lyon out of the way." RN achieved this goal. Lyon was in the process of promoting the new Concord Hotel and had financed it through the sale of stock to investors. In a hurry to get under way, he began construction prior to obtaining all the necessary funds from those investors. Meanwhile, RN had his architect, George Applegarth, prepare an excellent elevation of a competitive hotel for display. When Lyon's investors saw it their interest in purchasing stock in his project waned and construction funding dried up accordingly. In the face of increasing demands for payment from his contractors, Lyon then "made the same mistake many have made. He used the bank's money to make advances to his hotel company." In due course RN reported, "… word was dropped to the State Banking Department that it might be a good idea to see if the Bank of Concord was advancing money to the Concord Hotel

Company beyond its legal right." In consequence, Lyon was forced to sell his controlling interest in the Bank of Concord in the following year. His buyer? RN Burgess. Writing of his actions decades later, RN seemed to express some regret, saying "I was fighting back, but it would have been a better policy to have had a public relations man and made friends in place of enemies." RN was silent on the question of who made the call to the State Banking Department, but it seems likely that he or one of his agents would have done so.

The foregoing is interesting because it displayed a character trait that has been exhibited before. Lyon's actions in interfering with the Burgess opening-day events have to be assessed in light of then current business mores and standards. It was nothing if not a competitive environment and the Lyon group's conduct was aggressive, but whether it required the response engendered is another question. When hit, RN hit back, often harder than necessary under the circumstances.

In 1911, RN had several significant interactions with the town of Walnut Creek. Not yet an incorporated city (incorporation occurred in 1914), the town was growing, but it was subject to several serious constraints on its ability to further expand. The Pringle Ranch was a 300-acre parcel at the north end of town that RN had purchased with the intent to develop. Seeking to create a town site, an extension of the existing city, he had the property surveyed, graded the streets, and installed curbs, gutters, and sidewalks. Fire insurers had concerns about the amount and pressure of water available to combat fires, however, and announced they would not issue policies, nor renew existing ones, without improvements in water availability.

RN's company responded to this impasse by putting in a well on his San Miguel Ranch property and routing the water via a four-inch main two to three miles over to a 100,000-gallon water tank he had built on the top of Larkey Hill. He then extended the four-inch water main south along Main Street in Walnut Creek, installing fire hydrants that were still in use over fifty years later when he wrote the *Memoirs*.

RN was later approached by the town's only doctor, Dr. Leach, who advised him that a serious threat of a diphtheria epidemic existed because of all the raw sewage being dumped into the creek from an expanding supply of homes along the waterway, both in and outside the city proper. The threat of a quarantine by the Board of Health if remediation was not begun had brought Dr. Leach to RN's home to seek his involvement in the solution. In response to RN's question about why they had come to him, Dr. Leach responded, "the town is not incorporated, so there is no one in authority to act, but if someone like yourself will undertake to install a sewer system there will be many people to support the undertaking by paying for connection therewith…the cost can be largely recovered, but the undertaking requires a head, and someone to finance it."

This must have been a difficult request for RN to resist, so, as he put it, "Mrs. Burgess and I were launched in the sewer business." He reported in the *Memoirs* that in fact he did recover almost all of the investment via customer subscriptions, finally making a gift to the (then) newly incorporated town in 1914 of the unrecovered $12,000.

***

RN's ultimate nemeses would be his San Francisco financial partners acquired in those years before World War I. In the beginning, they were all impressed with him and with his ability to complete jobs, fulfill commitments, and, most of all, make money. He was a golden boy among men very senior to him, clever and on his way up. He was the kind of man that older men, with resources, sought relationships with because he could produce results and profits. An episode, occurring in 1911 or 1912, demonstrates the initial strength of his bond with these lenders, but also foretells difficulties ahead. John McKee was the Vice President and manager of RN's primary bank, the Mercantile National Bank in San Francisco, and on one occasion he summoned RN to his offices for a consultation. Arriving in McKee's glassed-in office, RN found a formidable group of men assembled there. Henry T. Scott was the President of the bank (as well as of the Pacific Telephone and Telegraph Company) and he was present along with several directors including H.C. Breeden, Wakefield Baker, and William G. Irwin, all prominent San Francisco businessmen and financiers.

The assembled officers and directors advised RN that they had asked him to come in as a result of a recent visit by a national bank examiner. The examiner had reviewed their loan book and found that all of RN's loans were secured by his real estate projects in apparent violation of Treasury regulations. His loan, for $75,000 was thus at risk and the question posed by the assembled group was what RN proposed to do about the violation?

In a now familiar pattern, RN responded to this threat of potential loss of his financing aggressively. "That is something for you to decide, you are running the bank, you made the loan, and accepted the security. I don't know the regulations you operate under. If you wish my reaction it will take me a few days to think it over. I will go out to Homestead and shoot squirrels with my .22 Cal. rifle…the answer will become clear." The group agreed to reconvene a few day later.

On the morning of the appointed meeting day, RN went to his office first and asked his secretary to assemble all the keys to his office files, doors, desks, cupboards, as well as to his various jobs outside and place them on a chain. The keys made an impressive bundle which he then took with him to the bank meeting at Mercantile. Standing outside the glass office, he could see that the same group was assembled and he realized that the group was the bank's Executive Committee, the senior staff group empowered to make and enforce the operating rules of the institution. As RN described it, on being invited to enter the office, he walked in, approached John McKee's desk, and dropped the key collection on the desk. Somewhat startled, McKee asked RN what the keys were for and RN responded, "They are all the keys to my office. You have just purchased a building and real estate company for I cannot operate without tools, and credit and cash are my most important tools." He went on to explain further that it would take a credit of $175,000 to complete his operation, presumably adding his anticipated profit and overhead to the value of his loans.

In describing this event, RN indicated that his ostentatious key drop was greeted with stunned silence by the group, saying that, "I had not been trying to be theatrical or to run a bluff, for I thought we would have to close up shop, and the logical thing to do was not to flounder hopelessly but to turn the business over to them at once." His demurral is disingenuous, as such theatrical presentation was stock in trade for him as demonstrated by earlier episodes in his life. It seemed to do the trick, however, as President Henry T. Scott intervened immediately, directing John McKee to visit each job site with RN and make the necessary arrangements (i.e., arrange the financing) to complete all the jobs. After their visits, McKee indicated to RN that he was clear to finish the work, saying, "Carry on your work as you have been doing, and you will get the necessary credit."

This story raises more questions than it answers, and the matter of bank regulations is something that would figure prominently in RN's story a few years later. If real estate really was insufficient collateral for Mercantile Bank's loans, how did it happen that he was allowed to continue? How frequently did bank examiners make such visits in those years, and how soon would it be before one returned only to find Mercantile in violation again?

RN's subsequent comments appear to shed possible light on these questions inasmuch as he suggests that, on literally the same day, he was contacted by Mr. William G. Irwin, a meeting participant, with an offer of a business relationship on the side. Irwin expressed a willingness to use some of the $5 million in US Government bonds he held in his safe as a source of cash to purchase RN's trust deeds on the condition that RN gave him 40% of his profits. In effect, he was offering the same deal that RN had concluded with Henry Morris back in Oakland in 1906. RN reported turning the deal down, explaining that he was already involved with other members of the Executive Committee as directors of his company or as stockholders, and "I am honor bound to carry on with them."

RN's older financial colleagues were so impressed with his business acumen and ability to execute his plans successfully that they were willing to look the other way on certain rule violations. Clearly the banking rules and regulations, as well as the rules of corporate governance, in the first decades of the 20th century were less strict than would be encountered today.

Others among this group of senior officers and directors also wanted to invest with RN. John McKee soon advised RN that Henry T. Scott would like to see him. On arriving at Scott's offices in the Shreve Building he learned that Scott wanted to place funds with him. "Burgess, your enterprises are developing into quite a business. I particularly like your financing receivables through R.N. Burgess Mortgage Company, and I am willing to invest $80,000 in R.N. Burgess Company." Scott's intention was to buy stock in the business, equal amounts of preferred and common shares, and to invest $40,000 for himself and $40,000 for his son Harry." RN welcomed the opportunity.

Scott's interest was soon followed by similar expressions of intent to invest by H.C. Breeden and Richard Pease, the latter the local manager of the Goodyear Rubber Company. Breeden initiated his offer with another meeting in his offices downtown. He purchased $20,000 of stock and shared with RN the fact that he had come West from New York where he had been a director of Standard Oil Company of New Jersey. A director of the Oakland and Antioch Railway, along with Richard Pease and Henry Scott, Breeden suggested to RN that he join them in an expansion of the road, saying "Let us expand along the Oakland and Antioch Railway and each make a million dollars." This must have been heady company for RN, a relatively young man in his thirties, and the offers of investment could have only cemented his confidence in his own ability. His relationship with the directors of the Oakland and Antioch Railroad would bear fruit in several years as he sought to extend rail lines into areas in which he planned subdivisions or other real estate enterprises.

RN's financial innovations were not original to him, though a reading of the *Memoirs* provides no attribution other than his own creativity. Henry Scott was familiar with an operation in New York City, Lawyers Mortgage Company, which was employing similar procedures and enjoying considerable success. He offered to visit them while on an upcoming trip east, to collect copies of their forms, and to become familiar with their practices with the idea of improving and enlarging the scope of R.N. Burgess Mortgage Company. RN agreed with the idea conceptually, but insisted on a name change if Lawyers Mortgage's practices were to be implemented locally. Sometime later the company became known as Western Mortgage & Guaranty Company. With these changes an expanded board of directors was approved, growing to fifteen men, and RN "found myself surrounded by a fine group of men, mostly friends of Henry T. Scott, and all but one old enough to be my father, if not my grandfather." The Board nominated RN to be President of the company.

He worked diligently at maintaining good relationships with his lenders and other influential men who played various roles in his growing businesses. In the years shortly after their marriage, RN and Anne lived in Berkeley and he commuted to San Francisco by ferry boat. In 1913 Anne asked that he build her a summer home on their new property in Diablo. He did so and she liked it so much that it became their permanent new home for the next ten years. The Homestead property, the original home that came with the purchase of the Rice Ranch in 1908, became a weekend home and a place for entertaining business associates.

Homestead was large enough to accommodate groups of four in its four bedrooms, and the family cook, Sing, was an excellent cook. The home was also well placed in the center of the many subdivisions RN was working on, so it became an ideal location for business entertaining. The group would meet at a pre-designated location in Contra Costa County and tour all of the properties under construction. When the property tour was completed, they would drive over to Homestead and spend the night.

RN's descriptions in the *Memoirs* of these evenings provide revealing insights into how he saw himself in those early days prior to the collapse of his business empire. The men he was entertaining after the property tours were among the elite of San Francisco's financial and business community and included, Harry T. Scott, President of Mercantile National Bank and of Pacific Telephone and Telegraph, H.C. Breeden, former director of Standard Oil of New Jersey, Richard Pease, local head of Goodyear Rubber Company, and John McKee, Vice President of Mercantile Bank.

A typical evening of business entertainment at the Homestead consisted of a mid-afternoon arrival after the property tour, time to freshen up, a two-hour cocktail interval, and dinner prepared by Sing, all followed by poker until well into the evening. RN kept a poker book recording each player's account and in later years it enhanced his recollection of those evenings. In his own words, "I notice that on April 2, 1912, H.T. Scott, H.C. Breeden, and R.H. Pease registered at Homestead…Sing prepared a roasted shoat for dinner that night - even the roasted apple in its mouth. After dinner we frequently had a game of poker. I did not ask these associates to sign the guest book after the original party as their record was in the poker book."

On one such occasion, Henry Scott proposed that the group purchase one of the properties they had toured that afternoon. "Gentlemen, it will take $80,000 to finance the land we just looked at. I am in favor of our each putting up $20,000; that is, if Burgess is willing to put up his $20,000." RN reports that he went along but notably had to borrow the $20,000 for his share from Scott's bank.

Henry Scott liked good scotch and had supplied the Homestead with ample quantities of McCallum's Perfection, his favorite. It is easy to imagine RN, a relative youth among these seasoned operators, but smart and shrewd enough in his own right to be accepted into the company of sophisticated money men of San Francisco. His demonstrated interest in the finer things of life must have come to the fore in these meetings and dinners. He was not a big drinker, by his own account, but on occasion the older men set him up for over-consumption.

On one evening when the group was assembled he left the house temporarily to visit his foreman and attend to his nursery and orchard stock, all on the land at Homestead. This stock was being grown for future transplanting to developments throughout Contra Costa County. His associates remained behind, enjoying their cocktails. He reported that his suspicion was that the older men felt he was ducking out on the drinking part of the evening's festivities. On his return to the house, he was greeted by Richard Pease and Henry Scott each of whom put an arm around his shoulders and, escorting him to the dinner table, announced that, "We never have to worry when Burgess is alone, we know he will attend to business, but we know it is cold outside and have prepared a double header for him." As he put it, RN felt that "this was a time for deeds not excuses," and responded to the men by asking where their drinks were, suggesting that "I can't drink alone." On their filling their glasses, he announced "bottom sides up," and finished his drink.

One is struck by RN's own reporting of his conduct in these evenings where, as a much younger man (he was thirty-four in 1912), he was in the position of entertaining men of prominence, and men with whom it must have given him much pride to associate. In later years, when he ran into serious financial difficulty with these men, difficulties which caused them to abandon him completely, these must have been rueful recollections.

Another anecdote suggests RN's impressions of his guests as well-connected men of affairs. One evening, in an effort to dissuade his associates from returning to poker after dinner, since his losses had mounted and he was fearful of another losing evening, he turned up the heater and kept the wine glasses full until, after the meal and much conversation, the guests were no longer interested in anything but retiring for the evening. Shortly after they all went to bed the telephone rang and RN picked it up. The caller was Templeton Crocker, one of two heirs to the Charles Crocker estate, for which Henry Scott was executor. Templeton was calling his executor to secure permission to make a $40,000 loan to a local shipping company. Scott replied that the bank had run a credit check on the firm and that it was not worth the risk. Templeton insisted, however, and Henry finally approved the funds. Scott's sense of the risk was accurate as Crocker subsequently lost all his money.

To a reader over a hundred years later these stories suggest RN's fascination with the lives and affairs of his business associates. These were men of whom he had perhaps read in his early business days in Contra Costa County, but with whom he would never have interacted in the absence of his business dealings. They were his means to rise in the world, to gain acceptance and recognition in his chosen profession. His emotional investment in them was far greater than theirs in him, as would become clear in a few years.

The properties that RN and his lenders were viewing during these afternoon tours were located throughout the central part of Contra Costa County and included land that he had coveted since his days in his aerie at the San Miguel Ranch as he dreamed of great subdivisions. During the years of 1912 through 1914, he bought large tracts of land, almost all financed with loans from the San Francisco bankers that he worked so hard to cultivate. The subject of his purchase of the Oakwood Stock Farm at Diablo will be the subject of a future chapter, but concomitant to that major purchase he bought large properties in today's Walnut Creek, Concord, Clayton, Moraga, Lafayette, and Diablo.

Under the R.N. Burgess Company name he bought 160 acres in Pleasant Valley (part of the Blackhawk Ranch), 240 acres of the Cope almond orchard north of Mt Diablo, 160 acres of the Bruce Stone Ranch, the 1,300-acre Brubeck Ranch on the north slope of the Mountain adjoining Ygnacio Valley, another 3,050 acres adjoining these parcels, a park of undisclosed size from George W. McNear (the son of the manager who sought his dismissal at CSBR&C during the Hookston days) and, most notably, a block of 15,000 acres which included the summit of Mt. Diablo from the H.H. Haight family of San Francisco. This last purchase included the right-of-way for the Mt. Diablo Scenic Boulevard.

After these acquisitions, RN began construction of a road to the summit of the Mountain. This job undertaken in 1912 was the first of two such extensive road construction and improvement jobs he would perform on Mt. Diablo. The second occurred three years later and was a condition of the contract he signed with W.R.

Hearst in 1914. An article in the December 21, 1912 edition of the San Francisco Call describes the urgency under which improvements were being made on the intercounty tunnel between Contra Costa County and Berkeley. The Call piece suggested that tunnel-improvement work was being done in anticipation of the pending completion of "Mt Diablo Boulevard" to the summit of the Mountain and the immense demand that new road would create for visits to the County. "The board of supervisors, which recently visited Mt. Diablo Boulevard …are planning to immediately fix the tunnel road from the intercounty tunnel to Bryant station. Chairman Trythall of the board is particularly anxious to see that the tunnel road is in first class condition in order to be able to handle the increased traffic that will come from the completion of this boulevard, which will be one of the most scenic drives in the state. The R.N. Burgess company, San Francisco and Oakland realty operators, who possess vast holdings in the Mount Diablo country, is constructing the boulevard at its own expense. The traffic over the tunnel road is growing daily, and, on the completion of the Mt Diablo boulevard it will increase tenfold." This piece from the Call, datelined Walnut Creek, was printed under the headline "Rushing Work on the Mt. Diablo Boulevard – New Road Will be Great Scenic Highway to Greatest Viewpoint in Bay Region," looked as if it had been written and placed by RN, but with no acknowledgement that it was an advertisement.

A log of the second Diablo road construction project is in the Museum of San Ramon and includes entries beginning on April 26, 1915 and continuing through the end of that year. The log was not written by RN but his name appears clearly as the man in charge of the entire operation, though not the day to day activities. Presumably, the writing was that of his foreman on the job. From RN's description in the *Memoirs* and the detail in the April 1915 logbook, it is clear that this job was more extensive and thorough than the earlier. RN directed the work from his offices in San Francisco and the log is replete with references to "Mr. Burgess's" periodic visits and his active participation in the project.

The road began on the 1,300-acre parcel he had purchased from

Brubeck in Ygnacio Valley on the north slope of the Mountain. The plan was to go from there to the summit, then back down two to three miles to the south gate junction and from there to the Oakwood Stock Farm site. To accomplish this work, RN purchased a Marion steam shovel and, because much of the surface was rock or shale, he employed substantial blasting work in the process. The log contains entries about running out of blasting powder and needing to go to Hercules for replenishment.

After the completion of the roads to the summit and to Diablo, RN arranged to have rail service extended to both the Ygnacio Valley North approach and to the Oakwood Stock Farm. In accomplishing this he was aided by his contacts with both Henry Scott and H.C. Breeden. In addition to being President of Pacific Telephone and Telegraph, the Mercantile National Bank, and the St. Francis Hotel Company, Scott was a director of the Oakland and Antioch Eastern Railroad, as was Breeden. Scott's influence at Pacific Telephone also resulted in securing a telephone exchange at the new Mt Diablo Park Company and lines to the residences. A final enhancement was designation of Diablo as a Post Office site. Important for getting the site included in local maps, this step was accomplished by RN's application to the Post Master General in August of 1916. By December of that year, Diablo had its own Post Office.

Another news article echoed the bullish reports of opportunity in "Diablo Country" as the area was called. On March 30, 1913, the San Francisco Call ran a piece extolling the benefits of the soon to be completed Oakland, Antioch and Eastern railway, indicating that scheduled operations would begin within thirty days. It also mentioned that three branch lines were being built in the Diablo Valley, presumably the lines that RN was pushing for improved Diablo access. As so many of these pieces seemed to have done, it goes on to talk about his extensive holdings. "When it was first rumored that this road was to be built the R.N. Burgess company purchased all the available ranches in the district until today, aside from the thousands of acres that they have resold in subdivisions, they own 35,000 acres. Practically this entire acreage is on this new road, and with the inauguration of train service will be opened and sold as income home farms." Once again, this feels like a planted piece by RN's publicist (perhaps himself) and there is no way to corroborate the size of his land holdings, but it is clear that his subdividing, homebuilding, and development business was among the largest in Contra Costa County in these early decades of the 20th century. The enhancements in terms of access to the mountain top, rail service to the new developments at Diablo, and postal service were all a preamble to a major chapter in RN's life, his association and contract with William Randolph Hearst.

RN and Anne with their first child, Robert Noble Burgess, Jr., born in the 2325 Piedmont Ave. home in Berkeley, 1910. Courtesy Burgess Family collection.

*Downtown Walnut Creek and a view of
the First National Bank, started by RN.
Courtesy Contra Costa Historical Society.*

Walnut Creek scene; RN's real estate office is just visible.
Courtesy Contra Costa County Historical Society.

Anne Fish Burgess with her first daughter, Frances Webster Burgess. 1914
Courtesy Burgess Family collection.

RN with first daughter, Frances Webster Burgess; September 15, 1915.
Courtesy Burgess Family collection.

Diablo home, April 1917.
Courtesy Burgess Family collection.

Driveway of Diablo home overlooking orchards which later became the seventeenth and eighteenth holes of the Diablo Country Club golf course. Courtesy Burgess Family collection.

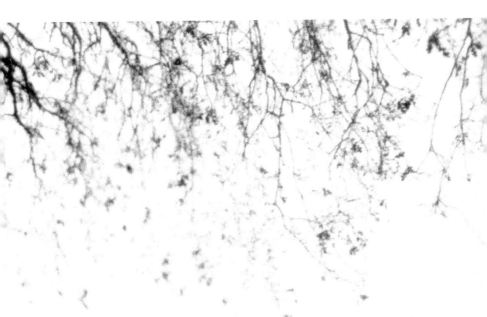

Band hired by RN to showcase his new Concord housing development on the day of his dispute with the President of the Bank of Concord. C-1911. Courtesy Contra Costa County Historical Society.

Completion of Mt. Diablo Summit Road in November, 1915.
Courtesy Diablo Country Club collection.

CHAPTER 11

"A Community with an Ideal"
William Randolph Hearst and Diablo

The Oakwood Stock Farm which RN had so admired in his youth from the vantagepoint of his home at Bonney Vista some three miles west had a rich heritage. In the 1870's the property was acquired by business entities known as The Western Development Company. This company was controlled by very powerful California investors, known to history as the Big Four. Leland Stanford, Collis Huntington, Mark Hopkins, and Charles Crocker were the fathers of the Central Pacific Railroad and, at its joining with the Union Pacific at Promontory Point, Utah in 1869, the West was opened to millions of Americans living in the East. The wealth amassed by the four men enabled them to acquire rich land throughout the state and among the parcels they added to their portfolio was land on the southwest slopes of Mt Diablo which became known as the Railroad Ranch.

In 1874 the four investors acquired a fifth partner when they brought in San Francisco attorney David D. Colton. Colton, who had prospered in the gold fields before returning to his home in the East to earn a law degree, was a remarkably accomplished man and, as a much younger partner of the Big Four, he could be counted on to run the ranch and continue to develop the improvements installed by the prior owner, William Cameron. Cameron had already made improvements, most notably building the first road to the top of the mountain from the south side in 1874.

In 1877, having decided to make the ranch his country home, David Colton moved with his family to Diablo. Mark Hopkins conveyed his interest to Colton who soon acquired the remaining shares of the original partners and by June of 1877 he owned the entire 1,600-acre parcel. Colton made new improvements to the property and began acquiring thoroughbred horses and other prized livestock with the intent of creating a world-class source of breeding stock. With these investments and Colton's active management, the Railroad Ranch became known as the Colton Ranch. Sadly, it was not destined to last. In July of 1878, David Colton was thrown from the back of a wild stallion, Don Juan, that he had captured in Arizona and had shipped to Diablo. The fall proved fatal and he died from his injuries the following October.

Colton's youngest daughter, Caroline, inherited most of the acreage of the ranch and, in the fall of 1879 she was married to another successful miner, Dan Cook. Cook and his older brother Seth, in partnership with John Franklin Boyd, made their fortunes with the Bunker Hill Mine in Bodie, California. Dan Cook came into his marriage to Caroline Colton a wealthy man. He and his brother, together with Boyd, had initially invested $67,000 in acquiring the Bunker Hill Mine and were reported to have extracted $10,000,000 of gold and silver from the diggings. Dan and Caroline Cook continued to improve the ranch. They expanded its acreage, installed a dairy and fruit orchard, and modified the existing estate house into a family home. On a hill behind the home they built a clubhouse, which, in a much-modified state, is still in use today as the Diablo Country Club. [1]

On the death of Dan Cook of tuberculosis in October 1882, his widow Caroline and their only child moved back to the family home on Nob Hill in San Francisco and Dan's brother Seth took over the management of the renamed Cook Ranch. Seth Cook, a fifty-nine-year-old bachelor, died in 1889 and left the then 4,700-acre property to his niece Louise Cook Arner who in 1883 had married his old mining partner, John Franklin Boyd. The Boyd's with their three children, lived and prospered on the once again renamed Oakwood Stock Farm during the 1890's until the death in 1901 and 1902 of two of their three children. The two brothers died of heart disease following bouts of rheumatic fever. The parents

[1] David Alan Mackesey with Linda Parker Hamilton, *From Country Estate to Country Club, The History of Diablo Country Club*, Cory Curtola Brett, Miller Brown, 2014, 23.

and their remaining daughter spent less and less time on the ranch, preferring their home in San Rafael under the circumstances, and Louise tried unsuccessfully to sell the property. [2]

RN's purchase of the Oakwood Stock Farm on June 17, 1912 was one of his largest land purchases to date and there are numerous references in the *Memoirs* about his interest in the property beginning in his early years. In his youthful farming days in Danville, he had met Seth Cook and knew of the land and its possibilities. When an opportunity to acquire it came along, he didn't hesitate.

The story of this purchase and of the creative tactics employed in overcoming the reluctance of the owner's attorney to sell represents another variation on some of the themes of RN's life. It began while he was on a driving tour of the southwest slopes of Mt Diablo on a summer afternoon in 1913. Stopping by the Oakwood Stock Farm he encountered a current tenant of the property sitting on the front porch and accepted the tenant's invitation to stay for a drink. The man told RN that he was very pleased with the ranch and in fact had tried to purchase it from his lessor, the owner, Mrs. John F. Boyd. RN had known Mrs. Boyd when, as a boy, he had worked on the Farm and his older brother Will was a tutor to the Boyd's only daughter, Louise. Indicating that the price had been set at $150,000, the lessee said he had communicated with Mrs. Boyd that he would accept those terms and buy the property. She in turn gave him a letter to give to her attorney to complete the transaction. For reasons unclear to the tenant, the attorney, Mr. William Humphries, refused to close the sale. The lawyer had apparently stymied similar such sales on several occasions in the past. Either he had personal intentions of purchasing the land himself or he felt it unwise for his client to sell.

Later, back in his offices in San Francisco, RN telephoned Mrs. Boyd and was invited for tea at her home in San Rafael. Accepting the invitation to tea, he made plans for overcoming the attorney's objection. Arming himself with a $10,000 cashier's check payable to himself drawn on the Crocker National Bank, he took the ferry to Marin for his three o'clock meeting. Mrs. Boyd was gracious,

2 Ibid., 35

recalling their earlier relationship and responding affirmatively to RN's question that she did indeed wish to sell Oakwood at a price of $150,000, with $50,000 down, and the balance due in three years at a 6% rate of interest. She acknowledged that she had received several prior offers but all were unable to meet her attorney's requirements and added that she wished RN better luck. To this, RN responded that he would buy the ranch at her price but would pay cash within thirty days.

While Mrs. Boyd was conferring with her secretary about the instructions to be written to her attorney, RN "hovered around and purposely dropped the $10,000 cashier's check" in a conspicuous place near her chair. On taking her seat, she saw the check and picked it up exclaiming "What in the world is this"? RN replied that he had brought the check with him with the intention of making a payment on account. Then, exclaiming over his own carelessness at dropping the check, he suggested that he endorse the check over to her and "then when Mr. Humphries is ready I will only have to pay him $140,000." On her agreement to that suggestion, RN said that a simple PS on the note she had written to the attorney, explaining that she had accepted the $10,000 payment on account and only $140,000 was now due, would suffice. As he left Mrs. Boyd, he told her, "You can now feel you have sold the ranch."

Back in San Francisco, RN had a Photostat made of Mrs. Boyd's note and proceeded to the office of her attorney. Mr. Humphries was in a meeting but interrupted it to come out of his office to see RN. To RN's statement that he had just purchased the Oakwood Stock Farm from Mrs. Boyd, the lawyer indicated, "You may think you have." RN then produced the documentation proving his ownership and Humphries acquiesced, realizing that his client had issued a valid contract of sale, in the form of her letter, at the moment she accepted the $10,000 payment on account.

RN certainly gets good marks for creativity in developing a strategy to overcome the resistance of the owner's lawyer. He is on less firm ground, however, in the interchange with Mrs. Boyd. The most charitable view is that the attorney was guilty of self-dealing with his client and, under this construction, RN's subterfuge went only to blocking the lawyer's efforts in his own behalf. Mrs. Boyd almost certainly did not know of the legal impact of her actions in following RN's directions and RN did not advise her. Would a more forthcoming posture on his part have killed the deal? Possibly, but it is difficult to evaluate actions taken a hundred years ago, in the light of today's business and legal mores. In today's world, failure of full disclosure as to RN's actions might have subjected him to charges of fraud should Mrs. Boyd have ultimately decided against going forward. But, from RN's description, she seemed genuinely interested in selling the property and he met her price, so a change of heart on her part was not likely.

***

The successful acquisition of the Oakwood Stock Farm from the Boyd's was big news in local real estate circles. A transaction of this nature could only have enhanced the growing reputation of RN's company. He wrote that since the early days of his real estate syndication and subdivision efforts, indeed since his boyhood in Danville, he had dreamed of controlling this piece of property and of creating a high quality and unique subdivision there surrounding an exclusive country club. During the next three years, RN would begin the work of bringing to fruition his dream for Oakwood. He envisioned an exclusive enclave on the slopes of Mt. Diablo, a world-class golf club surrounded by homes, orchards and spectacular scenery, all available an hour or so east of the suburbs of the near east bay and San Francisco. Added inducements included a telephone exchange to Diablo with a hook-up to each new home and a two-mile extension of the Oakland & Antioch Eastern Railway. When he bought the property, the railway terminated at today's Green Valley and Diablo Road intersection. His additional investment, utilizing his relationships with board members of the railroad, resulted in a new terminus close to the clubhouse.

His vision of a world-class golf club was facilitated by attracting a legendary Scottish golfer and club maker from his position at the

Claremont Country Club in Oakland. RN's friend and business associate, George McNear, a member at Claremont, helped in recruiting John Smith and his wife to relocate to new quarters at Diablo, thus facilitating the development of a championship course at the new club.[3] Also in 1917, he held a dedication ceremony for the new Chalet building on the hill above the Club Inn, designed by Arthur Burnett Benton. Benton, known for his restoration of the San Juan Capistrano and San Diego Missions as well as for his design of the Mission Inn in Riverside, California, was yet another in the group of prominent early 20th century architects who worked with RN on many of his projects. Interestingly, Benton, a lover of Mt. Diablo, would not accept a fee for this design work, instead writing and sending to RN an original poem, *On Mt. Diablo*, in 1918. The poem is included in its entirety in the *Memoirs*.

His dreams were now within his reach, but before RN could actually begin to bring them to fruition he was challenged by some former business associates who expressed irritation that he had not included them in the Oakwood deal. Not long after the deal closed in the summer of 1912, RN was invited to lunch in San Francisco by his former colleague, Senator Arthur Breed. With Breed at the Palace Court restaurant that day were his partner Harlow Bancroft, and another friend of Breed's, George Emmons, the owner of a local moving and storage firm. RN reported being "severely ribbed" by Breed and his colleagues for failing to invite them to participate with him in the Oakwood deal.

In 1906, immediately following the earthquake and fire, Arthur Breed had given RN one of his first breaks when he invited him to set up his new real estate practice in Breed's offices. At that point, Breed was a man on the way up in Oakland and in the intervening years, his star had continued to ascend. By 1912, RN must have felt that his affiliation with a man of such influence could only have helped him. Breed was born in San Francisco in 1865 and relocated to Oakland in 1883, a year prior to RN's arrival in California. A principal of the successful real estate firm of Breed & Bancroft, he began his public career as city auditor of Oakland in 1899 and was

---

[3] Ibid., 58

then elected to the State Legislature in 1912, a position in which he performed well enough to be named President pro tempore of the California State Senate, an office he held for 18 years. In 1953, on the occasion of Breed's death, Governor Earl Warren called him the "father of our state highway system," in recognition of his authorship of the California Motor Vehicle Act and the attendant gasoline tax which provided funds for the construction of highways in California. Breed also served as Lieutenant Governor on Frank Merriam's ascendancy to the governorship after the death of Governor James Rolph II in 1934.

A man of such political, social, and business prestige was hard to deny, and, from his account in the *Memoirs*, it appears that RN acquiesced to this pressure rather quickly. Rationalizing that Breed as a State Senator and prominent realtor, along with his partner Harlow Bancroft, and Emmons, also a prominent business man in the drayage business, might be useful as partners, he surrendered his majority interest by agreeing to take the three on as equal partners. In doing so, he violated his long-standing policy of retaining personal control of his business entities. Each of the three men bought a quarter share of the newly-named Mt. Diablo Park Company at a price reflecting actual cost and each was named a director of the company.

RN's decision to accept this offer of a partnership had critically important implications for the long-term chances for success of his dream community at Diablo. For one thing, the partners were never in agreement as to the basic strategic direction of the investment. As David Mackesey writes in his excellent *History of Diablo Country Club* RN's vision was not in line with that of his new partners. Emmons saw potential for pasturage for the mules needed for his drayage business and for sale to others. Breed and Bancroft had differing views as to the opportunity afforded by the property. Within the first year of the new partnership, on June 8, 1913, the San Francisco Call ran an article describing keen interest on the part of the Olympic Club of San Francisco in acquiring the property for a rural retreat and elaborate sports complex. A party for the entire membership was planned for the weekend of June

21-22, the intent being to expose the group to the new property. RN must have intervened aggressively on behalf of his dream, however, because the following month, the Call announced that the deal had not gone through because of inability of the parties to come to terms. What roles Breed, Bancroft and Emmons played in stimulating the Olympic Club interest in the property is not clarified, nor is any role RN might have played in these negotiations. But it seems clear that the new partners were not on the same page with respect to the future of Oakwood.[4]

Breed's seniority and experience quickly manifested itself as he nominated RN as President. But he also appointed George Emmons as general manager in charge of all farming operations at the ranch. This move rankled RN because he thought of Emmons as a moving and storage man, not a farmer, and because Breed apparently made the appointment without consulting the others. Breed's political clout and prestige, his experience, and his earlier mentoring role with RN must have conferred a senior role on him, but RN was not happy with the result and the move spawned tensions that would play out during the following year and be costly in terms of RN's strategic plans for the property. RN reported doubts from the start. "I had my first misgivings that it was a stacked deal. I realized that I had made a mistake and the line-up was three to one."

RN's apprehensions about the new partnership soon became justified in his mind when George Emmons moved in a board meeting to approve the purchase of 300 mules. As a drayage man, Emmons thought he saw an opportunity to profit from the acquisition of the mules at what he thought was a good price. RN's take on the investment was not charitable. He characterized them as "some of Santa's reindeer... sired by a mountain goat or reindeer." Emmons' plan was to pasture them at Mt Diablo Park for a year and then sell them to drayage operators. His prediction to the board was that they would realize a profit of $6,000 from the sale of the mules as well as an additional profit of $6,000 from the crops grown elsewhere on the farm.

Early in 1914 when the financial results for the prior year were

---

[4] Ibid., 40-43.

in, it became apparent that Emmons had badly misjudged the opportunity and a loss of $6,000 was realized instead of the expected $12,000 profit. As RN described it in the *Memoirs*, the partners were understandably upset at the unexpected loss but inexplicably blamed the result on him. The argument put forward was that RN, as President, should have seen the poor result coming and headed it off at its inception. In RN's view, "It was unreasonable enough to blame me when the farm manager was their nominee and the purchase of the mules also their nomination. Of course, I voted with them as it was customary in our companies to vote unanimously or else throw the motion out." These financial results and his reaction are interesting because they speak to RN's underlying need to be in control of his operations, a characteristic consistently displayed throughout his business life. The partners were described as being "upset at the unexpected loss." The surprise nature of the loss is understandable only by assuming that RN had total operational control, which seems likely given his role as president, and did not submit periodic financial status reports to his partners or communicate well with them. The $18,000 swing between a $12,000 profit and a $6,000 loss was probably unfolding throughout the year and he must have had insight into the likely results before they were produced by the accountants. For whatever reason, he kept it to himself. RN worked best alone, a trait first seen in his early days of fruit-buying in Concord and one that stayed with him throughout his business life.

This partnership disagreement ultimately spawned the breakup of the group, RN suggesting to the others, "Gentlemen, I can see that we will not get along together, and I will not be involved in a constant dogfight. Either buy my holdings or I will buy yours at a basis of cost plus the $6,000 loss."

Ultimately, the three partners did exactly that and the R.N. Burgess Company bought out their interest becoming once again the sole owner of Mt Diablo Park Company. It is difficult to comprehend RN's so quickly surrendering control in such an important real estate development and then acceding to staffing arrangements with which he strongly disagreed. Breed's influence seems to be the key to his acceptance of such uncharacteristic (for him) operating conditions at the bidding of the more senior and experienced man. Breed was RN's elder by thirteen years and was a successful State politician and sophisticated real estate operator. He had been a guest of RN's at the Homestead on at least ten occasions and the two frequently exchanged cards and letters. Perhaps of most significance, he had offered RN his first affiliation in the heady days following the 1906 earthquake and fire. A combination of loyalty, affection, and a sense that Breed's public persona might be helpful seem to have coalesced in RN's mind, driving him to accept what he otherwise might not have. Interestingly, in the Memoirs, RN commented that, "From then on the friendship between me and Breed commenced to deteriorate."

The Breed partnership was damaging to RN's prospects for success at Diablo because of the timing of other, non-related events during the next two years. The years 1913-14 were particularly important to the development of Diablo and time spent in a partnership with men not of one mind on the ultimate project goal was time lost irretrievably to RN. His hope of a once-in-a-lifetime marketing opportunity at the 1915 Pan Pacific International Exposition (P.P.I.E.) was frustrated by delays in 1913, the first year of the Breed agreement. Had RN been able to fast-track the project on his original time-line, he would have been able to expose it to thousands of potential buyers from around the country. The loss of this opportunity, coupled with other national and international events, essentially doomed his plans.

Had the events reported by the press in the spring of 1916 occurred a year earlier, attendees at the San Francisco World's Fair in March would have been reading in the Oakland Tribune about the commencement of marketing of the first 250 acres of the Mt. Diablo Park Club. Had RN's elaborately planned opening day, occurring on May 14, 1916, occurred in the prior spring, press reports and promotion would have appealed to a much broader audience, which would have included attendees of the P.P.I.E. In any event, the day of the opening must have marked a singular event in RN's mind as he reflected on his career to that point. A grand celebration was held at Diablo. Four specially scheduled trains brought prospective buyers from Berkeley, Oakland, and San Francisco to view what had been marketed as a unique opportunity to buy and own spectacular real estate in "Diablo Country." As David Mackesey described the day, "...guests wearing 'panama hats, summer suits, gaudy-colored silk jerseys, broad striped sports coats and millinery of every hue' gathered for an open-air concert on the tennis courts across from the clubhouse, delighting in arias from Madam Butterfly sung by popular soprano Madam Margaret Jelica...Visitors that day could join the Mt. Diablo Park Club for $60. If they bought a lot, the $60 would be refunded. Yearly dues were $20. Half-acre and acre lots sold quickly, with many purchasing two or three adjacent lots. Burgess sold $40,000 of lots that day." The high point of the day for the young developer may well have been the long-distance telephone call he received from William Randolph Hearst. As effusive in his praise as he was slow in honoring the terms of his deal to promote the project, Hearst was quoted in the San Francisco Examiner as saying, "I congratulate you on your magnificent enterprise. I believe that you are doing a splendid work not only for the great numbers who will be immediately benefited by this beautiful development...but for the whole state and the whole community. I believe that your development will make Mt. Diablo as great an attraction and as famous as a beauty spot as the Golden Gate, the Yosemite, the big trees and other world-renown attractions of our wonderful state."

RN's relationship with Arthur Breed may have deteriorated, but it did not end with the termination of the business partnership. Indeed, Breed, at a luncheon between the two shortly thereafter, gave RN what might qualify as the tip of a lifetime in terms of business associations. Apologizing for the way the Mt. Diablo Park partnership had ended, he referred RN to another real estate operator in a gesture possibly designed to soften the blow of the lost time and money of the failed partnership. Breed told RN that, when at times he found himself in need of competent real estate help he had gone to M.T. Minney, President of the M.T. Minney Real Estate Company in Oakland. Minney had enjoyed great success as a broker in Oakland, having sold $5 million worth of properties between 1906 and 1910 according to an article in the San Francisco Call. Breed characterized Minney as a man of many ideas who had often been helpful to him, but also cautioned that Minney, in his opinion, was a marketing genius but also a man of questionable character. "He is not a satisfactory associate."

RN's met with M.T. Minney not long after his lunch with Breed. They were scheduled to meet at the Mt Diablo Park location but inclement weather precluded this and the two met at the Homestead instead. RN began the session by lighting a fire and mixing a shaker of gibsons to break the ice and facilitate conversation. Minney proved a font of ideas and anecdotes about his alleged real estate successes. As the evening wore on, he indicated he had to head home as it was getting late and RN offered his chauffeur but first said, "Let us have another shaker of cocktails and see who can do the tallest bit of entertaining." He went on to relate that "I told the first yarn, and after Minney told his I realized I was completely outclassed as a yarnster." Minney's stories continued, describing an array of real estate successes and accomplishments which included sales of townsites, shopping centers, golf courses, country clubs, and race tracks. RN's reaction was that all this was too elaborate and detailed to have been a mere off-the-cuff recitation; it seemed as if it had been prepared and rehearsed. Feeling that the unwritten rule of such story-telling was that a story needed to have some basis in fact or justification, he challenged Minney as to the secret of his success. Minney's response was that he was able to accomplish all this because, "he had William Randolph Hearst as his publicity agent." Hearst "stood squarely behind him with his controlled papers and magazines that reached five million people daily."

RN's excitement was palpable. As he recalled it, "M.T. had just given me his outline for subdividing Old Mexico." The reference to Old Mexico is unclear unless seen in the context of RN's ambitions; he was saying that, with this idea and a relationship with a man like Hearst, his development prospects could span the state of California. He went to work on the idea immediately, sending

Minney home with his chauffeur and staying up the rest of the night composing a series of draft telegrams to William Randolph Hearst at his Los Angeles headquarters. Stumped at what he might say that would capture Hearst's attention in a telegram from a man he didn't know, RN finally decided on a strategy. He decided to make allusions to various things he knew about current events in Los Angeles which he knew would be of concern to Hearst and were a "thorn in his flesh." He drafted the telegram accordingly, sent it, and went to bed. Before mid-day the next morning, the following telegram arrived: Meet me at the Hotel Alexandria, Los Angeles, at 10:30 next Thursday morning. WRH."

***

The man that RN was about to go to Los Angeles to meet was, by this time, a major force in the newspaper publishing business in the United States. Born in San Francisco in 1863, the son of mine-owner and United States Senator George Hearst and Phoebe Apperson Hearst, William Randolph Hearst was to change the course of American journalism with the flamboyant, ostentatious, and often lurid style of reporting in his papers. After growing up in San Francisco, he attended St. Paul's School in Concord, New Hampshire, and Harvard College, from which he was expelled for misbehavior. In 1887, looking for something to do with his life, he was given a newspaper, the San Francisco Examiner, a publication that his father had won in a gambling debt. An aggressive and talented manager and identifier of creative talent, he soon prospered by bringing in writers such as Ambrose Bierce, Jack London, and Mark Twain. In the beginning, the politics of his papers were progressive and populist in nature.

In 1895, with financial help from his parents, Hearst moved to New York where he acquired the New York Morning Journal and promptly got into a circulation war with the major competitor for his brand of journalism, Joseph Pulitzer. Repeating the San Francisco experience, Hearst attracted excellent creative talent, including writers Steven Crane, Julian Hawthorne, and America's first color cartoonist, Richard Outcault. Outcault had created a color cartoon, "The Yellow Kid," while at Pulitzer's rival paper. Hearst later paid him an enormous salary to lure him to the Morning Journal and utilized his cartoon strip, "Yellow Kid," in sensationalizing stories to increase sales in a very competitive New York market, fathering the term "yellow journalism" in the process. He paid more than the going rate for writers and managed his newspaper in a fashion that contrasted well with the difficult-to-work-for Pulitzer. His success and growing reputation led to the acquisition of additional newspapers between 1900 and 1904 including the Chicago American, the Chicago Examiner, the Boston American, and the Los Angeles Examiner. His visibility and support of progressive politics soon brought him into the public arena as an office seeker. He ran successfully for the United States House of Representatives in 1902 and again in 1904, but the demands of his business activities contributed to a poor record of attendance and his constituents failed to grant a third term. Returning to New York, he ran unsuccessfully for Mayor of the city in 1905, for governor the following year, and again for mayor in 1909.

Hearst is remembered today for being the father of "yellow journalism." In particular, the role played by his newspapers in the declaration of war against Spain in 1898 is cited as being critical in creating nationalistic and belligerent attitudes towards that country among American voters. Reporting in his papers on this topic has been described as one-sided, short on evidence, and chauvinistic. The sinking of the battleship Maine in February was declared by Hearst's and other papers as sabotage without evidence to support the claim. To an American public incited by a jingoistic press, this was the last straw and a declaration of war followed in late April.

***

RN was on time and at the appointed place in Los Angeles for his meeting with Hearst the following Thursday. Calling Hearst from the hotel lobby, he was quickly invited to come to his room.

Hearst was engaging, putting the younger man at his ease immediately. Taking a seat on his couch, Hearst appeared to stare at a
blank place on the carpet in front of him as he invited RN to speak.
"Young man, spill it." RN talked for an hour, describing his plans
for the Mt. Diablo Park Company and pacing the floor in front of
an immobile and silent Hearst. Feeling that he had not convinc-
ingly made his case, he was preparing to make an exit when Hearst
exclaimed, "Hold on, we are not through. I will meet you next
Thursday morning at 10 a.m. at the Ferry Building, San Francisco,
and we will take a look at the Oakwood Park Stock Ranch." After
mentioning that his mother had a country home not far from Mt.
Diablo which could be seen from the summit, he concluded the
meeting and RN left.

On returning to San Francisco, RN immediately arranged for
one of the Key System's private ferry boats as well as for a private
rail car for the trip out to Diablo with Hearst, explaining that "It
seemed important to me to avoid strangers or busy-bodies and be
able to concentrate on the deal in view."

At the designated time, Hearst appeared with a party of three
women and three men. The names in his guestbook included Mrs.
Millicent Hearst, Miss Maddeine Podrane, and Nana B. Sigournay.
The men included Max Thomsen, manager of the Los Angeles Examiner, and M.T. Minney. Earlier in the day, RN had worked out
a plan with one of his men to leave the train early, prior to arrival
at the Club House, go to the stable and drive all but two of the saddle horses out of the main corral to higher pasturage up the Mountain. His idea was to ride the property alone with Hearst and to
accomplish this he needed all the available horses far enough away
that the others in Hearst's party would not have time to round
them up and accompany the two of them. Having heard the ladies
talking about making the horseback ride with them, he instructed
his associate to, "Post the stableman to be dumb, then hurry back
and entertain the ladies."

He was successful in this subterfuge and spent four hours on
the Mountain alone with Hearst. They began their ascent at Diablo
and were thus heading north and east as they climbed. Hearst

selected a building site and discussed plans for a two-hundred-foot wide boulevard planted on the sides with trees and shrubs selected with a view to their thriving at each elevation change, which began at 350 feet and ended at just under 4,000 feet. Hearst's thinking that afternoon was that, upon completion, "I will deed it to the University of California as an arboretum and have it endowed, and I will give some thought as to how to develop it further so it will be of educational importance." Listening to Hearst, RN realized that to do what he seemed to be suggesting, making gifts to institutions like the University, Hearst would need to be the owner of the property, not merely an investor as RN had been viewing him.

Stopping at a site on the southern slopes high enough to have an excellent view of the San Joaquin Valley and the southern Sierra Nevada Mountains, Hearst suggested that it ought to be the site of a collection of statuary pointing out the southerly views of valley and mountains. Continuing up, in a northerly direction now, they reached another high point from which they could see clearly the junction of the San Joaquin and Sacramento rivers and the northern Sierra Nevada Mountains. The views again caused Hearst to exclaim that more statuary was needed to enhance such a magnificent view point. On reaching the summit, Hearst, again taken by the stunning views, suggested it as the site of a hotel, a "castle-like building...worthy of Julia Morgan's skill."

RN's plan to engage and attract Hearst to his proposed development was a success and began a business association that lasted for half a decade, though never produced the ambitious financial results both had in mind. Their plans were nullified by a combination of RN's significant exposure to financial debt, Hearst's own complex and deteriorating financial situation, and history. Later that summer, the first World War began in Europe and, while it would take three years for the United States to become involved directly, the ripples of war began to be felt in this country over the subsequent years, affecting public confidence, the availability of financing, and business opportunities.

The arrangement the two of them reached involved the sale to Hearst of the 15,000-acre parcel recently assembled by RN extending from Ygnacio Valley Rd in the north, up the slope of Mt. Diablo to the summit, and then down the south slope to Diablo. The price for the land was $100 per acre, $1,500,000, and was to be remitted by Hearst in the form of in-kind advertising in his newspaper chain. The R.N. Burgess Company was to prepare advertising copy, reimbursable by Hearst, who would then publish it in 27 newspapers and magazines throughout the country for as long as it took to recapture the costs of the land and all improvements. In addition, RN was to complete the Club House at Diablo, the golf course, and complete the roads to the summit from both the Ygnacio Valley and Diablo ends. The R.N. Burgess Company was to act as sales agents for the estates and was to be paid a 20% commission. Hearst, however, delayed execution of the agreement for a year and then inserted a key modification, stipulating that no advertising or promotion would be forthcoming in his newspapers until repair and repaving of the Mt. Diablo summit roads was completed.

The nascent Burgess-Hearst agreement had the potential to become RN's largest real estate undertaking to date and, had it come to fruition, it might have been spectacular indeed. Among the initial steps indicated by their agreement was the purchase of more acreage to provide sufficient water to the project. As envisioned, it would draw upon the supplies at the Diablo Villa Homes site which were inadequate to the project as planned. Additional acreage would be needed to provide for more water. This came in the form of a purchase of the 8,000-acre Tasajarra Land Company parcel which connected the Diablo Villa property with the ample supplies in the Pleasanton basin to the south. Acquiring this additional land yielded a right of way for a water pipe within which to transfer the water to Diablo.

RN's dream community was not to be. Several factors coalesced to impede what seemed like a natural business arrangement at its inception. His own opinion was that a significant element was Hearst's delay in signing the agreement. The exact dates are unclear, but, the Diablo ride took place in the spring of 1914 and if the two had a meeting of the minds on an agreement by the fall of that year, Hearst's delay, as well as the addition of the significant new road-improvement condition, meant that the promotional aspects of the deal (the critical part to RN) would not have begun until early 1916. The last entry in the log of the road construction project is on January 11, 1916, suggesting that it was finished early in that year. The United States entered the war in Europe in April 1917, over a year later, and the Selective Service Act of 1917 (the draft) was enacted on May 8 of that year, so Hearst's delay in signing the agreement and insistence on the Diablo road completion were only part of a more complex story.

In early 1916, as RN finished the new roads to the top of Mt Diablo, Hearst's condition for initiating national promotional activities in his newspapers, the East Bay was anticipating a banner year for real estate sales. In spite of distant war drums and increasingly expensive building materials, the Oakland Tribune published a bullish article on the 13th of February touting the prospects for local real estate sales. Citing statistics reflecting year over year sales growth, the article goes on to suggest that, "The mortgage and loan market shows that there is a big movement under way which will result in many new developments during the next few months... Loans are plentiful and are being sought not only from the banks but from the small operators." The article cited the new, "back country" development at Diablo, reporting that "The meridian mountain has been linked to Oakland by a system of broad highways leading to the summit and has become a distinctive scenic asset to this city. And now, a syndicate of wealthy men have undertaken the establishment of the Mount Diablo Estate, which comprises 10,000 acres of hill and valley land, and which will be developed along community lines. Villa home sites will be placed on the market in the spring"

Presumably, this was indicative of the kind of promotion that RN expected Hearst to fund throughout his newspaper empire, though with construction of the Scenic Boulevard having just been completed, it had not yet begun. By the time of the opening day celebration, on May 14, 1916, it should have been well underway under the terms of their agreement.

A bigger problem for both men was that the bullish article from the Oakland Tribune in February of 1916 may have been close to the high-water mark for home prices nationally. They began to decline toward the end of that year, spiked marginally during the early part of American involvement in the war, and then fell precipitously through the early post-war period finally bottoming in 1920. Robert Schiller's long-term graph of American housing prices, dating to 1890, reflects a 33% decline. And, while there were rebounds during the 1920s and late 1930s, American home prices did not regain their 1916 level until just after the end of World War II. This post-World War I decline, spawned by America's entry into that war and by the flu pandemic, created one of the most severe declines in home prices in this country's history. A larger percentage decline did not occur until the 2007-8 financial crisis. This post-WWI price decline did not spare the Bay Area, and RN's life and business affairs were upended in the process. As he phrased it, "... the American people then were more concerned with the draft and taxes than with seeking a milder climate." [5]

The world-wide flu pandemic of January 1918-December 1920 also contributed to a significant fall-off in household formation in the United States. The pandemic infected an estimated 500,000,000 people world-wide, killing 3-6% of the world's population in the process. In the United States, 28% of the population were stricken and an estimated 500,000-675,000 died from it. Because of the nature of the virus it was particularly devastating to otherwise healthy young adults as it attacked the immune system, normally strongest in that segment of the population, while its impact was relatively lighter on younger and older victims. The most at-risk age group was also the most likely to marry and form new households with devastating implications for the home building industry.

A perfect storm of events, locally and nationally, thus consumed RN and his plans for Diablo. A short national recession resulting from the end of wartime production and excess labor availability from returning troops, depressed business activity

---

[5] Robert J. Shiller, *Irrational Exuberance*, 2nd Edition, (Princeton University Press, 2006).

overall. The delays in the marketing and promotion of Diablo caused by both the Breed partnership and Hearst's additional contract provision put his planned timing askew. The nation's preoccupation with World War I, during which Diablo seemed a frivolous local sideshow, exacerbated declining activity in real estate. A frightening, world-wide influenza pandemic, with unusually high mortality among those most likely to start families, further depressed commercial activities. Most ominously for a man accustomed to financing his activities with borrowed money, slow or nonexistent sales at Diablo, dropping home prices throughout his area of operation, and the attendant rising risk of default put RN and his lenders in a very precarious place.

With United States entry in World War I in April of 1917, events at Diablo slowed markedly and RN was in a holding pattern with respect to his dream community. His financial position would not improve under these conditions. He would have been watching home sales slow to a crawl in both Diablo and his other East Bay markets. He would have been making debt payments on his land purchases, buying scarce materials for whatever building he was able to do, and, most critically, not receiving the exposure throughout the Hearst newspaper empire that was the essence of their deal. His financial picture was spiraling downward with no prospects for improvement any time soon. Finally, on November 11, 1918 the War ended and the troops began to come home. But RN was far from out of the woods.

Early in 1919, Hearst sent a wire to RN asking that he visit him in New York when he was next in that city. The description of this visit is fascinating both for what it suggests about the state of their business arrangements at that date and for what insight it provides into RN's character. By this date, he had already spent considerable time with Hearst and, among other activities, they dined together frequently, meals often characterized by RN regaling Hearst with stories of business deals and personalities he had encountered in his affairs. In the meeting, at Hearst's home on Riverside Drive in New York City, the publisher was seeking RN's agreement to dissolve their contract. Business affairs were not going well for either partner at this point. In Hearst's case, rapid debt-fueled expansion of a never particularly profitable newspaper empire had him at the mercy of his creditors, and, although he was still ten years away from the apogee of his enormous empire, signs of his profligacy were beginning to appear. More ominously for RN, federal legislation relieving draftees of their obligation to make mortgage payments while serving, as well as the discovery that earlier state legislation modifying and tightening the conditions under which mortgages could be legally written and renewed, had him in a classic cash squeeze. The result was that neither man was in the financial shape he was five years earlier when they made the horseback ride up Mt. Diablo in 1914.

Finally, to gain liquidity, Hearst needed to sell some of his publishing properties and was advised that he would have to absolve himself of his obligations under the Burgess contract so as to be able to deliver clear title to prospective buyers. Although David Mackesey's research could produce no evidence that Hearst ever published one article about the project, his newspaper companies, under the agreement executed between the two men, were obligated contractually to provide the advertising RN and Hearst had agreed to. Under a prospective sale of any of the companies, such contingent liabilities would need to be removed. The Hearst Burgess agreement needed to be terminated.

Hearst's way of compensating RN for the early termination of their agreement was to publish a book he hoped that RN would write. His idea was that RN would write up the stories he had shared with Hearst during their dinners together. RN's ability to spin yarns and his creativity in describing his own business interactions throughout his career must have caught Hearst's ear and planted a seed of opportunity in the publisher's mind. When RN first met him on this visit, Hearst was carrying a book. RN described it as a "dummy book," entitled *"O.P.M. (other peoples money) and the Bottomless Trust Company."* Hearst went on to propose, "If you will dictate the experiences and episodes you have related to me at our suppers (and there are others you can add) I will get Mr. Wooster to edit it. I will publish it and our papers and magazines will review it favorably. It will be a success and I will give you all the royalties coming to the paper. With what you get direct (*sic*) there should be sufficient revenue to keep you for life. My reason for doing this is to leave you something to offset the losses you have made on advances you have made to Mt. Diablo Villa Homes." RN demurred, saying, "Mr. Hearst, I can't make my living by selling information given to me in confidence."

Thus, by the time of the 1919 visit to Hearst in New York, the Burgess-Hearst promotional agreement was moribund and in the process of being terminated. RN said in the Memoirs that Hearst "had OK'd the advertising bills before we decided it was useless to proceed while the war was on," suggesting that he was being paid for the promotional expenses he was incurring in the Bay Area, at least through early 1917. However, *national* advertising in the twenty-seven newspapers, which was the "currency" Hearst was to use to pay for the Mt. Diablo land and the substantial improvements RN had installed, did not happen. Hearst said to RN on that visit that, "Something will have to be done to clear up this matter. You have done your part and I feel I have done mine, but I have to stop my losses, and I am sure you are in the same fix."

RN's Diablo chapter was coming to an end and he would be forced in late 1919 to sell his position in the Diablo holdings. An event in the spring of that year provides more evidence about the conditions attending the end of the Diablo story. In April, RN was invited by Hearst's Mother, Phoebe Apperson Hearst, to a reception at her home in Pleasanton. RN described a reception line in which some three-hundred guests were lined up to pay their respects to Mrs. Hearst. RN was in line behind his business associate, lender, and competitor, P.E. Bowles, and when it was his turn to address Mrs. Hearst he felt her tug at his sleeve and whisper to him, "Wait until these people leave, I wish to see you." She offered to give him a tour of the home, its rooms full of antiques, and other items from her world travels. When, in the midst of their tour, she grew faint and asked RN to ring for her maid, she said to him, "What I particularly wished to ask you was to promise to look after Willie. As you are associated in the Mt. Diablo Villa Homes venture you will see much of him, and I do not expect to be here much longer."

Just how RN came to know Phoebe Hearst is not clarified in the *Memoirs*, but it seems likely that Julia Morgan might have been the intermediary. RN described building five homes designed by Morgan in the first decade of the century, a time when she was also Mrs. Hearst's client for the major improvements being made on the U.C. Berkeley campus. Whatever the source of their relationship, David Mackesey reports that RN was a favorite of hers and asking him to look out for William Randolph was an expression of that affection. On April 13th of that year, Phoebe Apperson Hearst died from complications of the influenza virus and RN reported of her request that, "I had the will to live up to it, but lacked the capacity…"

Phoebe's death appears to have been a critical event in W.R. Hearst's financial life. She had been the sole heir to the estate of her husband, George Hearst, but the senior Hearst had stipulated in his will that their son, William Randolph, was to receive only one half of the value of the estate on his Mother's death, the other half being distributable at his Mother's discretion. Presumably this provision was inserted as a mechanism for restraining a willful son, but it had the effect of binding Will to his Mother during her lifetime and of increasing the likelihood that he paid attention to her counsel and advice. With her affection for RN, this would have included honoring his deal with Burgess. On her death and his release from his filial obligation, he received almost the entire estate including her Pleasanton estate. His interest in Diablo began to wane at that point.[6]

The Diablo Villa Homes and Country Club projects occupied seven years of RN's long career. His purchase of the property in June of 1912 in fulfillment of a vision he had been nurturing for years began a series of events in his life, begun with high optimism but destined to have an unhappy ending. By mid-year 1919, he was facing bankruptcy and the loss of everything he had built with the exception of the one-hundred-fifty-acre parcel in Lake-

[6] Mackesey, *History of Diablo Country Club*, 45.

wood (Walnut Creek) he had gifted to Anne at the time of their marriage. Diablo would insure that his name remained in local history and it is indeed a remarkable story of vision and of a dream that is still being lived today. It was, however, only a part of his busy and long career and, before that career was destined to come to an end, he would be making more investments and deals throughout the Bay Area.

***

There is an important coda to RN's story of Diablo. His successor in ownership in the Diablo lands, local investor Walter P. Frick played a pivotal role in creating Mt. Diablo State Park.

Frick bought substantial portions of RN's holdings out of the bankruptcy after 1919, ultimately owning some 10,000 acres of the property which he incorporated as the Mt Diablo Company. Interestingly, Frick is never mentioned in the *Memoirs*, but he was a long-time associate and early business partner of RN's. Three years RN's senior, Frick came to California in the early 1890s and was living in Oakland after the 1906 earthquake and fire. His residence was close to the Athenian Nile Club, RN's residence at the time, and both men were members of the club and were young, aspiring land speculators and developers. In 1910, the two became business partners and two years later made a major investment together, buying 4,800 acres of Sonoma coastline. The property, a two by twelve mile stretch of coast was known as Del Mar Ranch and is more familiarly known today as Sea Ranch.

RN's role in developing and promoting the Mt Diablo Park Club, ultimately the Diablo Country Club, has eclipsed Walter Frick's key contributions to making Mt. Diablo the state park that it is today.

At the time of RN's bankruptcy and of Frick's acquisition of much of the land he lost, a movement was growing to have Mt. Diablo declared a State Park. In June of 1921, legislation was authored by State Legislator, Will R. Sharkey to declare Mt. Diablo a State Park and Game Refuge. On June 19th, some of the land was dedicated as such in a ceremony on the summit. The dedication came without funds to acquire the land, although a State Park Commission was formed, as was a local citizens group, the Mt. Diablo State Park Council. Both groups lobbied the state to begin making purchases of Frick's acreage. None of these efforts bore fruit, however until years later, when, in May of 1927, new legislation, backed by Governor Clement C. Young, created a State Park Commission and authorized a state-wide bond issue of $6,000,000 to be used to expand the park system. Approved by the voters in November of 1928, the bond issue required a fifty percent private match to supplement the public funds. By the end of the decade of the 1920s, however, Frick had been badly hurt by the stock market crash of 1929, leaving the state in a much stronger bargaining position in its negotiations for the land.

By early 1931, Governor Clement Young had been succeeded by Governor "Sunny Jim" Rolph, who agreed with Young's goal of expanding the state park system. Walter Frick was a personal friend of Rolph, the former five-time mayor of San Francisco, and by the spring of that year Frick had sold the first two parcels of his Diablo lands to the state. On the 21st of April, 1931, Mt Diablo State park was dedicated a second time, this time with actual acreage owned. In August of 1931, and again in August of 1932, Frick sold two more parcels to the state, and, as his financial situation further deteriorated in the Depression, he sold a fifth parcel in June of 1936. His final sale to the state occurred in February, 1937, just 26 days after his death on January 15, of that year. In all, Frick sold the state just over 2,000 acres of what by 1937 would consist of the 2,022-acre Mt. Diablo State Park.[7]

---

[7] Seth Adams, Who Was Walter P. Frick? *The Creation of Mt. Diablo State Park (Parts I and II)*, Diablo Watch – A Publication of Save Mt. Diablo, Vol. 37, Winter/Spring 2004 (5-7) and Vol. 38, Fall 2004 (3, 8-9).

In 1916, arrival by train from San Francisco and Oakland was typical.
Courtesy William B. Freeman.

Workers building RN's rail spur to the Mt Diablo Park Club.
Courtesy William B. Freeman.

Social hour on the veranda of Mt Diablo Park Club in 1916.
Courtesy William B. Freeman.

A Young William Randolph Hearst.
Courtesy Diablo Country Club collection.

Final hole of a golf tournament at the Diablo Country Club in June, 1918.
Courtesy Diablo Country Club collection.

The entrance to the South Gate Toll Road, C-1913.
Courtesy Diablo Country Club collection.

David D. Colton, the junior partner of Stanford, Huntington, Hopkins, and Crocker, the Big Four, of Central Pacific Railroad fame. Colton controlled the property which was to become the Diablo Country Club between 1877 and his death in 1878. Courtesy Diablo Country Club collection.

CHAPTER 12

With Jim Irvine II in Moraga

Remembering that RN was well into his eighties when he wrote the *Memoirs*, it seems equitable to make allowances for the unfinished nature of some of his anecdotes and stories. This chapter, in addition to describing his partnership with Jim Irvine II, contains a number of episodes in his life that are impossible to place precisely in time, leave the reader wanting more in the way of detail and closure, and seem of questionable relevance. There are numerous instances where RN's point in relating an event appears to be only to mention the names of prominent men of his time who were also involved and to showcase his own participation as a prime mover in the episode. Nonetheless, when placed in an historical context, they are interesting and reveal a character who was always striving to make the next deal and to advance his professional and social position.

The first half-decade after his marriage to Anne comprised some of the most productive years of his life. He amassed large quantities of land in Contra Costa County and began numerous subdivisions on that land, he undertook several significant commercial construction projects in San Francisco, he expanded his financing activities, and he rearranged his domestic living arrangements. He and Anne also had two of their five children by mid-year 1914.

RN's last large land acquisition, early in 1913, involved the purchase with partners of one half of what would become a 12,000-acre parcel between Lafayette, Moraga, and Oakland known as the Carpentier Grant. He had identified this parcel as one in which he had interest several years earlier. The property was held in trust for the owner Horace W. Carpentier by the Corn Exchange Bank in New York and was managed locally by Arthur Burton, Sr. Burton, a friend of RN's, advised him of its potential availability suggesting that he go to New York and call on the Bank trust officer who would inform him of how a sale of the property might be arranged. He went East, and met with the trust officer who told him that Mr. Carpentier did indeed wish to sell the property and that it might be purchased for $850,000. The trust officer further indicated to RN that Mr. Carpentier was planning a trip West to San Francisco and would be staying at the Palace Hotel, and cautioned RN to avoid trying to bargain with the owner as he was a "very sharp trader."

A deal of this size would need to be syndicated as RN didn't have the resources to do it entirely himself. In the *Memoirs*, he offers a listing of his extensive business affiliations at the time. He had controlling interests in the RN Burgess Company, Western Mortgage and Guarantee Company, Humbolt National Bank, Home Savings Bank of Eureka, the Bank of Concord, and the First National Bank of Walnut Creek. He also had a controlling interest in a vehicle called California Investment Company, the directors of which were James Irvine II, Guy Earl, and RN. It was to this investment company that he decided to take the Moraga deal, feeling that Irvine, an experienced and accomplished operator, would be able to handle a deal of this size.

James Irvine's family figures prominently in California history. RN's life was roughly contemporaneous with that of James Irvine II, or, more formally, James Harvey Irvine, Sr. Twelve years RN's senior, he inherited his father's wealth upon reaching the age of 25 in 1892. His father was a California Gold Rush pioneer, arriving in the state in 1848 after fleeing Ireland during the potato famine of 1845. Jim Irvine, I. bought into the wholesale produce and grocery business of his cousin, John Lyons, shortly after arriving in San Francisco. Investments in commercial property in and around San Francisco soon made him wealthy and in time he also acquired a silent-partner interest in the extensive sheep ranching and landholding operations of Thomas Benjamin Flint and Llewellyn Bixby in southern California. In 1864 and 1866 these partners had purchased the 49,000-acre Rancho San Joaquin and the 47,000-acre Rancho Lomas de Santiago respectively, amassing an enormous amount of acreage in what later became Orange County. On his inheritance, James Irvine II bought out the interests of his older partners and created the Irvine Ranch

RN and Irvine were not the only prospective buyers interested in the Moraga property. His old associate and sometime lender P.E. Bowles was also looking at it in partnership with C.A. Cooper, another land investor, and the competition for this very desirable parcel in Contra Costa County must have been intense. On the day that RN, Jim Irvine, Irvine's associate Mr. Crookshank, and Arthur Breed toured the property a discussion took place about how to approach the deal. Irvine wanted to control the negotiations personally given his record of accomplishment in Southern California. However, RN objected, suggesting that an offer at the asking price would secure the deal, but that, "You are wont to bargain, James, and will offer him less, and if you do so you will get into a game of auction. I know Mr. Bowles. He has been invited to join Mr. C.A. Cooper to purchase the property for $750,000." Cooper and Bowles had approached Carpentier prior to RN's trip east and were thus in first position with the seller with at least a tentative offer on the table for $750,000.

Disregarding RN's counsel of an offer at the $850,000 asking price, Irvine made an offer of $800,000. Within twenty-four hours Cooper and Bowles had closed their purchase for the 12,000 acres at a price of $1,000,000, all cash, leaving Burgess, Irvine, and Breed behind. Shortly thereafter, Cooper contacted Irvine through his son-in-law, San Francisco attorney Wellington Creed, offering to sell Irvine half of the acreage for $1,000,000. Which half was to be Irvine's choice, but his selection had to be of contiguous quarter sections. Surprisingly to RN, Irvine was interested in the deal even though at a price $200,000 higher than he was prepared to pay initially for twice the acreage.

RN felt that Irvine's interest at the higher price was stimulated by the fact that the Oakland and Antioch Electric Railroad was planned to run the length of the parcel. Irvine requested that RN and Arthur Breed conduct separate appraisals of each 40-acre quarter section and submit them to him before he went forward with the deal. They did this and when Jim Irvine asked them their opinion of the prospective deal, RN was not enthusiastic. Irvine was determined to go ahead, however, and RN then suggested that they obtain a legal opinion about a matter that had been troubling him.

Pointing out to Irvine's attorney, Guy Earl, that the seller (Cooper and Bowles) had reserved a right-of-way to contiguous points for purposes of building roads and would grant the buyer the same, RN's question to the attorney involved the definition of contiguity. Telling Earl that he wanted a legal opinion before he committed to the deal, he asked him to think of a checkerboard and asked if the black squares were contiguous. Earl's answer was that to be contiguous the squares only needed to touch at a common point, not parallel sides.

RN then advised Irvine that in his opinion the seller did not realize that the contiguous points essentially ran along ridge-lines by virtue of which road construction was going to be very expensive and difficult. He suggested to Irvine that if he went ahead and purchased the 6,000 acres with intent to sit on it and not make any improvements which might enhance the value to Cooper and Bowles, they would get discouraged and sell their acreage at a very advantageous price. He further suggested that Irvine finance the purchase with $250,000 down on a five-year due date with interest at 5%. Irvine proceeded as RN suggested and the deal closed.

A description of the deal appeared in the January 4, 1913 edition of the San Francisco Chronicle which mentions that several lawsuits, dating from litigation of original Mexican grants 30-40 years prior, had been dismissed by the court in Contra Costa County to facilitate Carpentier giving clear title to RN's group. "This tract, added to the present vast holdings of the Burgess Company in the Mt. Diablo country, means another big element in the immediate development of that fertile section... The Carpentier ranch lies in the Moraga valley, which is situated just over the Piedmont hills, and is the "closest" in holding of the Burgess company." The parcel was traversed by the main line of the Oakland and Antioch Railroad scheduled for completion in February of that year. On its inception, the new line would make possible 20-minute commutes from the valley east of the Oakland hills into Oakland and Berkeley. The San Francisco Call also noted enthusiastically that, "Among important projects of the Burgess company in this district is the promotion of a model suburban city, named Moraga, situated in Moraga Valley within a stone's throw of the city limits of Oakland." RN's vision of the opportunities inherent in the Carpentier land was an accurate one, and his prediction of an improved deal was about to come to fruition.

Within a "few years," according to the *Memoirs*, the attorney for the sellers returned with an offer to sell their acreage for $180,000. By that time, Cooper and Bowles had made a few improvements on the land, all of which inured to the favor of Irvine, Burgess, and Earl. The acquisition thus turned out much better than it initially appeared and RN opined that "I always felt someone in Mr. Creed's office overrated the value of the word 'contiguous.'"

From what he wrote in the *Memoirs*, RN appears to have known Jim Irvine relatively well. A San Francisco native, Irvine had left the Bay Area after the 1906 earthquake and fire and relocated to the Irvine Ranch south of Los Angeles. RN describes multiple visits and experiences with him, walking and riding over his extensive holdings. He characterized the ranch "as over 100,000 acres of hills, valley, and ocean frontage, with 10,000 acres in oranges and walnuts." Irvine liked to challenge his guests, taking them on long walks over his property in contests of endurance, and RN said that his host never became tired. They would take their rifles and hunt quail and rattlesnakes, all the while enjoying the impressive views offered from various spots on the property. Recalling such a trip, RN recounted a walk the two enjoyed together when RN asked about bright lights in the distance and was informed that he was looking at Santa Ana. Further up the hill, questioning the source of more, brighter lights in the distance, RN was told that it was Los Angeles harbor. RN's response was typical, "Jim, when we reach Santa Barbara I think we better turn around and go home."

***

RN's reputation and growing list of successes increased the demand among landowners and other interested parties for his services in all manner of land use problems throughout the state. He was hired to review a 40,000-acre site in West Sacramento, a project of the Mercantile Trust Company. He wrote of the George Roeding, Sr. properties in Fresno, a large tract of orchard stock that he was hired to appraise, also for the Mercantile Trust Company. Like RN and his father-in-law Lafayette Fish, Roeding was progressive in his land cultivation practices, preferring to only plant a parcel once and acquiring additional land for new planting. By proceeding this way, RN suggested that Roeding avoided many problems associated with pests, disease, and over-planting.

In one humorous anecdote, he writes about a pro bono appearance as a friend of the court in a matter involving the Peoples Water Company of Contra Costa County in a dispute with Claus Spreckels, the founder of Spreckels Sugar Company. RN was asked to testify as to how he would value watershed land which included both ridges and surrounding canyons. Once again, RN had known the opposing attorney since childhood in Danville. Charles Wheeler, Sr., an attorney in San Francisco, had been an associate of Joshua Chase Burgess and would visit him at the Danville home occasionally and so knew RN as a boy. RN's role in the trial was to appear on behalf of the court and provide testimony as to recent land sales, their size, value, characteristics, and terms.

To Wheeler's valuation question, RN responded that, for watershed purposes, he valued ridge land the same as he valued canyon land as the combined terrain served as a catchment, or area for the capture of rainfall over a natural drainage area. To make his point, RN held out his hand, palm up, analogizing between ridges and valleys and the fingers and palm of his hand. If dammed for the collection of water, both the high ground as well as the valleys would have equal value. On questioning by Wheeler, who intended to debunk his valuation theory (on behalf of a client who was seeking lower water rates) by holding *his* hand out palm down, RN responded that with the palm-down illustration all the water would be lost, "for if the back of your hand represents the storage basin there would be no catchment...you have reversed your hand in using my illustration." RN reported gales of laughter in the courtroom at this remark, something of a putdown to the attorney. Catching up to RN as he left the courtroom, Wheeler said, "Robbie, little did I realize when I used to have you on my knee, that you would grow up to give me such a rebuff."

RN's attitudes concerning issues of social justice in his time, as well as his views of those in the power structure higher than himself, are further illustrated in his account of the 1911 State Constitutional amendment concerning worker's compensation. He recounts a meeting, which Henry T. Scott had arranged with Will Crocker, the subject of which was a campaign to defeat the proposed Worker's Compensation Act in 1917. The focus of the session was the assignment of sectors of responsibility to individuals who were to manage the campaign to defeat the measure. Will Crocker directed RN that he was "to take charge of the campaign in Contra Costa County and Solano County." When RN protested that the amendment "was as good as passed," pointing out the fruitless nature of the assignment, Crocker responded "You attend to the job allotted to you, for if this bill passes it will stifle our industry in California. Important men can make important mistakes." RN's comment about Crocker ("He could throw his weight around.") indicated no love lost between the two, but his own earlier experience with a job-related injury on one of his projects probably predisposed him against taking part in this campaign. A driller on the Walnut Creek water supply expansion several years earlier had hit a power line and been thrown to the ground incurring serious injury. The man had a wife and four children and RN claimed that his company did what it could for him, but the experience left in him a residue of sensitivity for the plight of the working man.

The *Memoirs* contain a humorous episode, probably around 1911, on the occasion of the opening of a new hotel in Klamath Falls, Oregon. RN had been hired by the developers of the hotel,

Herbert and Mortimer Fleishhacker, San Francisco bankers, and Orie Johnson, a northern California lumberman and railroad builder, to review, appraise, and inspect the project. A celebratory banquet, replete with a special photographer brought in from San Francisco by the sponsors, was planned for the grand opening of the new, state-of-the-art facility. A six-story building, advertised as fire-proof, and heated by local geyser water, which on opening night failed to work as advertised, made for a very cold and subdued celebration in the new dining room.

The San Francisco-based sponsors of the project had big plans for the community and for the development of the surrounding farmland. They intended to modernize Klamath Falls with new water mains, a new sewer system as well as utilities all of which would substantially upgrade the town. The problem they encountered was that many of the citizens, particularly the older among them, were not interested in the kind of progress envisioned by the Fleishhackers and Johnson, and were vocal in their opposition.

At one of the banquet tables, occupied with guests from the Bay Area and numerous local dignitaries, Anne and RN were seated with sixteen other diners. His understanding was that the owners expected him to entertain the local guests at his table, presumably selling them on the advantages contemplated for the town. He reported buying six rounds of champagne for his table mates, getting everybody well-oiled in the process. At about midnight, a note arrived at his place from Mortimer Fleishhacker indicating that "You will be called on next as a large rebuilder of towns, and asked what have you found to be the most essential thing." As RN described it, "Mortimer gave me an exaggerated build-up, then called on me… his party was not going very well. They were getting less than no cooperation from the local people. I felt there was too much 'soaping up' and not enough fact-finding." RN's short speech, doubtless lubricated by too much champagne, must have startled the assembled guests. "I have not much latitude, so will keep to the question asked of me - What have I found the most essential thing in rebuilding an old town? My experience is that it is a wholesale funeral for the old-timers who are obstructing the development."

Back in their room, Anne, described by RN as mortified, told him that she was hoping a crack in the floor would open up and swallow her! A cold room had grown even colder after his comments and Anne later said "Robb, you must have been tight to have said such a thing; I never was so mortified." Responding that they had best not cross their bridges until morning and a new day revealed the reaction, RN went to bed. Around mid-morning the following day, Mortimer Fleishhacker phoned their room, apologizing to RN for seeming to ignore them, but saying that he had been floored by RN's comments. "We were all depressed, and your bombshell finished us off. But what you did was the thing needed. Already we have signed up this morning four of our greatest obstructionists; and they came to us and volunteered their help and have told us of others that agreed to cooperate."

In his telling, the shocking remarks offered by RN moved the reluctant old-timers to drop their opposition and become enthusiastic supporters of a makeover of Klamath Falls. Whether or not this is what actually happened, it is not difficult to picture RN arising from his seat and offering his caustic observations after a long and uncomfortable dinner. Once again, he employed shock to get attention and suggested the unthinkable, a vintage performance.

RN related another interesting interaction in Washington DC between himself and Josephus Daniels, Secretary of the Navy under President Woodrow Wilson. In an undated anecdote in the Memoirs, he reported a loan application to his firm, Western Mortgage and Guarantee Company, for a $600,000 loan the security on which was to be the land in Alameda, subsequently used as the US Naval Air Station. The prospective borrowers, a group of twenty investors, intended to buy the property in hopes of making a killing when, as rumored, the United States government later purchased the property for use as an air station. As RN reported, understating the issue, "it was of the upmost importance to know if the United States government had actually purchased the site for a naval base."

RN called on an acquaintance, San Francisco attorney and

active participant in affairs of the Democratic Party in California, Gavin McNabb, seeking McNabb's intercession in his behalf in obtaining a meeting in Washington DC with the Secretary of the Navy. McNabb instructed RN to go to Washington and call on the Secretary, indicating that he would make the necessary arrangements to get RN an audience. McNabb's influence in the Democratic Party was sufficient to get RN in because when he arrived in a waiting room full of people, the desk clerk advised him that it would be impossible to see the Secretary that day, but that he had received a wire about "that other matter" and RN should follow him out into the hallway. A side door just down the hall entered directly into the Secretary's office and RN shortly found himself in the presence of the Secretary of the Navy.

After exchanging pleasantries and shared stories about Gavin McNabb, the Secretary asked what he might do for RN. RN indicated that, "I told him that I wished to know if the United States had selected the 600 acres at Alameda, purchased it and was going to build a Naval base there..." Secretary Daniels responded that, "There is no one in this world that knows that but me; my deciding report is in my pocket, and in a few minutes I leave with President Wilson for White Sulphur Springs to give him this report and I couldn't tell you before I tell the President. Just where is Alameda anyway?" Then, walking to a nearby wall, he pulled a large map down, and placing his thumb over Alameda, he said, "Observe this area carefully. I think it is remarkable that I can cover with my thumb the area that is to become a great naval base in San Francisco Bay."

RN wrote that his next bill from attorney NcNabb included "a $10,000 item that was well covered by the expenses allowed by the borrowers." Apparently, McNabb's influence not only got RN into a meeting with the Secretary of the Navy, but also included persuading Daniels to share what must have been a fairly sensitive secret with a man he had barely met. Further testing the reader's credulity is the fact that the United States government didn't actually acquire the base until June of 1936, prior to which time it served as a municipal airfield. The United States Army had used the field in the early 1930's, but the actual federal government purchase didn't occur until mid-decade. RN's anecdote is undated, but must have occurred between 1915 and 1917, so almost two decades, and three successors to President Wilson, had passed before it became United States property.

The anecdote makes a good story, though it places the Secretary of the Navy in an unflattering light. Josephus Daniels, a Wilson appointee and former newspaper publisher and editor from North Carolina, on RN's telling was hardly circumspect, revealing state secrets to a man with whom he had an untested political connection. In concluding his story, RN goes on to name a number of then prominent men in finance and banking who were among the thirty guarantors, including the presidents of several large California banks and the president of a large life insurance company. Once again, his story leaves a number of questions unanswered: did they close the deal; inasmuch as it was not sold to the U.S. Government for almost two decades, did this investment group hold on for the duration or sell it to someone else? Like other stories, absent closure on the actual outcome of the deal, it makes the anecdote seem merely a vehicle for positioning RN in a group of very prominent financial men of his time, and the reader is left wondering about the outcome of such a potentially rewarding, though apparently miss-timed, deal.

RN's experience with the US Navy and his experience in doing business with the government in general began about this time. He developed considerable expertise and understanding in the sometimes maddeningly slow workings and red tape involved with government contracting. On one occasion, in 1915/16, he became involved with an experimental research laboratory in Chicago doing work for the government. Timing on these experiences as related in the *Memoirs*, is imprecise but the names of prominent men are mentioned, usually only the last name. In one instance, he described a nutrition issue that might place the timing during WW I. He wrote of many trips to Chicago, to the laboratory in question. In his words, "I remember one item the government advertised. It was short 17,000,000 pounds of fat annually." A byproduct of rice milling and processing was apparently the loss of a large amount of fat. "This, and the research on developing a way to preserve whole rice so it would not become rancid required that I go to Washington and meet Mr. Wiley, Pure Food Administrator."

Harvey Washington Wiley was appointed Chief Chemist in the United States Department of Agriculture in 1882 and later became known for his involvement in the passage of the Pure Food and Drug Act of 1906. As an early advocate for research into, and the regulation of, food and drug manufacture in the country, he was appointed to administer the Act after its passage, continuing in this role until political enemies forced his resignation in March of 1912. RN said that he met with Professor Wiley, and later with another official, Professor Shepherd of Boston, in a luncheon at the Willard Hotel in Washington.

These trips and meetings were apparently about a possible contract with the U.S. Navy for the purchase of rice, then considered a desirable food in the tropics for the avoidance of beriberi which had become a problem due to the shortage of fruits and vegetables. Rice, however effective as an antidote to beriberi, was of little use to the Navy because of its tendency to become rancid in a very short time. RN said that Professor Shepherd introduced him to the Navy where he "got first-hand knowledge of RED TAPE." His recommendation to the government that they try whole (brown) rice was met with the suggestion that "We will put out a requisition for 100 tons of whole rice and you can bid on it, if you are the low bidder you will get the order." He was offering RN the opportunity to build a $1 million processing plant for a *chance* at selling 100 tons of processed rice, an opportunity RN was only too happy to pass on. His reaction was typical, "I felt the high devotion to Red Tape far exceeded the interest in the health of the men."

RN related another anecdote involving attorney McNabb demonstrating the rather cavalier attitude towards conflict of interest considerations in existence at the time. Sometime in 1914 or 15, he was visited in his San Francisco office by Mr. Willard Williamson, and two southern California friends, William T. Summers and Mr. Diblee from Santa Paula and Santa Barbara respectively. The purpose of their visit was to inquire into the potential for acquisition of a controlling interest in the Merchants National Bank with local offices in San Francisco.

Merchants was controlled by John Spring and some associates, but the controlling block of shares was apparently tied up and unavailable for sale. Shortly thereafter, attorney Gavin McNabb arrived at RN's office and dropped a bundle of stock certificates on his desk indicating that the shares represented the controlling interest that Williamson was seeking. McNabb who had served on the Merchants' board for years, as a colleague to John Spring and other board members, felt that in his position he could not sell the shares. He instructed RN to prepare a receipt for them and either buy them himself, or sell them, at his choice. Saying that he would return in a week, he told RN to either return the shares or pay him $100 per share.

This is clearly a view into a regulatory regime much different than what we would recognize today. McNabb was able to circumvent his fiduciary duty as a board member by merely leaving the shares with RN, asking for a receipt, and indicating that he (RN) was free to either buy them or sell them at his choice. RN wrote that he purchased the shares himself but later sold them all to William Summers. This change of control apparently occurred sometime thereafter because a trade journal, the Coast Banker, listed W.T. Summers as President and T. Wilson Diblee as Vice President of Merchants National Bank in a 1917 issue.

The Burgess home life at this time, roughly the years between 1914 and 1918, appears to have been busy, very social, and characterized by numerous business trips on RN's part. He wrote that he would often be called to New York, Chicago, or Boston on short notice and would accordingly telephone Anne in Diablo asking her to bring his suitcase and formal wear to the rail station in Port Costa to meet the afternoon train east as it passed through. Occasionally, she would accompany him and he described a little black book in which they kept a record of all their domino games played while on such trips. Anne was frequently unable to accompany him because of responsibilities at home including young children, her aging mother, and RN's aging father. When unable to meet him at the train, she would dispatch Hartwell, their chauffeur, with what he needed for the trip.

Having built Anne a home at Diablo at her request after a summer trial in 1913, RN soon found it difficult and inconvenient to commute from his home there to his office in San Francisco on a daily basis and a residence in San Francisco was established. In the Memoirs, he wrote that he initially moved into the Clift Hotel, but his time there must have been short as it was not opened until early 1915, in time for the opening of the Pan Pacific International Exposition. Thereafter, they moved to the St Francis when Henry T. Scott asked that RN consider an offer that would make his availability to Scott easier. The bank (Scott was President of the Mercantile Bank as well as of the St Francis Hotel Company) had selected quarters on the tenth floor for RN and Anne, would install all improvements for them, and would pick up all his business entertainment expenses. Scott instructed RN that he should pay the monthly bill upon receipt and then submit it to the hotel. Within an hour, he would receive the hotel's check for the difference between his bill and $75, his monthly rent at the Clift. All his expenses were charged to the hotel's advertising budget. As Scott explained it, "It is worth that to the hotel to have you with us. I will tell the Maitre (*sic*) to reserve the table next to mine for you until 12:30 each day at noon."

***

RN's very busy and productive years in San Francisco coincided with important national events, one of which was the completion of the Panama Canal. In anticipation of that event and in response to a petition by San Francisco's Panama Pacific Exposition Company and its board of directors, President William Howard Taft signed a resolution designating the city as the future home of the exposition in February of 1911. In San Francisco, the post-earthquake rebuilding was progressing rapidly and by way of memorializing this progress and of showcasing the new canal with its implications for expansion of commerce between the two coasts, a World's Fair seemed appropriate recognition for a city rising from the ashes of its 1906 catastrophe. In the years leading up to its opening on February 20, 1915, the city was busy with all manner of preparation for the thousands of visitors expected. RN played a small role in this preparation via his finance company, Western Mortgage and Guarantee Company.

He recalled that sometime in 1913 he was approached by Henry Scott in connection with the then under-construction Clift Hotel. Noting that work on the planned 300-room hotel had apparently stopped after completion of the steel frame, Scott asked RN to look into the matter to verify that financing issues may have caused the work stoppage. This RN did, lunching shortly thereafter with George Applegarth, the project architect. Applegarth confirmed that the owner, Frederick C. Clift, had indeed begun construction before having his financing lined up. Clift, a San Francisco attorney and member of a family from the Sierra foothills that had inherited the land underlying the project, was apparently inexperienced in dealing with a project of this scale and had become stalled accordingly.

Clift had been scouring the financial community for a loan but had been unsuccessful to date, although he was in final discussions with the San Francisco Savings Union on a deal. RN described the terms of the loan Clift was seeking as generous: The hotel would issue $600,000 of 20-year, First Mortgage Sinking Fund Bonds with a 5% interest rate. The bonds were to be offered to the underwriter at a price of $950 (that is five points less than the $1,000 par value). RN told George Applegarth to tell Clift that Western Mortgage & Guaranty Company was willing to commit to the deal as described immediately and would keep his offer open for forty-eight hours. RN did not indicate that he in fact closed this deal with Clift, though from the context in the *Memoirs* it seems likely.

Next, Scott advised RN that he was having difficulty obtaining financing for a new wing on his St Francis Hotel. The firm he was dealing with, Bond and Goodwin, had expressed interest but had thus far been unable to provide a commitment. The terms were similar to those of the Clift loan except that proceeds were to be $1,500,000 and it was being offered at $930, a slightly larger discount to the face value of the bonds. RN told Scott that he would accept the deal, but only on condition that two changes were made. He insisted that the real owners of the property, the Crocker heirs, Jennie and Templeton Crocker, guarantee the loan payments as they became due, and, in the event of a takeout by another underwriter, that Western Mortgage be properly compensated for its release. Apparently by way of a challenge as RN's firm had not handled deals of this size before, Scott asked, "Burgess, do you think you can handle it?" RN's response, indicative of his confidence in his own abilities up to this point, was "I know I can." Within twenty-four hours Western Mortgage had a check in hand for its release (from whom it was not specified, but probably Bond and Goodwin, the competitive underwriter) and Henry Scott had his loan commitment. It appears that RN didn't get the deal for Western Mortgage, but his willingness to make a rapid commitment in place of a slower underwriter accelerated the commitment needed by Scott, and presumably enhanced his growing stature in the older man's eyes.

George Applegarth, from whom RN obtained information on the financing status of the Clift Hotel when construction had stalled, was yet another in a list of prominent California architects with whom he collaborated on a variety of jobs throughout the Bay Area. He worked with Julia Morgan early in his career. His work with George Applegarth involved numerous Burgess projects including the Bank of Concord, the First National Bank Building in Walnut Creek, the Humbolt Bank building in Eureka, the Burgess home in Diablo, a major retrofit of the Homestead house in Walnut Creek, and design of the club house and other buildings at the Diablo Country Club. Applegarth was also the Acting Architect, working under Bernard Maybeck on the development of the town of Clyde on behalf of the Pacific Coast Shipbuilding Company in 1917. RN also worked extensively with Arthur Benton, the designer of the notable Riverside Inn in Riverside, CA, on other improvements at the Diablo Country Club, including its chalet building.

The Pan Pacific International Exposition in San Francisco opened on February 20, 1915 and closed nine months later on the 4th of December. The world changed during the course of that event and it closed on a much different international situation. World War I began in Europe in August of the year prior, and what had seemed a distant conflict with little interest or implication for Americans was becoming almost daily a matter of increasing domestic concern. In May, 1915, the sinking of the British passenger liner Lusitania brought home to Americans the risks of neutrality represented by an aggressive Germany. Although the country did not enter the war for another two years, the newspapers were full of stories of the carnage on the Western Front and it was becoming difficult to ignore the sense of potential threat to the United States. The events and changes wrought by World War I would bring change to RN's life as a Bay Area real estate developer and financier and would have important subsequent implications for his career and his social position. Before those events, however, he had one more new business avenue to pursue. He would become, like his Great Uncle Rufus, a shipbuilder.

Moraga town site, C-1913.
Courtesy Contra Costa County Historical Society.

Burgess sales brochure, Lafayette California. C-1913.
Courtesy Contra Costa County Historical Society.

James Harvey Irvine, Sr., RN's business partner
and loyal friend through his most difficult times.
Courtesy R.N. Burgess Memoirs.

CHAPTER 13
The Youngest Shipbuilder in America

R N's association with Henry Tiffany Scott of the Mercantile Bank was critical to the next role he would play in life. Scott was his patron in many ways. As President of that bank, he and his Vice President, John D. McKee, helped the young builder get started in the City in the fall of 1908 by accepting his financing plans and creating the necessary trust bank under the Mercantile umbrella. As a member of a world-famous shipbuilding family he was in a good position to oversee RN's entry into that business. Also, as President of the St. Frances Hotel Company, he arranged for an apartment for RN and Anne on favorable terms so as to make him more available for business meetings and frequent lunches. It is also likely that Scott was involved in RN's admission to the Bohemian Club, whose records reveal membership between 1918 and 1924.

Henry Tiffany Scott and his brother, Irving Murray Scott, were names prominently associated with a company known as the Union Iron Works during the last decades of the 19th century. The Union Iron Works was founded by an Irish immigrant, Peter Donahue, in 1849, when Donahue and his brothers opened the first iron casting foundry in California. The firm built numerous local buildings as well as much of the mining machinery used in the gold country. Donahue sold the business in 1864, using the proceeds to open a gas works, the forerunner of PG&E. Prior to selling the business, Donahue had hired Irving Scott, an engineer who became the firm's senior manager after Donahue's departure. Irving's younger brother, RN's patron Henry Tiffany Scott, was put in charge of the business affairs of the firm, allowing Irving to concentrate on the technological aspects of shipbuilding. With the decline of the mining business in California and Nevada, Irving Scott, recognizing the growing importance of seaborne trade to the west, became interested in developing a large shipyard. After an exploratory trip around the world visiting numerous shipyards to acquaint himself with current practices, Scott returned to San Francisco in 1883 and relocated the new yard to recently-filled land at Potrero Point. [1]

Scott's efforts to build a world-class yard on the west coast succeeded and it launched the Arago in 1885, the first steel-hulled ship on the West Coast. Irving Scott had political as well as engineering talent, and he persuaded decision makers in Washington that his yard could handle the production of modern warships as well as any eastern yard. The first major government contract was for the cruiser USS Charleston and it was soon followed by numerous additional agreements. The Spanish-American War followed and Admiral Dewey's Flagship, the USS Olympia, was a product of the Scott's Union Iron Works. The first two battleships built on the west coast were built by the firm, including the Oregon and the Ohio (the launching of which was attended by President McKinley, a friend of Irving's). The two Scott brothers had a nephew, John Thomas Scott, also a marine engineer, who followed them into the business at Union Works, becoming a superintendent in 1895. In the early years of the new century, Irving Scott's health was in decline and he passed away in April of 1903, leaving only Henry and his nephew John in the business.

The prior year, 1902, the Union Iron Works was absorbed into a combine known as the United States Shipbuilding Company which was trying to buy several other shipbuilding firms in the United States. This unsuccessful merger was followed by three years of litigation and, ultimately, receivership in 1905. Charles M. Schwab, representing the Bethlehem Shipbuilding Company, bought the assets of the Union Iron Works for $1,000,000 as the only bidder on the courthouse steps in 1905.

After the death of his older brother, Henry T. Scott concentrated

---

[1] Wilson, Ralph. "History of Potrero Point Shipyards and Industry." Pier 70 San Francisco. pier70sf.org/history/p.70_history_html (3 November 2017).

on other business and banking interests while his nephew John teamed up with Robert S. Moore and Moore's younger brother Joseph to create the Moore and Scott Iron Works in 1905. The partnership purchased the National Iron Works at the intersection of Main and Howard Streets in San Francisco and began to operate that business. Waterfront access in San Francisco increased their interest in ship repair as an additional business and they began to undertake such work. In 1909, however, the loss of its rented dry dock facility caused Moore and Scott to purchase a small yard owned by the Boole family in Oakland at the foot of Adeline Street to which it then moved. Henry T. Scott remained in the shipbuilding business through service on the Board of Directors of the new company. [2]

The United States Shipping Board was established by the Shipping Act of September 7, 1916. The Board itself consisted of five commissioners appointed by the President, subject to confirmation by the United States Senate. Given broad powers, it essentially controlled all American shipbuilding. Early meetings took place in Washington D.C. in January 1917 and by the end of that month it was formally organized and under way. In the years leading up to World War I American shipbuilding had steadily lost ground to European interests and by the beginning of the War only 10% of U.S. trade was carried on domestic ships. With the outbreak of War, most of European shipping was impounded for the duration, producing significant shortages in numbers of vessels. Initially empowered to purchase existing hulls, with the start of war the Shipping Board established the Emergency Fleet Corporation (EFC) on April 16, 1917, expanding its role to include the issuing of contracts to build new ships.

***

RN's association with Henry T. Scott thus put him in a position to engage in shipbuilding in the company of seasoned profession-

James Rolph Moore, *The Story of Moore Dry Dock Company*, (San Francisco: JAM Securities 1994).

als a few months prior to the United States entry into World War I. In the *Memoirs*, RN described a meeting, the date and location of which are undisclosed, with J.F. Carlson, the President of the Central Bank of Oakland. It is likely that this meeting occurred in late 1916 or early 1917, and the topics under discussion were the enhanced financial opportunities available in shipbuilding with war in Europe, as well as the potential for a new yard somewhere in the Bay Area. RN brought up the possibility of a yard in Bay Point in Contra Costa County, close to his property purchased seven or eight years earlier from Foskett and Elsworthy. To Henry Scott's objection that it lacked deep water access, RN responded that an adjoining 233-acre parcel, owned by the Crocker Land Company, did indeed have such deep-water access and he was confident he could acquire a 60-day option, at a purchase price of $40,000, to acquire that acreage. The discussion in the meeting then turned to the benefits that might accrue to the acreage already owned in the area, the potential for expansion of the Oakland & Antioch Railroad, and for employment opportunities associated with shipbuilding.

Henry Scott, apparently convinced that the idea deserved exploration, responded that his nephew John Scott was available and that RN "...might get the figures together and go to Washington and see what you can do." John Scott's availability was due to the fact of the prospective buyout by Moore of the Scott interest in Moore and Scott Ironworks which ultimately occurred in June of 1917, with Moore thereafter being known as the Moore Shipbuilding Company. The Moore buyout of Scott was followed by the incorporation, the following month, of the new Pacific Coast Shipbuilding Company (P.C.S.B.) by Henry Scott and some associates with Scott named as president. With John Scott no longer needed at the Moore yard, he was free to go with RN to Washington. Henry Scott then offered to set RN up with a Washington lawyer, Clarence de Night, an "old hand" in the Capitol in the event RN needed help. He also told RN to draw $3,000 in expense money, indicating that "You will need it with the crowd you will mix with."

With that, RN and Anne left for Washington D.C. in the company of John T. Scott. Henry Scott's send-off, as recalled by RN, said nothing about obtaining a contract from the Shipping Board for ships, and indeed his instructions sounded like nothing more than an exploratory visit. Nonetheless, RN came back with a contract for ten 10,000-ton freighters, a significant accomplishment for a man of 39 with no experience in the field. Scott's involvement was as the technical man; his experience and knowledge of all the details of acquiring contracts and building ships was essential to the undertaking. As RN put it, John Scott's role was to "browse among the sub-contractors and machinery men," and a separate room was rented at the Willard Hotel "for anyone John had to butter down to find out what was doing."

RN, a finance man with no experience in this new business, needed Scott's help and experience on this mission. His personal comments in the *Memoirs* are interesting in this light. RN had met Robert S. (Bob) Moore through his relation with Henry Scott and Scott's service on the Moore and Scott Board. He liked Moore, "He was well-liked and I found him most agreeable." Henry's nephew, John T. Scott, however, was "a disturbing factor, always scheming and trying to push someone aside to his own advantage." John Scott was thirteen years RN's senior, possessed an upper-class pedigree which was out of RN's reach, and, as a member of a famous shipbuilding family, may have been problematic as a forced partner for RN. But he was Henry's nephew, he had critical knowledge and expertise that RN lacked, and, when it was suggested that he accompany RN to Washington, there would have been no resistance on RN's part.

Ensconced in Washington with his wife and new partner, RN went to work. He called on the U.S. Shipping Board and dropped off the plans and specifications for a new shipyard. These had been prepared for him prior to his departure from San Francisco by Golden Downing, the corporate secretary and treasurer. The Shipping Board needed time to review these so RN and Anne went up to New York for some relaxation and shopping. After a successful shopping day during which she surprised him by buying a new coat, Anne announced a second surprise. She was going home to be with the children. She said his schedule was incompatible with her continued participation because he was in meetings and dinners almost every day and she was bored. On RN's return to Washington, after her departure, John Scott, citing loneliness, also told RN he was returning to California. RN was thus on his own as he navigated the intrigues and shoals of wartime Washington.

Prior to returning to California, Scott had done his part by reviewing the technical plans for the new yard with personnel at the Shipping Board and obtaining commitments for various necessary pieces of shipbuilding machinery. There was, however, one glaring exception. He had not been able to line up 3,000-horsepower turbines, essential to the specifications drawn up for the ships they were to bid on. The government had placed a hold on all plants that manufactured these turbines and those with larger capacity. But, to Scott's credit, "he had picked up and buttered down" the President of The Kerr Turbine Manufacturers of Connecticut. Kerr's firm manufactured a 2,700-horsepower turbine to government specifications. In discussions with Kerr it developed that he wanted to expand his plant's capacity and needed $100,000 in additional capital to accomplish the job. RN inquired as to the possibility of his increasing the size of his turbines to the required 3,000-horsepower. He thought he might be able to do so, but needed a day or so to verify this with his plant which he subsequently did. RN then offered to finance the $100,000 plant expansion through his Western Mortgage and Guarantee Company subject to two conditions: First, he (RN) must be awarded the shipbuilding contract he was seeking in Washington, and Second, Kerr would need to give RN first call on his entire output. These conditions agreed to, the two entered a written contract.

On his return to the U.S. Shipping Board, RN was introduced to Admiral Land. In the *Memoirs*, RN often did not include first names, but it is probable that the Admiral Land to which he was referring was Vice Admiral Emory Scott Land. Admiral Land was a naval architect, specializing in submarines. During his association with RN, he would have been serving on the Board of Devices and Plans with emphasis on submarines and it is unclear what, given his specialization in submarine warfare, he would have been doing at the Shipping Board. In any event, he interacted with RN right away, asking him if he was acquainted with Mr. Hand, the General Manager of shipbuilder Cramp & Sons. RN responded that he had met Mr. Hand through Robert S. Moore but was not a close friend. The Admiral then asked him if he would go to Mr. Hand's yard and borrow their estimating file for a few days. This seemed a curious request and when he told Mr. Hand the purpose of his visit, the General Manager laughed, explaining that such a request "is an old Navy Trick. It's like sending you out to get a half-round square."

The General Manager of Cramp & Sons was more than hospitable. He called on Cramp, Jr. to give RN a tour of their yard and then take him to the clubhouse for a cocktail. After their tour, the two went to the boardroom, decorated at either end, over two fireplaces, with oil-painted portraits. Pointing to one, young Mr. Cramp proudly announced "My Grandfather, founder of Cramp & Sons." Walking to the other end of the room, RN examined the second portrait and exclaimed, "Rufus Burgess, my cousin and co-founder of Cramp & Sons." RN described Rufus Burgess as "the largest builder of wooden ships in New England" and shared with Cramp his memories of his cousin visiting the family in Danville while he had forty sailing vessels at anchor off Port Costa in the freshwater awaiting barnacle-clearing so they could load grain at that port. The younger Mr. Cramp, apparently impressed with RN's shipbuilding lineage, urged RN to tell Mr. Hand, the General Manager, of the connection. Hand's response was that this news "puts a different face on your request for Admiral Land. Now you will have to return to the club and have another drink while I prepare an estimating file that will make the Admiral's hair curl if he ever uses it. It will sink the Navy... but Burgess, you are now dealing with the high brass and you must deliver it with a long face and with no suggestion of a smile. He will ask you how you got it. Tell him you just asked for it."

Returning to Admiral Land's office, RN submitted the estimating file and the Admiral instructed him to return the following morning. At the appointed hour the following day, Land indicated that he was prepared to give the Pacific Coast Shipbuilding Company the contract he sought, subject to certain requirements. He first asked RN if he was married and if he had any children. To RN's affirmative answer the Navy man then issued a sobering warning. "I feel it my duty to tell you that if you take a contract to build ships there is a possibility that a muck-racking congress will send you to the penitentiary for an estimated 700 years. These contracts are a violation of the United States constitution in that they have not been let out for competitive bids and there is no completion bond required, but God help America if we can't find able men who will take that chance. Are you willing to take that chance?"

RN responded that he was and the Admiral went on, "All right, if I give you the contract you will be the youngest shipbuilder in America and that puts a responsibility on me should you not perform." The Admiral then asked him if he would be able to furnish 3,000 horsepower turbines, knowing that the government had requisitioned all plants that produced such equipment and adding that it will "be impossible for you to secure them." Responding, "that Uncle Sam must have overlooked something when that requisition was issued," RN said he was willing to tell the Admiral how he could get the turbines on condition that he be allowed to use them to fulfill his obligation under the prospective contract. On Land's agreement, RN then told him about his deal with Kerr Manufacturing and his commitment to finance their $100,000 plant expansion in return for the turbines. Land then suggested that the Government would take over that agreement, advance the $100,000 to Kerr, and provide RN the turbines he needed, adding that "You seem quite resourceful."

One additional step remained between RN and a contract with the United States Shipping Board for the construction of ten ships. It was standard practice for the Government to require a character bond in the amount of $75,000, guaranteeing a full accounting for the $2,500,000 advance for equipment and materiel which was part of the contract. RN responded that he would seek such a bond immediately. To accomplish this, he had in mind the Maryland Casualty and Fidelity Co in Baltimore and he planned to travel there the following day in an attempt to secure the bond. At a two o'clock appointment the following afternoon, RN sized up the Maryland Casualty directors who had to approve his petition describing them as old men most of whom had long grey beards. In spite of their apparent age, however, they also had "pep and decision" and, after a few questions, one of them suggested that they move the process forward saying "Let us get along with it. We have got to win this war. I move we grant the bond as requested." The directors did grant RN the bond, charging him a premium of $7,500 for the coverage. He related his later surprise on learning that his had been an unusually quick approval; most appellants required extensive investigations and one or more endorsers for what RN obtained on his own. Presumably, wartime emergency had something to do with this result. Although RN didn't date many of these episodes in the *Memoirs,* the comments by the director and reference to the war emergency place the events shortly after United States entry into the War on April 6, 1917.

On his return to Washington, P.C.S.B. was awarded the contract for the ships. The agreement, which he described as a $20,000,000 contract, was for ten steel freighters each of 10,000 tons. He wrote that he also received an advance of $2,500,000 to be used as seed capital for equipment, supplies, and raw materials for the new yard. However, RN's account is not supported by an accounting made after the War indicating that this advance was in the form of a check issued on November 16, 1917 to Pacific Coast Shipbuilding Company for $1,384,020, of which "$700,000 was to be used in the construction and equipment of its plant...the balance to pay labor and materials bills." [3]

The Shipping Board agreement also had very specific conditions for raising the additional capital that would be required. RN and his associates (the Scotts and others) were to put up equity of an additional $500,000 and use the combined Shipping Board

---

G.L. Downing to R.N. Burgess, et. al. 29 January 1919. Letter of Financial Conditions as of December 31 December 1918.

advance, and private equity funds ($3,000,000), to collateralize loans for an additional $2,500,000, providing a total of $5,500,000 in initial capital to begin the shipyard construction work. An additional provision to the contract was inserted, presumably to protect the private investors from dilution of their investment profits through Shipping Board change-orders and subsequent changes in labor rates. Quoting RN in the *Memoirs*, "The Board could change the rate of pay on the payroll schedule and alter the plans and specifications, but if they did either we had the right to require the Board to repay our $500,000 and to pay us five percent profit on the cost of the ships." This provision, which offered seemingly iron-clad protection to the private investors in the deal, was never exercised and those investors got either a minimal or no return on their investment.

After obtaining the Shipping Board contract in Washington, RN returned to San Francisco to begin construction of the new yard in Bay Point, a small community on the shore of Suisun Bay west of Pittsburg. The firm had been incorporated as the Pacific Coast Shipbuilding Company (PCSB Co) under California law in July of 1917 with Henry T. Scott as president. In a January 19, 1918 Board Meeting, Henry Scott resigned his position, claiming personal stress and other commitments, and moved that RN be elevated to the position at a salary of $20,000 per annum. Scott retained his position on the board. Simultaneously, John T. Scott was named vice president at compensation of $15,000. A unanimous vote of approval followed these motions and both appointments were effective retroactively to January 1, 1918. Within three weeks of his 40th birthday, RN was thus given responsibility for the erection of a new shipyard and the fulfillment of a $20,000,000 contract with the Shipping Board to build ten ships to support the war effort in Europe.

With a Shipping Board Contract, partial financing, and responsibility for the entire operation, RN next proceeded to secure the land needed for the site of the new yard. He had indicated to his partners before going to Washington that he had lined up the land purchase by securing an option on the 233-acre Bay Point parcel (adjacent to his own property) with a $40,000 purchase price. His land purchase didn't work, however, at least not the way he had envisioned. When he presented his check for $40,000 to Samuel F. B. Morse, Manager of the Crocker Land Company, Morse was overruled by his employer William Crocker who had decided the value of the parcel demanded a price of $250,000, not the $40,000 Morse had earlier agreed to.

Samuel Finley Brown Morse had arrived in California in 1907, settling with his new bride Anne Thompson and a recent large inheritance in Visalia. He came from Massachusetts, was educated at Yale (where he captained the undefeated 1906 football team), and was a distant cousin of Samuel Morse, the inventor of the telegraph and of the Morse Code. Soon after his arrival in California, he went to work for William H. Crocker, a son of Charles Crocker, the founder of the Central Pacific Railroad, running the Crocker Huffman Ranch in Merced. His relationship with the Crocker family was fortuitous and in 1916 he was named manager of the Pacific Improvement Company, a Crocker firm charged with liquidating a significant portion their holdings. To acquire the Crocker family holdings on the Monterey Peninsula, Morse, with the backing of Herbert Fleishhacker, formed the Del Monte Properties Company, a firm which he ran from 1919 until his death in 1969. The Morse Fleishhacker purchase ultimately included 7,000 acres on the Monterey coast, the Del Monte Hotel, Pacific Grove and 11,000 acres in the Carmel Valley, all for $1,300,000. During the time that RN was trying to purchase the Bay Point property in 1917, Morse had not completed his purchase of all the Monterey properties and was still working as an employee of William Crocker.

RN had initially approached Crocker about the $40,000 option price. Crocker sent him to Morse indicating that "whatever Sam did would be final." Sam Morse had then approved the deal as initially struck. When Crocker changed his mind, RN was furious but in no position to back away from the deal, given his commitments to the Shipping Board contract and his investors, so he paid the $250,000 purchase price under protest with full intention to sue Crocker for the $210,000 extra price plus damages. RN's character was such that Crocker's actions did indeed drive him to take legal action, but he was ultimately dissuaded from that course through an intervention by Alexander Francis Morrison of the firm of Morrison, Dunn, and Brobeck, attorneys for Crocker.

Morrison telephoned RN a day or so after the transaction, acknowledging RN's right to pursue legal action under the circumstances, but urging caution because of "the harm such a suit would be (*sic*), particularly at this time." In RN's account, Morrison pleaded with him not to bring suit, indicating that he was ashamed of his client's actions, but that there was more involved than he could reveal. RN capitulated, writing that, "I let the matter rest. The implications made by Mr. Morrison, a very fine man, worried me very much when added to the other things that were surfacing. At that time, I was working eighteen hours a day and did not feel it possible for me to go through the strain of a long, drawn-out suit that affected the title to our plant. And, of course, $250,000 was not an excessive price to pay for the property for the purpose it was acquired…The Del Monte Property Company, headed by S.F.B. Morse was really dominated by William H. Crocker, and Sam said that if put on the stand his testimony would be that he had given me an option on the property for $40,000 under proper authority and in good faith. He was very much put out."

The proposed capital structure of the new company contemplated the issuance of bonded debt to supplement the original Government advance, private equity, and short term private borrowing. An advertisement and prospectus dated August 1, 1917 describes this offering and includes a $1,000,000 initial offering (the first of an eventual $3,000,000 total offering) of First Mortgage 6% Serial Gold Bonds. These securities were being offered in three tranches of $300,000 each maturing in 1920, 21, and 22, and $100,000 maturing in 1923. Further, in the section of Management and Directors, RN's name does not appear at all. Henry T. Scott is listed as President, John T. Scott as General Superintendent. The absence of his name reflects the fact that at that point, in mid-1917, RN was acting in behalf of the Company through his Western Guaranty & Mortgage Company, as a sales agent for the offering.

He would take the bond issue to New York and attempt to sell it in the capital markets there. The Management and Directors section of the document lists all of the men with whom RN had extensive business relationships at the time. In addition to the Scotts, the Directors included H.M. Robinson of the Merchants National Bank of Los Angeles, H.C. Breeden, Alden Anderson, A. Christeson of Wells Fargo Bank, and John D McKee of Mercantile Bank.

RN's description of the challenges he encountered while trying to locate and contract with an underwriter for this issue of bonds in New York is both entertaining and puzzling. On his first day in the city, he found very receptive interest in his sale with various underwriters expressing interest in the issue. He said that "he found shipbuilding financing was reasonably popular with the public on account of its being a necessary war issue." On his first call on one underwriter, he obtained a verbal commitment and was told to return the following day to work out the particulars. This happened twice more and he must have been optimistic when he returned for his follow-up appointments. In each case, however, the sales were turned down on the following day with no apparent reason for the change of heart. Using an existing banking relationship from California, he called on a friend at Chase National Bank and was advised that, "Someone doesn't want you to succeed in placing these bonds." The friend then directed RN to a man he described as the "Sage of Wall Street," John W. Simpson. In 1884, Simpson, along with William Barnum and Thomas Thatcher had founded the securities law firm today known as Simpson, Thatcher & Bartlett.

RN liked Simpson right away and related his experiences with the several underwriters who had turned him down. He suspected that his adversary in selling the bonds might have been Charles Schwab, Director General of the Emergency Fleet Corporation, and also a competitor back in San Francisco as President of the Bethlehem Shipbuilding Corp. Simpson said that he doubted that Schwab was behind RN's troubles and, after telephoning the security houses RN had visited unsuccessfully, he became convinced that someone else was trying to obstruct the bond sale.

Simpson advised RN to return to his suite at the Waldorf Astoria and then come back the following day for another appointment. He also suggested that he check periodically to see if he was being followed. As RN described the exercise, he was to act naturally, occasionally stepping onto a doorway to light his cigar and, "casually look up and down the street and register the figures you see in your mind's eye...try to note what they are wearing, the color, etc." The following day, at lunch in Simpson's office, RN described a man of medium height wearing a brown suit and a derby hat, to which Simpson responded with laughter that, "You are right. I had you followed. That was my man... I can now tell you definitely someone is determined to prevent you from making a sale of the bonds and you stand no chance of marketing them in New York. Do you have any other contacts out of the city?" RN indicated that he had a relationship with Tillitson & Wolcott in Cleveland, Ohio.

Simpson then planned an elaborate ruse to enable RN to leave his hotel and the city, unnoticed by any adversary. Well known at the hotel, Simpson called the Waldorf and arranged for an additional room around the corner from RN's current space, a room that would mask his entry and egress, allowing him to leave undetected. Simpson told the desk clerk that he needed to rent the room adjacent to RN's current room as well as the room around the corner. "I wish you to give the keys to my friend, Mr. Burgess, I will stop in and register and do not give out any information about him." He instructed RN to make his usual calls from his original room, but to use the new room for any calls to Cleveland. Further, if he was able to make an appointment in Cleveland, he was not to get his reservations or tickets at the Waldorf. He was also to conceal his exit from the hotel, using the service elevator and staying out of the main lobby.

RN was successful in obtaining an appointment in Cleveland with Tillotson who had expressed interest in his bond issue during their telephone conversation. Following Simpson's instructions, he was able to exit the hotel without being noticed and made his appointment in Cleveland the next morning. The meeting was successful and RN left with a commitment on the deal, subject to verification of his representations. He also expressed to Tillotson that "there seemed to be some jealousies or prejudices" associated with the issue and that he (RN) wanted all his cards on the table from the start as he didn't wish to "go to all this trouble and then be tripped up. After all, we were trying to win a war." Tillotson responded that he first wished RN to meet two of his bankers and then, subject to their favorable opinion, he would send his associate John Milligan back to California with RN to verify everything and make a final commitment to PCSB Co.

Everything went smoothly for a while. Milligan came to California with RN and stayed at Diablo as a guest in the Burgess home while doing his due diligence. His final step before returning to Cleveland was a courtesy call on Herbert Fleishhacker president of the Anglo and London Paris National Bank in San Francisco. Something in the Fleishhacker meeting was not right, though exactly what it was is not expressed in the *Memoirs*. As RN described it, Milligan returned from his visit with Fleishhacker with "his Irish all the way up." Angrily challenging RN, he asked what he had been led into. RN responded, "John, you have been living at my house while on this job. Apparently, it was a mistake for you to come to San Francisco, but I believe you have located the source of my trouble." He then pressed Milligan on his intention to fulfill Tillotson's commitment on the bond issue, "are you going to carry out his instructions or not?" Milligan responded, "I am, but I am going to take every precaution. I won't even put the trust with your friends in the Mercantile Trust Company (Henry Scott's trust bank), but with First National Bank, and you had better live up to all your commitments, or else." RN's response was that "It doesn't sound good, John, but if that is the way you wish it, o.k. You know we have a war to win and you are only adding to the hurdles." He reported that Tillotson underwrote the loan and sold the bonds, as promised, and that all bondholders were "paid in due course."

This episode in the *Memoirs* suggests numerous questions. Who would want to bury the PCSB Co bond issue, and why? His suspicion of Charles Schwab is not implausible because Schwab, as Director General of the Emergency Fleet Corporation, occupied a position of authority in the Shipping Board and was therefore in a position to give direction to RN; the two later had a disagreement over yard capacity questions. Schwab's position as both a competitor and an authority figure precluded a close relationship between them. More likely, however, the problem lay elsewhere. RN's interchange with Milligan and his comment about the latter's revealing the "source of my trouble," seem to point at Fleishhacker. RN's writing, taken literally implies that Fleishhacker turned Milligan off on the PCSB bonds because of reservations about RN himself. If so, what these reservations had to do with, or from where they came is not clear. RN's description of his relationship with the Fleishhacker brothers in the Klamath Falls hotel-opening anecdote mentioned earlier leaves the impression that, at that time (1911), things were fine between them. If Fleishhacker was indeed seeking to wreck the PCSB bond issue, perhaps RN did not reveal the full story of the events in Klamath Falls, or else something had gone wrong between them during the intervening years. On the other hand, the root of this could have been nothing more than an abrasive and combative style of doing business. As acknowledged by himself earlier, RN was not a particularly adept organization man. He seemed to have had an almost innate dislike of authority figures, and of people higher than himself socially, and, in becoming part of a large organization in a business in which he had little or no background, he may have found much to struggle with compared with his former free-wheeling and uninhibited style of operation. It is certainly probable that RN, an outsider to the well-established networks of San Francisco finance, could, through his style, have made his share of enemies. Indeed, the impression created by his anecdotes is of a network of assailants, often unidentified, trying to upset his plans on a number of fronts throughout his life. We are left to guess at the source of these difficulties.

Another anecdote puts his earlier suspicions about Charles Schwab into better perspective. From the context, this occurred later in the War, probably in 1918, but prior to the Armistice of November 11th. It again highlights RN's resistance to authority and to prominent persons who were in a position to affect his life. Charles

M. Schwab was a leader of the American steel industry who began his career working in one of Andrew Carnegie's mills in Pennsylvania. He ascended the ranks in Carnegie Steel and later engineered its sale to several New York financiers in an acquisition spearheaded by J.P. Morgan. The United States Steel company was the surviving entity of this deal and Schwab became its first President in 1901. In 1903, Schwab left U.S. Steel to join the Bethlehem Shipbuilding and Steel Company in Pennsylvania. As we have seen, Bethlehem had acquired shipyards in California, Delaware, and New Jersey through its involvement with the ill-fated United States Shipbuilding Company, which Schwab was able to buy out of bankruptcy in 1905. Under Schwab's leadership the company developed a new steel beam, the H Beam, which facilitated the construction of office buildings, ushering in the era of the skyscraper.

During World War I, Schwab was named Director General of the Emergency Fleet Corporation and it was in this connection that he and RN interacted in the San Francisco Bay Area. RN described a day in which he was scheduled to meet with Schwab as well as with Charles Piez, Vice President and General Manager of the EFC. He described being taken by boat from the Ferry Building to the Bethlehem Yard in South San Francisco at which point they transferred to a private yacht of the Moore Shipbuilding Company and, traveling on the Moore yacht, they crossed the Bay and visited the Moore Yard at the foot of Adeline Street in Oakland. From Moore's yard in Oakland they cruised up river to the Pacific Coast Shipbuilding yard at Bay Point.

After visiting the Bay Point facility, they were returning to San Francisco on the Moore yacht when Charles Schwab approached RN and asked him about the status of a request for plans and specifications for a yard expansion submitted earlier by Schwab to RN. RN responded, "I have written you that I was not attempting to prepare such an estimate as it would be a waste of money and there is no chance of success because we could not get enough men to carry on our present operation up to capacity." Schwab's retort, in a fashion which, without context, seems a little peremptory was, "You do as you are told or you will be indicted and probably sent to jail." RN's response was, "I have no fear of jail-I would get some much-needed rest. I have been working for over a year for more than eighteen hours a day. It is physically impossible for me to do any more, and there is no competent help available to assist me." Schwab ended the conversation by suggesting, "you have your orders, and we will see what will be done about it."

Later that evening, after dining together at the Bohemian Club in San Francisco, Schwab approached RN again and relented, saying, "You have an advocate in Mr. Pillsbury (A.F. Pillsbury, District Officer, EFC, San Francisco). He thinks you are right and says all the shipyards in his area are understaffed and can only make necessary changes in their staff when they require technical men by stealing them from one of the other yards, so I guess it is best to forget about doubling the plant." Schwab thus backed off, but the story echoes a side of RN's makeup that has been described before. At that time, with respect to questions of national shipbuilding policy, Charles Schwab was as high as one could go in the hierarchy, and for RN, a local shipbuilder, to get in the spat he recounts seems improbable without thinking of him as an aggressive challenger of almost all authority. Irrespective of his style, however, if the discussion occurred as RN recounts it, he was correct. The early end to the war suppressed demand for new ships, and the labor constraints RN complained of were fortuitous in preventing a destructive addition to ultimately unneeded capacity.

The construction of the shipyard in Bay Point in early 1918 was a singular success. Under the experienced guidance of John T. Scott, ground was broken on January 6 for eight shipways, a plate shop, and auxiliary buildings and all were brought on line in record time. These accomplishments were duly recognized by the Shipping Board. The July 7, 1918 issue of the San Francisco Chronicle described awards presented to three Bay Area shipbuilding yards by Schwab. The Moore Shipbuilding Company, the Bethlehem Shipyard, and the Pacific Coast Shipbuilding Company were all given recognition for outstanding performance during the preceding month. In the morning, Moore and Bethlehem were both presented pennants for efficiency as yard bands played martial music. Later, EFC Vice President, Charles Piez, made a similar appearance at the Bay Point Yard of PCSB Co to observe the laying of its fourth keel after beginning construction only six months earlier.

As the Chronicle described the proceedings, "The celebration at the Pacific Coast Shipbuilding plant across from Benicia set what is believed to be a six- month ship construction record. Six months ago yesterday ground for the big plant on Suisun bay was broken. Since that time the yard and its buildings and ways have been constructed and four keels laid down." The attendance at affairs like this typically involved local leadership of the Shipping Board and Emergency Fleet corporation as well as management of the yard. In this instance, Piez was accompanied by General Council of EFC, Chester Cutthel, District Officer of the EMC, Captain A. P. Pillsbury, as well as RN, John Scott, and George Radford of the company. Finally, a telegram was read by Vice President Charles Piez from General John Pershing on behalf of the American Expeditionary force in France in which Pershing said, "All ranks of the Army in France send their congratulations and heartfelt thanks to their patriotic brothers in the shipyards at home. With such backing, we cannot fail to win. All hail American Shipbuilders!"

Earlier in that week, another press notice appeared in the Oakland Tribune (July 4 edition) in which John T. Scott was honored, again by Charles Schwab, but this time in the company of three other Bay Area shipbuilding men "who have been instrumental in making possible the winning of the honor flags and the speeding of the shipping program." Among the honorees were President George Armes of the Moore Shipbuilding Company, Daniel Hanlon of the Hanlon Drydock and Shipbuilding Company, Joseph Tynen, General Manager of the Alameda and San Francisco plants of Bethlehem Shipbuilding Corporation. The omission of any reference to RN as president of the company in this context highlights his role as a financial and business leader as opposed to a shipyard operator.

Another trip to Washington, this time in pursuit of steel with which to produce the ships, revealed additional insight into how

RN viewed himself. Anne accompanied him on this trip and the two of them took the train up to New York to call on the United States Steel Corporation. On their first night in town, Anne had other commitments which left RN on his own for dinner. In the dining room of the Ritz Hotel he ran into George McNear, Jr., an acquaintance from California from whom he had purchased a large portion of his Diablo land. The two of them dined together and the conversation produced an opportunity for RN to describe his approach to business and to contrast it with McNear's. McNear began the conversation by saying, "Bob, I have the sole rights to the new diesel engine in the United States and have three months in Washington and did not get to first base. Meantime, you have secured a $20,000,000 contract for ships and a $5,000,000 contract for side arms. Just how do you do it?"

RN's answer to McNear reveals much about his perceived social standing in relation to McNear's (whose Father was the successful grain exporter with whom RN had difficulties during his Hookston Ranch days) as well as about his pragmatic approach to doing business with the Government. "Well George...you try to make your commitments on a social basis, but you are not socialized enough to get to the right teas or cocktail parties. You spend your time at the country club perhaps playing (golf) with the secretary of whatever you are after. In my case, I stay in town and take the secretary's clerk, who writes up the documents, to some obscure upstairs place where we can get a wonderful, juicy steak. As you know, there is a definite restriction on meat, and if you are a meat eater as I am, you have to patronize the black market. These office chaps do not have that kind of contact, or the money to avail themselves of it. Well, when you get through playing golf with the secretary he goes to the office and his head clerk says 'Mr. Secretary, here are the papers for the day's commitments. Sign here, and here,' and among the pile is my allotment. Washington seems to me to operate very much in that order. You are not in line for any contracts, just an appointment to play golf."

These sentences accent RN's character. He had come from nothing and harbored resentment about those of his peers who came out of a life of luxury, position, and privilege. He contrasts his "street smarts" with the approach to business of a man who has access to the clubs and relationships he lacked when he began. His success spoke for itself, and McNear, the scion of a wealthy California family who could not match his accomplishments, was seeking his advice. A biographer has few questions about RN's audacity, or his energy, resourcefulness, and brains. Less clear are his inner attitudes about himself. Much of his writing in the *Memoirs* reveals an attitude suggesting a union of superiority and inferiority, superimposed on an underlying layer of aggression in his approach to interpersonal situations.

Another interesting insight accompanies the McNear anecdote. During the course of their dinner, RN noticed W.R. Hearst entering the dining room at the Ritz with an entourage of twenty or so associates. With Hearst was Judge Elbert Gary, the President of United States Steel. Inasmuch as RN's mission in New York was to obtain steel under conditions of extreme shortages, he thought of approaching Hearst for a letter of recommendation to Gary, but rejected the idea. "I had a feeling if one got things through his own strength he was better off than making the approach through someone else."

Elbert Henry Gary (1846-1927) was a Chicago attorney who represented railroad companies through the mid-west in the late 19th century. He served two terms as Du Page County, Ill. judge between 1882 and 1890 and served as the first mayor of Wheaton, Illinois when it became a city in 1892. The title of judge stayed with him throughout his life and he was known as Judge Gary when he became President of Federal Steel Corporation in Chicago, retiring from the law to devote full time to the steel business. When Federal Steel merged with other steel companies in 1901 to become U.S. Steel, Judge Gary, who formed the new company by joining with J.P. Morgan, Andrew Carnegie, and Charles M. Schwab, was its first Chairman. U.S. Steel moved its headquarters to New York in 1900 and became America's first billion-dollar corporation. During World War I, Judge Gary was appointed chairman of the committee on steel of the Council of National Defense, a role in which he worked successfully to improve cooperation between the U.S. government and industry.

RN arrived at the offices of Judge Gary at United States Steel at the appointed time. In the waiting room, when asked how he might be helped, he produced one of his business cards on which he wrote, "I wish to purchase 500,000 tons of steel." Judge Gary admitted him immediately, and, after small talk, asked RN if he was unaware that the U.S. Government had requisitioned all the steel plants in the country and suggested that he go to the government directly for his steel. RN acknowledged that he had heard this news but that he also suspected that the government would not be able to operate the plants without the help of the current owners and that, as business would soon be back to normal, he wanted to place his order with US Steel now. Indicating that, "I have the contracts and the shipyard will be ready by the time we can get the steel; and the ships are needed." Gary's response reflected his own background. "Do you know I reached this position by way of the legal route and never sold a pound of steel in my life? However, I will take you upstairs to a man who has sold steel to all the crowned heads of Europe, and he may be able to fix you up."

After climbing the stairs to the top story of the headquarters building, Judge Gary introduced RN to James A. Farrell, saying "Mr. Farrell, I want you to meet my new friend Mr. Burgess...he wants to buy 500,000 tons of steel. Treat him kindly." Farrell, the President of U.S. Steel from 1911 to 1932, apparently liked RN because he soon prepared a draft of the steel order for RN's signature, commenting that, "I will get off the steel for a couple of keels as soon as you send me the details, and the balance of the order will follow along. Now, let's see, I believe you are the youngest shipbuilder in the United States, and I am going to invite you to be one of Farrell's Boys... as one of my 'boys,' you are entitled to call on me in any emergency, except one - that has to do with money. I can't help there, but there are many things that come up in a large business I can help with. Anyway, should you need help, try me." RN later commented that he never imagined how quickly he would avail himself of that offer.

With his steel order in hand, RN and Anne left New York that evening, heading for Chicago. Between Chicago and Omaha, Nebraska, Anne became quite ill and RN had to wire ahead for an ambulance to meet them in Omaha. On arrival, she was unable to walk and RN was forced to carry her off the car to the waiting ambulance which took them to their hotel suite and a waiting doctor. The doctor advised that her condition was not serious but would necessitate bed rest for at least a week. Her recovery was faster than expected and RN began to search for a reservation with which to resume their trip to California. With the war on and full-scale mobilization of troops throughout the country, train transport was exceedingly difficult to arrange and RN lacked the status to break through this logjam.

One morning while waiting in the hotel, he noticed an article in the local newspaper announcing the departure for San Francisco of a local telephone executive, George E. MacFarland. MacFarland had been offered the Presidency of Pacific Telephone and Telegraph in California and would soon be leaving Omaha to begin his new assignment. His new boss would be Henry T. Scott, RN's mentor, who would move up to the position of Chairman of the Board. RN felt it would be appropriate for him, as an associate of Scott's, to make a courtesy call on MacFarland which he did. RN's short visit reminded MacFarland that he had forgotten to secure his reservation for the trip out to the coast and, in RN's presence, telephoned the Pullman Company, securing a reservation on the spot.

MacFarland's success, in the face of the repeated denials of available space that had met his efforts, made RN angry and his next call was at the Pullman office. To their continued denial of availability, he exclaimed in a loud voice, "That is a dammed lie," repeating his recent experience in Mr. MacFarland's office. In the middle of his explanation a nearby office door opened and a man advised him that he had to leave because, "we don't allow such language in our office." RN responded, "I will leave as soon as you take my wire to Mr. Farrell president of the United States Steel Company." He then proceeded to dictate a lengthy wire to Farrell at US Steel advising him of his predicament. He explained that he had been trying for a week to make a reservation, that his wife was ill, and that he needed to be back in San Francisco for an imminent stockholders meeting.

On his return to their hotel, Anne greeted him in a happy mood indicating that two wires had arrived during his absence, one from James Farrell and the other from Judge Robert S. Lovett, the President of the Union Pacific Railroad. The Union Pacific had called her indicating that a special Pullman car was being added to the Overland for six am departure for California and that a limousine would be around to pick them up and transport them to the station the following morning.

The trip back to California, in a Pullman car on the Union Pacific Line all courtesy of RN's newfound sponsors and helpers, was uneventful except for one anecdote revealing his contempt for what he felt were overly pompous men, often in positions of authority. On what he described as a comfortable trip home, one in which the Union Pacific expended unusual efforts to insure Anne's comfort, he had an encounter with a man of some prominence whom he apparently offended. A lifelong cigar smoker, RN liked to lounge in the parlor car with his cigar after meals. In this instance, the man offended by his cigar smoke was George Woodward Wickersham, a former Attorney General of the United States during the William Howard Taft administration between 1909 and 1913. At the time of the trip RN described, Wickersham would have been serving on the War Trade Board, an organization vested with control over wartime imports and exports, as a Woodrow Wilson appointee.

As RN relaxed in the observation car one afternoon, a young man in the adjacent seat began a conversation. The man was on his first trip to the west coast and was full of questions for RN about an area of the country he had never visited. Another man, somewhat older, seated next to RN's interlocutor, had only moments earlier arisen and left the car, apparently in irritation at the cigar smoke emanating from RN's seat. Introducing himself to RN, the younger man explained that he was the private secretary of the departed traveler, Mr. George Wickersham. The younger man, whom RN remembered as Mr. Prince, explained that the two were on their way to Honolulu for a break from their wartime duties. RN continued in his *Memoirs*, "Well, I began to haunt the parlor car after meals to have my smoke, but I particularly enjoyed upsetting Mr. Wickersham. Every time I entered, he would get up and leave. If my presence offended him, I thought less of him than a stuffed shirt."

The conclusion to this story occurred on the platform at disembarkation in Oakland when the porter, as he brushed RN's suit off, observed, "I guess youse is the most important man on this train, with a special car, etc. I guess Mr. Wickersham is the next most important man." As the porter spoke, RN glanced across the platform and caught Mr. Wickersham staring at him. Writing that the scene was too good to pass up, he gave the porter a ten-dollar tip. RN's attitude towards prominent men he didn't like seemed always aligned with the goal of popping inflated balloons, of pricking stuffed shirts. In this case, he seemed to take perverse pleasure in deliberately irritating the man with his smoke and in taking great joy in being perceived (by the porter) as the most important man on the train.

Upon arrival in California RN discovered that John Scott had called a meeting of the board of directors of PCSB Co without notifying him. At this stage, Scott had no duty to tell RN of his plans. He was an officer of the company (Superintendent), his Uncle Henry was the President, and RN's formal role at the time is less clear, but might best be described as problem-solver-at-large. As Henry Scott's energetic and creative protégé knowledgeable in many aspects of business, RN was able to accomplish things in the non-shipbuilding arena that would have been beyond John Scott's capacity. But RN's attitudes about the younger Scott are quite clear in his writing. Regarding the meeting, he reflected that "the courteous thing would have been to let me know in advance, and to inform me of the matter to be discussed. However, that was not John's way. He was combative, crowding for his own advantage through embarrassing me. He really wished to be president and he defeated himself." Reading these words, the competitive nature of the relationship becomes obvious and RN might have been describing himself. As far as the formal title was concerned, RN ultimately won the competition, but Scott had the shipbuilding name and experiences that RN lacked and would never obtain. The tension between them had to have reflected all of these considerations and added to the wartime production pressures to which both men were already subject.

The next crisis both men faced came to a head in the boardroom and reflected the fact that, although Scott's expertise was manifest in getting the new yard built on time under difficult conditions, he could still not build the contracted ships without the necessary steel. He announced as much in a board meeting, presumably in full knowledge that obtaining the steel was RN's responsibility. The problem was that, though the steel had been ordered and partially shipped, it was stuck on rail sidings in Bay Point. The short rail distance from the sidings to the yard crossed over a terrain feature known at the time as the "sinks." These were extremely marshy areas into which traditional rail cars loaded with steel plates would subside (to the point of being unrecoverable) unless what RN described as "very heavy steel rails" were installed. The only local rails of such character were owned by the Southern Pacific Railroad and were unobtainable, being reserved exclusively for snow shed use.

Ever resourceful, not to mention dramatic, RN left the table and went to the telephone in the director's room to make a call to the railroad. William Sproule, President of the Southern Pacific Railroad between 1911 and 1918, had been an occasional visitor to Diablo and was therefore known to RN. He asked Sproule if it would be possible to borrow some of their rails and have their engineering department install them. Noting that the distance between their tracks and the new yard was just over two and a half miles, Sproule invoked a Railroad Commission wartime ruling precluding rail construction of over two miles. Further, he explained that any violation was subject to a penalty of five years in jail or a $5,000 fine, or both. RN's retort is characteristic. "Mr. Sproule, I was told in

Washington that the penalty for taking ship-building contracts such as ours, if it came up before a 'muck-raking congress,' would be about seven hundred years in jail...God help America if we can't find men who will take the chance. It seems to me I am forced into one situation after another that is transgressing the law 'to save America.'" At that, Sproule promised a call back in a half hour. When the call came the message was that the necessary rails were being loaded and the men would be on the job the following morning to install them. As RN reported the outcome in the boardroom, "that took a little of the wind out of John's sails, but he always had a comeback." The next comeback concerned the problem of insufficient housing for shipyard workers.

The problem of housing for a rapidly growing population of US shipyard workers preoccupied planners in Washington as they tried to grapple with massive increases in war-related shipping needs. In early 1917, the United States had a total of 50,000 shipyard workers. By the end of that year the shipbuilding population had grown to 150,000, and by the Armistice in November of 1918, it numbered 380,000 workers. [4]

Existing yards and potential new yards throughout the country had to be brought on line quickly and put into production. Skilled and unskilled workers numbering in the tens of thousands needed to be located, hired, and housed. The government responded to the housing challenge by incorporating the United States Housing Corporation as a unit of the Department of Labor in July of 1918 and within two years of its inception had 83 new projects under way in 26 states. By the end of the War, in excess of 5,000 acres of land had been developed into housing for 170,000 shipyard workers. Many of these industrial sites were near existing communities while others required a substantial commute to get workers from their homes to the sites. Reports from the period tell of accidents occurring as overloaded streetcars and electric trains with workers hanging from the rails carried men back and forth to work.

William J. Williams. *Accommodating American Shipyard Workers, 1917-1918.* The Pacific Northwest Quarterly, Volume 84, No 2 (April 1993), 51-59.

Frederick Law Olmstead reported in The Monthly Labor Review that skilled workers, often older men with families, were in high demand as being critical to yard operations and refused to live in sub-standard housing. Less skilled labor often commuted or were housed in on site-dormitories. [5]

RN's description of the role he played in the construction of the town of Clyde, just south of Bay Point (today's Port Chicago, as renamed in 1931) on the shores of Suisun Bay, evokes many of his other anecdotes about his ability to overcome obstacles and succeed where others had failed. Predictably, serious conflict often occurred. Dean L. McLeod in his History of Bay Point relates an interesting set of circumstances that are not found in the *Memoirs*.

As we have seen, RN had purchased and subdivided the Foskett and Elsworthy ranch (a portion of a larger parcel originally known as Government Ranch) a number of years earlier and had suggested it as the site of a new shipyard, subject to his ability to acquire an adjacent deep-water site owned by the Crocker Land Company. The parcel was a good site for a town within which to house the shipyard workers. After PCSB Co obtained the contract to build the ten ships, the local community of Bay Point sought access to government funds with which to build a residential community of their own for the anticipated workers. That community, some two miles east of the Clyde site and much closer to the proposed shipyard on the water, sorely needed housing and wanted the government funding to come to its community. This would have provided housing within easy walking distance to the yard for workers. RN, however, did not own that land and he wanted the town built on land he controlled. He was the person who got the housing contract and was thus in a position to site the new community where he wanted it, inciting pushback in the local newspapers about his ability to get funds from the U.S. government to subsidize Clyde. McLeod concluded that "Clyde was thus born of one man's shrewd ability to tap onto Federal grant

---

[5] Frederick Law Olmstead. *Lessons from Housing Developments of the United States Housing Corporation.* Monthly Labor Review (Vol 8, May 1919): 27-38.

programs." [6]

In RN's account, he had no sooner solved Scott's problem of rail access than the Superintendent began complaining about lack of men to staff his operation, saying, "We are having trouble getting enough men and should have housing." Dating these events is difficult, but this must have been in the first half of 1918, in any event prior to the establishment of the U.S. Housing Corporation in July because RN mentioned that there were rumors about government financial help on the housing problem but that leadership for the position had not been finalized. As he put it, "So I was to leave for Washington and see if I could get housing money..." He wrote that the office of the man who would soon be appointed to run the new agency was in Philadelphia and it was there that he went first.

He arrived at the office in Philadelphia and found it to be alive with the kind of frantic activity one would expect under the wartime conditions then in existence. While RN was seated in his waiting room, the new head of the proposed agency (RN did not name the man) rushed in and, after a peremptory introduction in which RN stated his mission, asked him if he knew anything about the construction of bunkhouses and barracks. Acknowledging that he did, based on his experiences at the California Beet Sugar Refining Company, RN proceeded to describe the barracks he built for his Japanese laborers and the particulars of construction details. The new agency head asked RN if he could write specifications for such construction, indicating that, "I can build a 12-story building, but I do not know a damned thing about bunking men cheaply and must meet with the organizing board and lay down a plan. If you can write up the plan and specifications you will just about save my life." RN responded that if the man could get him a "room and a good stenographer" he would prepare the plan for presentation to the board. "Do that, and I will see that your housing requirements are taken care of" was the grateful response.

After RN completed the plan, the agency head reviewed it and

---

[6] Dean L. McLeod, *Images of America, Bay Point.* (Arcadia Publishing Co. San Francisco, 2006). 37.

asked him to return the following morning for his housing contract. RN reported that the following day he picked up a $2,500,000 check payable to the Pacific Coast Shipbuilding Company, a check he characterized as the first loan by the US Government for housing construction anywhere during the War. RN's recollection on this matter is not consistent with documentation on the subject obtained elsewhere, however. In a copy of a partial letter obtained from the papers of the PCSB Co at the San Francisco Maritime Museum National Park dated July 6, 1918, the Shipping Board wrote, on the topic of the construction of Clyde, "We shall assist in the development of this housing tract by making a loan of $750,000, secured by first mortgage on the houses and one hundred acres of the improved land." Whether or not it was the first such check is impossible to say, but clearly the episode occurred in the early stages of the new housing program, given its July, 1918 formation. Once again, RN had gone East on a mission and employed his knowledge and creativity in getting results where others were not as fortunate.

When he later ran into Henry Robinson, the President of the First National Bank of Los Angeles, and was asked how it was that he succeeded in obtaining a housing contract so rapidly when delegations of men from Los Angeles, San Francisco, and other large manufacturing centers, were all competing for the same federal largess, RN's answer reflects the self-assurance, bordering on hubris, that we have seen before. "Well Henry, I was on the spot when needed. I presume it would be called appreciation."

RN's description of his role in the construction of the new town raises questions in light of a review of the historical record. In the *Memoirs*, he wrote as if the project was his alone to run and he described several initial steps. The new village was to be named Clyde, after the world-famous shipbuilding center on the river of the same name in Scotland. RN described grading and graveling the streets, setting the mud-sills for 100 new houses, and creating plans for a hotel to accommodate 80 men. All of this came to an abrupt halt with the arrival, from Minneapolis, of an architect to whom RN refers somewhat mysteriously as "Mr. Apple." Apple was apparently the government officer in charge of building housing under the contract that RN had arranged. RN's comments about Apple are such as to create the strong impression that there was tension between the two. He quickly overturned all of RN's construction activities to date as well as his financing arrangements. How all this might have occurred is not clear. Presumably, RN must have known that a government employee or contractor was scheduled to come to the site and assume responsibility for the construction, that the government was not going to simply write checks to private operators and then not insist on some level of supervision of the final product. If he did know these things, why did he let himself get so far along without coordination with the new man?

The financing arrangements were among the first to be undone by Apple, although the *Memoirs* do not make clear how he in his role as the housing manager was able to impede or interfere with the provisions of the underlying shipbuilding contract. To review, the initial capitalization of the shipyard contemplated the $2.5 million advance for seed capital to initiate yard construction, another $.5 million in private equity raised among RN's associates, and another $2.5 million in debt (all prior to a planned bond issue). Apple initially attacked the private equity portion, one part of which included a $50,000 piece from Henry Morris, RN's former mentor. Another provision included agreements by various sub-contractors on the prospective job to invest 10% of the value of their individual contracts, all contributing to the $500,000 equity portion. Apple cancelled all these subscriptions, causing problems with PCSB Co.'s lenders in the process. RN did not explain just how the equity financing was obtained in view of these cancellations. The required $500,000 equity was raised, so presumably replacements were found for the lost investors.

Apple also ordered all work on the housing stopped, insisted on the regrading of the streets, directed the installation of sewer and water mains, and ordered underground installation of street lighting conduits. RN's contempt for Apple's approach and propensity to spend money was palpable as he wrote, "...Oakland or Berkeley or like cities had nothing to compare with it. Then he appointed a committee of seven architects to prepare plans for 100 cottages and for an 80-room hotel with showers, dining room and kitchen equipment on the standard of first-class modern hotels and a color scheme drawn with imagination - the architect Mr. (Bernard) Maybeck was chairman and he included all the colors of the rainbow. Well, that damned monstrosity is there yet and cost about $250,000." Actually, the Housing Corporation named Bernard Maybeck Supervising Architect, and his number two, George Applegarth, RN's friend and collaborator, was given the title of Acting Architect.

RN went on to relate how, after the war, when the shipbuilding was completed, the homes were sold for 15% of their cost, the hotel was unsaleable at any price and became in turn a night-club, a dance hall, a road house, and a boot-leg joint. His pique was in evidence when he wrote about his enlistment by management to insure attendance by the yard workers at the grand opening of the new hotel. The workers were not inclined to participate in the events feeling the production, which included speeches by Shipping Board officials, architects and other notables, was "too ritzy" for them. RN arranged for a keg of whiskey and free beer to be delivered to the yard to soften up resistance to attendance. With that inducement, the yard workers attended the opening celebrations.

RN concluded his remarks on what he saw as a very wasteful investment on the government's part by saying, "I don't know how many times, if ever, the like was carried out, but I do know that it was deliberate, wasteful, foolish. The overdone housing defeated its purpose. It was the product of a man intoxicated with authority. Of course, it was all charged up to the shipbuilding company and definitely put the skids under it."

In these comments, RN is clearly laying the blame for financial results which were worse than expected in the lap of the US Government, suggesting that the wasteful spending he described used precious dollars that might have been saved or used more appropriately elsewhere in the operation. In the end, though, all ten freighters were delivered as contracted for and he wrote that all the bondholders were paid. In his recounting, the equity investors did poorly. "The stockholders who put up the original $500,000 got nothing, or at best little on their investment."

The Pacific Coast Shipbuilding Company fulfilled its obligations under the contract with the Shipping Board. On November 30, 1918, the first ship, the USS Diablo was launched to great fanfare at the Bay Point yard with Anne Fish Burgess as sponsor. This must have been an exciting day, but, with the war now over, probably the greatest impediment to profitability was timing. The Diablo slipped down the ways just nineteen days after the armistice was signed in France on November 11. With the end of the war, shipping demand was destined to collapse, while other, post-war economic challenges loomed on the horizon.

RN's *Memoirs* suggest that his work on the new town of Clyde was interrupted by the arrival of Apple, the architect representing the US Housing Corporation, and that Apple took over the job from that point on. There was more to it than his description, however. A Sunday, June 30, 1918 article in the Oakland Tribune describes the hiring by PCSB Co of L. M. MacDonald, a banker from Livermore, to manage the construction of the town. The article includes a good description of the plans for the village and the progress of the shipbuilding to that point, though it has no mention of Apple, and leaves open the question of how, if at all, RN interacted with MacDonald on the ultimate construction of Clyde.

How did the shipbuilding enterprise fare financially? The overriding answer to this question is that the war ended too early for the investors to achieve the return on investment initially contemplated. All ten ships were built and delivered according to RN's original contract, though on a time line somewhat slower than planned. The prospectus for the bond offering of August, 1917 made reference to a potential profit stream to bond investors continuing through year-end 1923, so, initially, a significantly longer duration was contemplated. The date of the launching of the last ship was in early 1921. An article in The Pacific Marine Review of April of that year suggested that, when the freighter Natasha was completed, in June, the Bay Point facility was to be closed. The article goes on to say that the future of the plant and equipment of the yard was uncertain, but that the town of Clyde had a bright future, possibly as a home for disabled veterans.

The contract, as it was initially conceived, was almost certainly a lump-sum agreement (81% of the ship-building agreements at the time were such), envisioning ten 9,400-ton ships for which the US Government would pay a price of $168 per dead-weight ton, or $15,792,000 for the lot. [7] RN described the agreement as a "$20,000,000 contract," leaving a margin out of which to repay debt and equity investors of $4,208,000 ($841,600 annually). The August, 1917 prospectus projected a net earnings stream close to that number over the period between 1919 and 1923. At the inception, this must have seemed a reasonable proposition to the investors because wartime demand for shipping was expected to be very strong, and because of the Scott's history and competence in the shipbuilding industry. However, a war of nineteen months barely allowed the producers of large capital-intensive products like ships to get started before it ended, leaving them with huge investments in plant and equipment which it was going to be difficult to recapture.

After the Armistice, the Government began reviewing all its ship contracts to determine which of them would be economic to cancel and such cancellations occurred at a number of yards. PCSB's contract was not cancelled, but its challenge would have been that the Bay Point yard was building ships into a market with collapsing demand. To make matters worse, early in the war, when all equipment and materials were being ordered for the construction of the vessels, demand for materials was at its highest and top dollar would have been paid for these critical materials. So, they began with high, demand-driven resource prices, but quickly (nineteen months later) evolved into a surfeit-driven market, competing with hundreds of other yards doing the same thing.

RN wrote that the bond investors all got paid off. But a combination of higher-than-expected materials prices, excessive invest-

---

[7] Third Annual Report of the United States Shipping Board. 30 June 1919. (Government Printing Office, Washington D.C. 1919). 62.

ment in the town of Clyde, and other factors difficult to identify at this distance, reduced the $500,000 investment of the equity investors to a zero, or almost zero return, as RN reported. Who were these equity investors? RN identifies Henry Morris as one. Presumably, many were members of the PCSB Board of Directors, which would have included Henry Scott, John Scott, H.M. Robinson, H.C. Breeden, Alden Anderson, A. Christeson, and John D. McKee. There is evidence that Robert Marsh, a Los Angeles real estate investor and fellow listing agent with RN on the Diablo Homes project, also made a substantial commitment.

The impact of his shipbuilding activities on RN's personal financial situation is more difficult to discern. It was certainly one of the more challenging undertakings of his life to that point, but obtaining insight into his financial picture is challenging. Because his primary business was real estate and real estate development and because he almost always used borrowed funds with the attendant reward or punishment associated with positive or negative financial leverage, his position at any time is not clear. His compensation as President of the PCSB Co was initially $20,000 per year. This was increased to $25,000 in mid-1918, but then reduced by order of the Shipping Board to $5,000 in March of 1919 in a move which reduced all executive salaries dramatically after the Armistice. As compensation for his efforts in securing the initial USSB contract and his other accomplishments, he was given 30,000 common shares of PCSB Co common stock, a nominal value of $3,000,000. Half of this was to be held as treasury stock, however, so his shipyard-related wealth in early 1918 (he was named President effective January 1st of that year) would have consisted of the PCSB Co shares, $1,500,000, on which he may have received dividend income, and any of his salary he might have saved. In addition to this, he of course had interest in, and income on, various real estate projects, which unfortunately were declining in value precipitously during this period.

What is clear, however, is that 1917-1919 were three years of almost continuous deterioration in his financial picture. The next chapter will look in detail into the implications of his position as a lender during times that can only be described as catastrophic for commercial and residential real estate, and it must be said that he was ill-prepared for the buffeting he would receive during those years.

An intriguing question lies in the circumstances underlying the failure of the shipbuilding firm to lay claim to significant funds due it under the provision mentioned earlier which allowed PCSB Co to make claims against Government-initiated change orders as well as changes in labor rates, both of which occurred during the life of the agreement. This clause in the contract, under which the equity investors would have been made whole and the Company awarded a five percent profit on all ship construction, was never invoked. RN described a lunch in Los Angeles with G. D. Reed, the Shipping Board District Auditor, some three years after his resignation from the Company. Reed, who had also left his position at the Shipping Board some time earlier, asked RN what happened to his shipbuilding company, indicating that, "Before I left they accepted the plant as part payment at its appraised liquidating value, when according to your contract you had the election of receiving back your $500,000 and five percent on the volume of business if we changed the specifications or the rate of pay to the laborers. We did both, so you were entitled to your $500,000 and at least $1,000,000 for your services, and that is what we expected to pay. The only two contracts we had with that provision were negotiated by you, and we thought it the fairest to everyone." RN offered, by way of explanation, that he had been out of the company for the past three years, to which Reed responded, "Well, that accounts for the odd settlement. I was sure from your stand when the contracts were negotiated that you required your people to be protected to some reasonable extent, so I could not understand your throwing the sensible provision overboard."

Nothing in RN's character as we have come to understand it thus far in his life presents a reasonable explanation for this failure to invoke a fundamental provision in the agreement which would have protected his investors and provided a cushion to whatever profitability the enterprise achieved. The next chapter in his life will present a series of circumstances which created his ultimate financial failure, leading to a declaration of involuntary bankruptcy. The nature of these circumstances was such as to cause an almost total separation between him and all of his financial and business relationships up to that point in his life. Powerful forces were at work and his otherwise inexplicable failure to persuade his former colleagues to seek the protection of that clause may be explainable only in this light.

After the Armistice and the resultant collapse in demand for new ships, RN's writing in the Memoirs reflects the strain he must have been under as other areas of his financial empire grew increasingly pressured. He described the hiring of a new Vice President at the yard, Colonel D. C. Seagrave, whom he described as, "A West Point man who was recommended as a rugged fellow who would put on jeans and get to the bottom of things. In my opinion, he was very good at occupying an office chair." The specifics of any problem RN had with Seagrave are never mentioned, but the Army man had longevity in the firm much greater than RN enjoyed. He was mentioned in a news article in 1941 in which the possibility of reusing the PSCB Co site was discussed in the context of then growing likelihood of another war.

On November 15, 1919, RN resigned as President of the Company. George Radford, another senior officer, also resigned the same day. Board Resolutions attest to both of these departures and to residual compensation voted for each of them by the directors, as well as funds owing each as the result of the Company's being unable to make its preferred dividend the previous August. No correspondence was available in which a description of events predicating these departures was offered. Was RN asked to leave his position as President? He remained on the Board for some time suggesting an amicable parting, but there is no record of why the decision was made. A speculation may be offered that seems reasonable under the circumstances then at work in his financial life. With shipbuilding in decline, no longer the opportunity that it had once seemed, and with his real estate businesses also failing, the resignation may have had more to do with a need for rest and a need to focus attention on other priorities more closely aligned to his lifelong interests. By 1919, the housing collapse was well underway with lenders insisting on payments that were probably in arrears and the PCSB Co may have been a distraction he was unable to devote more time to.

Thus ended a chapter in RN's life which included experiences unlike any others he had encountered in his forty-one years. He had stepped away from his real estate financing specialization and entered a world entirely different from that which he had known. The evidence he presented in his *Memoirs* described some singular successes, particularly early in the experience. The period between 1916 and 1919, however, spanned a time during which the geopolitical and economic outlook of the Country changed dramatically and his fortunes were not unaffected by these changes. The optimism of 1916 had faded to a much darker picture by 1919. The early end to World War I had left shipbuilding companies with too much capacity in the face of very little demand and had shattered the sanguine investment outlook of the early months of the War. RN entered this period on top of his game so to speak, but left it, in late 1920 as a bankrupt. The confidence that emerged from his writing in the *Memoirs* in his early years had disappeared by the 1920s and he was left to begin all over again. The final piece of this collapse is the subject of the next chapter and it will describe the events which ultimately undid his meteoric rise from his farm boy-beginnings to the shipbuilder he became at age forty.

Anne Fish Burgess, sponsor, with two unidentified participants at the launching of the USS Diablo. Courtesy Contra Costa County Historical Society.

The launching of the USS Diablo, the first ship completed by the Pacific Coast Shipbuilding Company, on November 30, 1918. Courtesy Contra Costa County Historical Society.

CHAPTER 14
Collapse

Speculate only when you have more money than you need, never when you need more money than you have. Hindsight can be so valuable in guiding you in the future, but it is not so easy to see ahead, even though surrounded by experienced and successful bankers.

—RNB

In January of 1919 the war was over and the troops began to arrive home to welcoming receptions, parades, and recognition of the service they had provided in France. San Francisco hosted parades and celebrations and in one such instance, RN was in the city participating in the festivities. In the *Memoirs*, he described a raucous evening at an Italian restaurant in North Beach and a potentially serious accident that preceded the party. As his party of five proceeded, by automobile, down a very crowded Market Street, awash with soldiers and sailors recently home from the war, a group of soldiers on the sidewalk to his right began wrestling and one of them fell under the wheels of his car. He described the car as a "four-door Winton, very heavy." As the man fell, he hit his head on the radiator and continued down under the front wheels. RN, feeling that if he stopped the car, the soldier might have been pinned under the wheels, continued driving, taking the wheels over the man twice, rendering him unconscious on the street. The San Francisco police soon arrived, put the man in their automobile and left for the station instructing RN to follow. By the time they reached the station, the man had regained consciousness and refused to press charges against RN, saying "Hell no, it was not his fault. We were horsing around and I jumped in front of his car." RN was free to go, stopping only to leave a ten-dollar bill with the officer for the man, instructing him to "Give him this to help make up for lost time."

The joy felt by Americans at the conclusion of the war contrasted with the very difficult economic conditions returning soldiers encountered on their return. As we have seen, RN's business life was affected by a variety of macro-economic conditions over the years, and the period of his financial collapse was no exception. In the waning months of World War I, with inflation raging in Europe and wartime production beginning to slow in the states, a recession hit America. The duration of this slowdown was seven months, between August of 1918 and March of 1919 and it was exacerbated in the United States by growth in the labor force represented by returning troops and a consequent increase in the unemployment rate. This event was followed ten short months later by a relatively short, but quite severe depression, lasting from January of 1920 to July of 1921. The short duration of this depression belied its ferocity in terms of price declines; wholesale prices declined an estimated 37% during its life. RN's attempts to re-start his building and lending businesses after the conclusion of the war were accordingly thwarted by factors well beyond his control.

The events that led to RN's financial collapse amounted to a perfect storm of adverse conditions over which he was powerless to exercise much influence. Geopolitical, macroeconomic, and public health issues all coalesced, in the years leading up to and ending immediately after the First World War, to create an environment that spelled the end of a period of significant accomplishment for him. A reader might fairly ask whether hubris played a part in his downfall. RN was a complicated personality and that conclusion is probably justified. With his eighth- grade education, he was bright enough to grasp financial concepts beyond the perspective of his peers in the farming community in which he came of age. He seems to have understood intuitively the concept of financial leverage through which the use of borrowed funds can enhance the return on investment far beyond what might be realized with cash-only investments. He also must have understood the downside of this leverage, which can magnify losses in equally dramatic fashion, but his initial experiences with leverage were, for the most part, characterized by great success. There were, for him, no significant failures which might have served as learning experiences or warning signs tempering his enthusiasm for borrowed money, or served as cautionary lessons tempering his unbounded confidence in his own ability. He had been able to obtain bank loans, using his real estate assets as collateral, all with the expectation that, in the growing economic climate of a new and expanding California, commercial and residential property prices would continue to rise, boosting the value of his collateral and facilitating additional borrowings. He had never been caught short, and had prospered accordingly. World War I, recession, depression, and the influenza epidemic combined to bring that decade-long string of successes to an end.

The genius of his original financing idea, his greatest strength in an era of rising commercial and residential prices, became a sword of Damocles when war and economic conditions changed so dramatically in 1917-1919. The details of these changes are the essence of his financial destruction, and they unfolded in a context which placed RN in a precarious position within his group of newfound associates and friends. This was the group of men who RN had striven mightily to affiliate with, and to emulate, when as a young man, he returned from his inspection of the San Francisco earthquake and began planning his future. In the end, these relationships did not serve him well; his friends abandoned him, breaking relations and distancing themselves from anything to do with the brash young man from Contra Costa County. The circumstances that precipitated this crisis within his peer group are the subject of this chapter.

A short review of his arrangements for financing the construction of residential and commercial buildings will be helpful in laying out this picture. In 1908, with his affiliation with the Mercantile Bank of San Francisco, and the subsequent creation of his mortgage company, Western Mortgage & Guarantee Co., RN established the mechanism under which he could continue to build houses and commercial buildings with an ever-revolving source of new capital. As he built and sold new starter homes to young people he could finance a new house, valued at say $10,000 with a 10% down payment and the balance carried for ten years with payments of principle and interest at regular intervals along the way. When the term had expired, the mortgage could be renewed or paid off, depending on the circumstances of the parties to the transaction. RN expressed his perspective on his strategy in this way, "We specialized in selling to young folks at ten percent down and the balance over ten years, representing it as good insurance of a future competency based on the last ten years of increase in real estate values in California." It was that critical assumption of continued increasing real estate prices that became the weak link in his plans and his approach to the market. He was not alone. His friends in the banking community shared, at least initially, his optimistic view.

The dramatic national slide in housing prices beginning in 1917 was described in Chapter 11. For builders, and for the bankers who financed them, this was a critical problem. For a builder, whose bank had syndicated his loans throughout the country to correspondent banks, the exposure was even greater. Mercantile Bank had done just that with the certificates of participation RN was generating with his Western Mortgage & Guaranty Company. These certificates were now held not only by Mercantile Bank in San Francisco, but were held by numerous correspondent banks elsewhere in the country.

An example may help clarify the magnitude of the problem ultimately faced by RN and his bankers. Assume that in 1912, RN had built and sold a $10,000 home in Oakland to a young couple, financing it under an installment contract for $1,000 down, with a $9,000 ten-year loan at 5% payable annually including interest on the unpaid balance. This loan would have been sold to Western Mortgage & Guaranty Company, which in turn would have deposited it in the Mercantile Bank Trust Company, all of this under the Mercantile Bank of San Francisco umbrella. Western Mortgage would then create a certificate of participation which included a guarantee from the trust bank that such certificate was in an amount 90% or less than the face value of the original $9,000 loan, insuring its "safety." The resulting certificate of participation, a binding contract under the regulations of the State Insurance Commission, would then have been sold to a bank or other investor. Because of RN's relationship with Henry Scott and the Mercantile Bank, a great volume of these instruments went to that bank, which in turn syndicated them throughout their correspondent-bank network.

This system worked well but depended on continuing strength in the housing market. If the $10,000 home purchased in 1912, became a $6,000 home in 1917, because of the nationwide decline in home prices, at the expiration of the contract the investor or bank holding the certificate of participation was in possession of an instrument not worth its face value. The certificate as originally issued guaranteed that it's underlying collateral was worth not less than $8,100, 90% of the original $9,000 loan. The collateral was now worth only $6,000, however, and, at its expiration could *only* be renewed as a new instrument reflecting current values. Such renewals became very problematic for the issuing institutions.

RN described a meeting with Henry Scott in which these difficulties began to become clear to both men. Scott advised RN, "We are having trouble at the bank, and on top of it all, several of our correspondent banks to whom we have recommended investments in Western Mortgage & Guaranty certificates, are demanding that either we refund their investment or have the underlying mortgages renewed, and they hold a very substantial amount." He went on to say that, "if the mortgages are renewed, the certificates will be legal for them to hold and they will be content." RN then advised Scott, apparently for the first time, that the mortgages were non-renewable because of "retroactive State legislation" which brought the Mortgage company under the jurisdiction of *both* the State Banking and Insurance Commissions. As he described it to Scott, we are not allowed to "renew mortgages on hand and any new loans must be appraised by an appraiser approved by both the banking and insurance commissioners who are appointed to appraise all loans." Further, RN explained, the law was being aggressively enforced with penalties for each offense of "a $5,000 fine and a five-year jail term." He anticipated a very likely chance of Western Mortgage & Guaranty Company failing its upcoming compliance examination. Concluding, RN told Scott, "at this time there is no chance of getting bank loans to replace maturing loans." And, he added in a huge understatement, "Indeed, I do not know how the values will stand up under present depressed real estate conditions." Scott responded that, "We have simply got to find some way to renew those mortgages, so we will have six months or a year to adjust our bank to the demands of the Treasury Department...You work out a plan and you can depend on me to get any resolutions passed that will assure your protection for doing a very necessary thing." And then, ominously, "Get your plans ready as quickly as possible. Time may be very short."

The exact date of this meeting with Scott is not identified in the *Memoirs,* but it seems likely it occurred in late 1918 or early 1919 as the recent war's ending was bringing into focus the solution to another difficult problem both men were facing. In March of 1918, the United States Congress had passed Moratory and Stay Legislation, known as the Soldiers and Sailors Civil Relief Act of 1918, granting persons serving in the military relief from their obligation to make contracted payments on indebtedness. By staying the remedies normally available to a creditor in the event of default, the Government protected borrowers from foreclosure actions while they were in the service of their country. The moratory was to remain in effect until six months after the termination of the war which meant that it would expire in May of 1919 and creditor remedies would again be available. What was understandable and appropriate legislation for the protection of American military personnel, was catastrophic for builders and lenders struggling with all of the events we have described during the period.

RN and his bankers thus faced two very significant hurdles to their business objectives during the war years: Service men to whom he had sold houses subject to installment sales, or on which he had placed mortgages, were forgiven the obligation of making their contractual payments for the duration of the war. Also, widely syndicated certificates of participation, issued by his Western Mortgage & Guaranty Co, were based on loans on which the market value of the securing property had declined to a level often substantially lower than the face amount of the original loan. And to compound the problem, as RN understood and explained it, as contract expirations came due, they could not be renewed legally in California.

These are complex topics, and RN's *Memoirs* were written at a time long after the events he described, and by a man then in his mid-eighties, so following the trail he described is far from easy. But it seems likely that Henry Scott, highly concerned with the declining quality of the collateral underlying his bank's book of business, as well as that of its correspondent banks, instructed RN to take action to renew the mortgages in (apparent) contravention of the law. RN described an almost tragic set of circumstances under which he posited the conflict they faced as a clash between obeying the law, and allowing the mortgages to expire, potentially risking the failure of multiple banks throughout the State and elsewhere in the country, and renewing the mortgages illegally - risking the considerable penalties RN described attending that course - but saving California's banks in the process. As he put it, "It was quite impossible to refinance the mortgages, and it was against the law for the bank to hold certificates unless the mortgages were renewed, and renewal was prohibited by the law. The choice was break the law and save the California banks; or obey the law and face the closing of all California banks." He went on, significantly, to suggest, "It is apparent that the commissioners (i.e., State Banking and Insurance Commission regulators) considered the course adopted was the better of two evils for the State of California, for they never called RN Burgess before them, and there was never any suit filed against me," implying that the mortgages had indeed been renewed, or reinstated in some fashion, but that the regulators had looked the other way.

In 1919, the United States Federal Reserve system had been in place for only six years and memories of bank runs must have been fresh enough in banker's minds to cause considerable apprehension.

The idea that Mercantile bank and its correspondents were holding multiple millions of dollars of valueless paper in their vaults would have been just the circumstance to create a panic situation, stimulating a run by depositors on an institution with insufficient capital to stave it off. This was made clear in a conversation RN quoted about a meeting he had with Frederick Lipman, an old San Francisco friend and neighbor.

Immediately after his discussion with Henry Scott, RN went home to Anne at Diablo where the two of them sat up most of the night discussing his predicament. Deeply in debt, with demand for his product almost non-existent, his mortgage company under risk of civil prosecution if maturing mortgages were renewed illegally, RN must have felt out of alternatives. In their conversation, Anne suggested that he seek the counsel of an older man who might be familiar with the conditions he now faced. "Robb, it would be a dreadful situation for the children if anything happened to you. I would like you to talk it over with some experienced men." One such man was Fred Lipman (Frederick J. Lipman, President of Wells Fargo Bank). Recalling that he had known Lipman as a child growing up in San Francisco, RN determined he would call on the older man for counsel.

On arriving at the Wells Fargo banker's office in the city, and revealing the purpose of his visit, RN was surprised when Lipman arose from his chair and indicated that he was not inclined to discuss the topic in his office. Rather, he suggested that the two of them meet on the ferry boat to Berkeley, disembark at Dwight Way and talk in private on their way to their respective homes. This they did, and as they made their way up Dwight Way, Lipman expressed initial surprise that Mercantile Bank was in difficulty, but upon reflection realized that signs were abundant that should have provided hints. To the extent that local banks at the time had significant exposure to real estate lending, the housing market difficulties would represent risk for all of them, and apparently Wells Fargo was no exception. Lipman expressed that apprehension by voicing the opinion that, "Should it (Mercantile Bank) close it will start a panic here (at Wells Fargo) and although this bank has a cash reserve to over fifty per cent, we would have no chance to stave off a run. It would ruin us." Lipman also mentioned that he had recently been a participant in an effort to shore up the Bank of Italy (which later became the Bank of America), because of similar dangers, in which an application to the Federal Government for a $50,000,000 real estate loan had been made, in the success of which he expressed confidence.

The older banker went on to opine that RN was in a difficult spot, but that it was his responsibility to do everything in his power to help Mercantile because, "Should any important bank in San Francisco close, the resulting panic would close every bank in the state. It would put the development of California back fifty years." This counsel, coming from a far older and more experienced banker, must have been sobering indeed to RN. Lipman then counseled complete secrecy, saying that, "One thing is absolutely necessary, and that is not to reveal the trouble facing your company. Already four people know, and I feel you should close ranks and take no one else into your confidence...there is no necessity of explaining about the reason for renewing mortgages." Then, in what may have been the first such attempt on the part of senior banking officers in RN's group of older associates, Lipman warned the younger man to, "Keep away from me. I do not wish to know any more. Don't ask our bank for any loans. If in need of money presently, remember you have many friends in country banks."

RN's description of the meeting with Frederick Lipman is fascinating both for what it expresses about the depth and scale of what was becoming an intractable problem, and for RN's position within the banking community in San Francisco. Heretofore, RN had been a young man on the way up, a kind of fair-haired boy in San Francisco financial circles, to whom older men had frequently given money to invest because of a track record of competence and success. Lipman's words paint a much different picture and reflect the significant changes in the business and banking climate which had occurred during the war years. If RN was indeed directed by Henry Scott to tell his loan servicing department at Western Mortgage & Guaranty to renew or extend expired mortgages, in violation of State Banking and Insurance Commission laws, such action on his part would have put at serious risk the directors of both his mortgage company and of Mercantile bank, under whose umbrella it operated. The penalties for renewing the mortgages, and the scale of the problem at Mercantile Bank, would have meant that Scott, and the officers and directors of both organizations (WM&G Co and Mercantile Bank) would have faced serious personal risk of prosecution. Under these circumstances, it is easy to see how they might want to distance themselves from him.

When RN shared his Lipman conversation with Henry Scott, his older mentor was not happy to learn of Lipman's opinion, but agreed with the Well Fargo banker's insistence on confidentiality under the circumstances, suggesting that "We must close ranks and positively make no explanation of why the mortgages were renewed...in an effort to keep the directors out of litigation that could be interminable. And, as I have to work with the directors, I must not become involved in any way that will require explanations. The directors are in my age group. Many have been close friends for many years, and we will need that friendship to hold the line." In these comments, Scott seemed to be setting the stage for insulating himself and his directors from the problem while isolating RN and setting him up as a fall guy.

But he didn't abandon him completely because his next question in that meeting was to inquire what RN felt he needed for his own protection under the circumstances. RN responded with three requests. First, he sought a procedural change within the trust department of the Mercantile Bank by which the trust office would write a letter to his firm, WM&G Co, requiring that any future assignments to the trust company have attached appraisals signed by three non-director officers of the bank. This first request seems to be a request to both facilitate expeditious handling (RN traveled frequently and was out of the state often) and to keep information about new appraisals associated with (illegal) mortgage renewals beyond the knowledge of the Bank's directors.

His second request was to call on both the State Insurance and Banking Commissioners and suggest that they assign a state appraiser, in addition to the private appraiser, to certify the value of loans and renewals. Acknowledging that such a request would double appraisal costs, he argued that "it was well worth the price to have the departments aware of what we are doing as we go along. They are aware of the present unstable real estate values and the necessity of a liberal policy to prevent a panic." Adding that, as the two Commissions were each short of work, he felt both would go along with his request, and, by instituting this cautious and prudent approach to valuation, Scott's leadership of his directors would be enhanced.

RN's final request in response to Scott's inquiry about his own safety was about protection for himself and his family. He allowed as how his income was going to decline precipitously and he needed, "dependable assurance that the certificate holders will be paid in full by the mortgage company, and that imposes a considerable responsibility on you." Scott's reply speaks volumes about the scope of the challenges faced by his bank. "...I feel the commissioners will hold the directors individually responsible for the payment of all certificate holders, and while that will be hard on the directors, it is a situation beyond our control. I can assure you the certificate holders will be paid in full. Our great concern is to not stir the directors by making any explanation as to why it was necessary to renew the mortgages." He concluded on a more ominous note, saying, "...there may come a time when we will have to end our association. We will speak of that if and when the time comes."

RN suggested that he sell his interest in Western Mortgage & Guaranty Company and resign as president, saying he was "bound to come under criticism." Scott agreed to this and discussion followed as to potential candidates to replace RN, although no decision as to who his replacement was is reported in the *Memoirs*, and it appears as if he may have remained for some time longer in his role as president.

Subsequently, and RN wrote that it might have been as much as a year later, WM&G Co was examined by Mr. Barry, an examiner for the State Insurance Commission. Upon completion of his examination, Barry announced at a board of directors meeting that the firm was seriously undercapitalized. RN didn't specify this in the *Memoirs*, but it is highly probable that the company was failing to meet its required capital standards because its capital base included too many problematic loans, the victim of delinquencies among protected veterans and a declining market for residential housing. It had also written and sold a great quantity of certificates of participation which failed to meet the legal standard then required. As the directors meeting continued, after the departure of the Insurance Commission examiner, RN described extreme unrest among the directors amidst which Henry Scott approached him, informing RN that, "It is now every man for himself. You tell McKee (John McKee a Vice President of Mercantile Bank)." RN also quoted an anonymous speaker at the meeting as saying "It is time for each of us to get our attorneys in to unscramble this mess." Going to the Mercantile Trust Company, RN Advised McKee as directed and McKee called in the trust officer Mr. Sims. After the ensuing discussion, which RN did not record, he wrote that, "That was about the last I saw of Scott, McKee or Sims. they seem to have arrived at an understanding (and the directors too), to by-pass me. I guess they figured my role was to take all the blame."

RN's allusions to the possibility of a bank run, or runs, in California are interesting in light of an absence of any historical reference to such bank panics at the time. Bank runs have existed through the history of the United States, and in many other locations across the globe, notably during severe economic depressions, but the record does not reflect any in California during this post World War I period. RN's recollections, recorded in the *Memoirs*, seem to suggest a high likelihood of occurrence of the phenomenon if mortgages remained un-renewed, but may suggest only that his perception of the widespread nature of problems in residential real estate lending were overstated. Certainly, there existed a real estate housing price decline of significant proportion as we have seen, but it is possible that Mercantile Bank's exposure was not representative of other prominent banks. RN's aggressive, and initially successful, foray into real estate finance had resulted in an elaborate organizational set-up within Mercantile Bank which may not have been mirrored in other lenders. In addition, other major lenders may have confined their own such operations to their state-wide operations and not encouraged the investment by correspondent banks the way Mercantile did. The evidence for his suggestion that the regulators, being aware of widespread problems with residential loans, allowed illegal mortgage renewals to go uncontested or un-prosecuted, is supported only by his statement that he was never personally charged after apparently renewing multiple mortgages held by the firm of which he served as President. Other reasons for his escaping prosecution may well also exist, but remain unknown to us one hundred years on.

Assuming that RN oversaw the renewal or extension of mortgages held by Western Mortgage & Guaranty Co, he, and the officers and directors of his mortgage company, and of the Mercantile Bank, were in violation of state law and subject to the stringent penalties described. This was the case, of course, even if he did so at Henry Scott's direction, and at the encouragement of Fred Lipman his personal friend and Wells Fargo Bank officer. These actions, taken as suggested by RN to "save California's banks," were illegal and he was at risk of going to jail for his actions. In writing about these events in the *Memoirs*, he is silent on the question of who actually directed the renewals, although a plausible construction of his words is that he followed Scott's suggestion in the initial meeting and initiated the action himself. In any event, that seemed to be the view of others within his circle of associates. He described one incident in which he sought to retain the services of his personal attorney, Winfield Dorn, to help him navigate the situation. Dorn's response is interesting, and suggests a common perception of RN's personal guilt in the matter. "Bob, I will represent you if you will make a complete confession." RN's response, suggestive of his characteristic combativeness, hints at the isolation and sense of being set up for a fall he must have felt. "'Win, you have come to a conclusion without knowing what this is all about. I will not require your services,' and that is the last I saw of him."

RN's relationship with Henry Scott during this period is

difficult to understand. Scott was, as we have seen perhaps RN's most important mentor throughout the period of his rapid rise to success. He had provided the platform on which RN assembled the financing mechanism which underpinned his entire business enterprise. He had facilitated RN's entry into the shipbuilding business, when war-related opportunities loomed large in 1916, and RN's aggressiveness, skill, and audacity had launched the enterprise with a Shipping Board contract. A much older man than RN, he had taken the young entrepreneur under his wing, embraced his ambitions, and facilitated his entry into the highest circles of San Francisco's banking and financial community. Now, in the face of unprecedented problems, he seemed to be on the verge of abandoning him. Scott's suggestion that, "...there may come a time when we will have to end our association," certainly speaks to a motive to distance himself from RN amid activities which had the potential to expose himself, his board members, and other associates to prosecution for violating state law.

At this point, both men were hard at work trying to control the actions of the members of the board of directors of WM&G Co. The risk, as they saw it related to the possibility of serious internecine conflict among the members of the board which would erupt should the directors learn the truth of the situation WM&G and Mercantile Bank were in. Both Scott and Burgess wanted, above all, to keep a low profile regarding the mortgage business, and a visible and acrimonious law suit would frustrate that objective.

Shortly thereafter, RN described being summoned to a legal conference wherein the attorneys representing the directors (of WM&G Co) assembled in what must have been an attempt to sort out the positions of their clients. RN was asked to come to the session with counsel, to which he responded, "I will not require an attorney to represent me." RN's account of this meeting is fascinating because it describes a convocation in which various attorneys threatened him, suggesting that he had committed a crime and was therefore subject to potentially serious penalties. He was unimpressed with the preparation of these lawyers for the session, suggesting that they did not appear to have a good grasp of the issues which had resulted in the risks facing their clients. They asked him numerous questions to which he responded that the answers were in the minute books of the corporation. At one point, one of the lawyers asked RN if he realized that he might spend a long time in San Quentin? RN's response reflects his calculation that if he was guilty of anything, he was far from alone in his guilt, "If so, the men who used to play poker at Homestead with me will be my companions. They are also directors in our Mortgage Company and Land Company and bank where we do business."

He was then asked if he would consider going to Mexico for five years, reflecting the suggestion that it might be cheaper for the directors to pay for such a vacation, "while they are settling up the Mortgage Company affairs." The questioner then said, "They *might* pay you $250,000." To RN's response that he wouldn't consider the offer, another offer followed, "They *might* pay you $500,000." RN pushed back at this, writing in the *Memoirs* that he felt there had been no such offer from any of the directors, and he intended to, "stay here where I can keep in touch with developments. There were certain assurances and promises made that I wish to see kept, some prompting may be necessary."

This legal conference was the last one RN attended on the affairs of WM&G Co. At the conclusion of the session, he was asked if he would send the books of the company, along with his letter of resignation, to the firm. Sometime thereafter, RN submitted his resignation as president and director of the company to Henry Scott, ending his association with the mortgage company that he designed, founded, and operated for more than a decade. What began in the excitement of a post-earthquake San Francisco building boom in the fall of 1908, was dying in the aftermath of World War I and the seven-month recession that straddled the November armistice.

When one considers the fact that the events described above all occurred concomitantly with the pressures of RN's shipyard work, the end of the War, the recession and later depression, filling the years of the late teens and early twenties, the pressure under which he must have been working becomes clear. By late 1919 he was broke, reduced to telephoning Anne in Diablo, asking her to drive to Oakland to fetch him at the ferry terminal after discovering that his car had been repossessed a half an hour before he arrived.

Sometime after the last meeting with the lawyers for the WM&G Co directors, he happened to be in the San Francisco and went to the Palace Hotel for dinner. In the lobby he encountered Mr. Barry, from the office of the State Insurance Commissioner, and the two agreed to dine together. Barry commented on the strain under which RN must have been operating during the past few years, and allowed as to how he felt that RN could let up a little. Referencing the State Insurance Commissioner, Barry indicated that, "The Commissioner feels you have done more good than harm, and our course is to require the directors to make good any losses to certificate holders as they develop. There will be no proceedings against you. We would like you to tell us who masterminded the renewing of those mortgages." RN responded that, "there is nothing more that I can tell you than what you found out from the books and the minutes," going on to say parenthetically that "I did not tell him I had been assured the certificate holders would be paid in full." RN reported this exchange as his last with either the State Insurance Commission or any of its representatives.

In the end, RN was not charged with any violation, nor was he sued by any member of the WM&G board of directors. He wrote that numerous rumors swirled about him as a result of these activities for some time, but felt that the absence of charges against him amounted to proof of his innocence of any violation. Once again, his accounts leave more questions than they answer. Did Scott actually direct him to renew or extend the mortgages, and did the two agree that there would be no record of the decision in the minute books, as his writing seems to suggest? How did the two of them square that with the risk he was actually taking? Were the thousands of holders of the certificates of participation all actually paid off and made whole on their investments? Whatever the outcome for the investors, and the other officers and directors of WM&G Co, RN's real estate lending career was over for the time being.

In reading RN's own description of the events in his long life a few salient characteristics reappear time and again and help us to develop an intellectual construction of what kind of man he really was. Certainly, he was ambitious and wanted to rise in the world and make something of himself. He was smart, a quick study, and brash enough to often advance his agenda when others might hesitate. His commitment to hard work as the necessary mechanism to achieve his goals was unwavering, reflective of his Calvinist background. He was also somewhat combative, quick to take offense and to fight back if he felt he had been wronged. Was he arrogant, was hubris at the root of much of what happened to him? Were his world view and his interpersonal relationships such that it was difficult for him to make close friendships outside of his family that were characterized by warmth and affection? These questions are unanswerable from a reading of the *Memoirs*, but his descriptions of countless events and anecdotes leave an impression that he was a difficult man to become close with. His fall from grace was so precipitous, so complete, and so total that one is left wondering if he had any professional friends to fall back on when the bottom fell out of his world. His colleagues in the world of finance were eager to distance themselves from him in the mortgage-renewal crisis as we have seen, and, with one exception, he reports no further relationships with any of them throughout the rest of his life.

Jim Irvine was his friend as well as his business partner. Irvine may have seen reflected in RN many of his own qualities and abilities. RN's descriptions of their times together on his ranch and at Irvine's home in San Francisco hint of something more than a merely professional relationship. Whether shooting rattlesnakes together or discussing Irvine's romantic interests, as we will see in a coming chapter, there appears to have been a real friendship underlying this relationship.

Shortly after the end of the mortgage crisis, RN reported an exchange between John McKee of Mercantile Bank and Irvine. McKee had telephoned Irvine, as a creditor of RN's, seeking his payment of the balance-due of an earlier, larger note RN had signed in the

Bank's favor. McKee suggested to Irvine that, "I thought you might like to take care of a balance of $8,000 Burgess owes us on a $40,000 note before we sue and attach as you are his largest creditor." RN reported that Irvine's response was unequivocal, "No, I will not do that, as I am trying to help Burgess pay all his indebtedness, and I feel if his creditors give him a chance he will be able to pay everyone." Irvine thus stood ready to help RN when others had abandoned him during his most difficult trials.

When RN returned a telephone call from Irvine at his office shortly thereafter, he was surprised and angered to learn that Irvine and their third partner, attorney Guy C. Earl, had put him into involuntary bankruptcy earlier that day. Jim Irvine and Guy Earl were RN's partners in the California Investment Company, the holding company for all of his stock in numerous California corporations, including the R.N. Burgess Company, Western Mortgage & Guaranty Company, the First National Bank of Walnut Creek, the Bank of Concord, the Humboldt National Bank, and the Home Savings Bank of Eureka.

An involuntary bankruptcy is an unusual variant of normal bankruptcy law in which the petition is filed by one or more creditors not by the debtor. It is typically employed as a mechanism for creditors to get access to business debtors who have assets that may be accessed to satisfy claims. RN wrote that Irvine and Earl, feeling it was not equitable for he and his family to be persecuted, had acted with his best interests in mind. Initially angry at his partner's actions, he wrote that on reflection, "...it was the very best thing for me. It gave me a fresh start, though I had to start at the bottom rung of the ladder. I had no car for the next few years, but had a family to support, my wife and four children, no capital-no funds."

RN's bankruptcy occurred under the jurisdiction of the Southern Division of the United States District Court for the Northern District of California. The original file was located in the national archives in Kansas City. These proceedings occupied just over seventeen months of his life commencing with the initial filing on December 10, 1920. They continued with his discharge by Judge

Jeremiah Neterer on April 30, 1921 and the closing of the case and release of the Referee, W. J. Hayes, on May 29, 1922. Interestingly, his mention in the *Memoirs* of Jim Irvine and Guy C. Earl and any role they played in placing him in this status is not confirmed in the actual bankruptcy papers, which contain no mention of either of them.

By the end of 1920, RN was essentially penniless. His assets in the file are listed at $75.00, all in bills, notes, and securities. Not counted were $150.00 worth of household goods and $200 of clothing and other personal property. His liabilities, on the other hand, were considerable and consisted of $129,520 of secured claims, $39,671 of unsecured claims, notes and bills of $5,144, and accommodation papers (i.e., papers signed to accommodate a prospective loan) of $52,000. All this totaled $226,333. In 2018 dollars his assets would have been worth $963 while his liabilities would exceed $2,905,000.

The file also contains information about the required notice to creditors and the newspaper in which such notice was placed. An advisory in the Courier-Journal (then serving Danville and Walnut Creek) is part of the file, as is a form reflecting the specific days on which the notice was to be run: February 4th, 11th, 18th, and 25th of 1921. The notice also scheduled the first meeting of RN's creditors on February 24th, 1921. Such a relatively small newspaper raises the question as to why a larger newspaper was not used and may provide the answer as to why repeated newspaper searches for his bankruptcy records produced nothing. Was the placement of bankruptcy notices a reflection of a desire to keep the proceedings quiet? This is, of course, unknowable, but the file does reveal names of many of RN's business associates as described in the Memoirs and adds numerous names and businesses that were not part of his recollections.

Irvine offered him the management of the Moraga Ranch, but he declined feeling that the best thing for him was to "get entirely new surroundings." RN's work on the Moraga Ranch development with Jim Irvine was extensive, involving initial development work, surveying, subdivision planning, planning and planting the orchards, and managing the leases. It is not clear if he put cash into the development, but he certainly had a good deal of sweat equity in the operation, and ultimately a ten percent position. At some point, he had assigned that ten percent to Irvine, and, after Irvine and Guy Earl put him in bankruptcy he asked Irvine about that portion. Irvine's response was that he did not want the issue brought up during the bankruptcy proceedings, but indicated that, If the operation proves successful someday your account will be credited with your one-tenth less advances and interest. Until then, you will have to trust me." RN wrote that "James was the one man I could and would trust absolutely."

Many years later, in 1947, James Irvine II died, unexpectedly, on his ranch in Idaho, and RN wrote in the Memoirs that Arthur Breed, another ten per cent holder of the Moraga Ranch property, and by that time an old man, invited RN to have lunch with him. He brought up the subject of RN's share and its then current worth, estimated by Breed to be about $350,000, and advised him that he should pursue a claim. RN, indicating he had not one scrap of evidence beyond the oral conversation with Jim Irvine of many years prior, and did not want to make trouble for the Irvine family, said he would not do so.

As noted, bankruptcy proceedings required that RN present in detail a delineation of all of his assets and liabilities, which he did. In the *Memoirs*, he mentioned $55,000 worth of notes due him for loans he had made to friends and family in recent years. His assessment was that they were all worthless and he burned them. He described his final discharge meeting in bankruptcy court as being attended by a large contingent of attorneys, mostly those representing directors in Western Mortgage &Guarantee Co. He does not provide a date of this important session but the federal bankruptcy file places it in April of 1921. An issue that came up was the ownership of the Homestead property, not listed among his assets. When he initially acquired this parcel in 1908, he had carved out 155 acres and gifted it to Anne so as to protect her and his children in the event of just such a catastrophe as had befallen him. Several attorneys for the directors challenged his discharge because of this exemption and the judge asked RN about it. When the judge asked RN for evidence of this exemption, he produced the recorded deed proving the gift and the judge granted the exemption and his discharge from bankruptcy. He recorded this important moment in his life in the *Memoirs* in this way: "When I stepped off the stand all the attorneys came up and shook my hand and wished me well except for one from Brobeck's office, and I felt more cheerful."

RN was now 43 years of age, had completed his bankruptcy proceedings, and was embarking on a new life. His life up to age 38 or 39 had been characterized by a long record of continuous success. He now faced the second part as a bankrupt with all the difficulty and stigma that status conferred. Attitudes toward bankruptcy in the United States would moderate, but not until the growth of the consumer credit boom beginning in the 1950s and 1960s. In RN's time, bankruptcy still carried significant stigma and his attempts to get back on his feet would encounter that problem, a significant issue for RN because it meant that he would be unable to fully participate in the strong economic recovery from the depression following World War I known to historians as "The Roaring Twenties." Times were going to be good again, but not for RN Burgess for many, many years. [1]

When he began all over again, RN had very little of what he had built during the first forty-three years of his life. By 1916, at the apex of his short career to that point, he had accomplished great things in a working life that spanned everything from farm operations and real estate development and sales to and sophisticated financing operations. He lived a life that displayed all the accoutrements of those successes. He had an apartment in the St. Francis Hotel in the City, lived in a beautiful home at the Diablo Country Club, had at his fingertips another fine estate at the Homestead in Walnut Creek, was a member of the finest golf and gentlemen's clubs available in the Bay Area including the Diablo Country Club, the Claremont Country Club, the Athenian-Nile Club in Oakland, and the Bohemian Club in San Francisco. His fall

Theoretical Inquiries in Law. *The Evolution of Bankruptcy Stigma*, Rafael Efrat. Ed: Alon Klement. July 2006.

from grace was total, involving a loss of social position, prestige, and respect. All of those status-conferring memberships were abandoned, and he was alone, in his home with his family. A particularly painful aspect of that fall must have been his abandonment by his former associates, poker partners, and friends from the heady days of his land development activities in Contra Costa County. He had gone from golden boy to goat in a relatively short period of time, and had been stigmatized in the process because of the nature of the problems in his finance company. In a wistful comment from the *Memoirs*, he wrote, "A situation arose in which we, with others, were deeply concerned. It originated more from acts of the California legislature in the distant past than from any acts of ours. There seemed nothing to do about it, but to wait developments. In the end we found we were deeply involved." That involvement was the catalyst that ended the first part of a very productive life and ushered in the second half.

A final question remains in trying to fully understand RN's fall. To what extent did his own unique character contribute to his financial collapse? Were arrogance and hubris inextricably wrapped up in his make-up to the extent that they precluded help when he most needed it? We touched on this question earlier in the context of describing a relationship which seems truly to have been genuine friendship, with Jim Irvine II. But if Jim Irvine was the exception, was it a combative nature, a tendency to take offense quickly, a need to always be the party with the correct answer, the first one, always, with the correct solution, to a problem, that prefigured such a dramatic fall from prosperity to impecuniousness? Was it the case that when RN needed help and guidance, he found that his social capital was evaporated, the victim of a personality which made true relationships difficult to establish and maintain? Like so many questions, these are unanswerable today, but the *Memoirs* contain numerous hints of a complex personality, buried in a man driven by ambition, who found it very difficult to establish the close relationships which might have buffered his decline.

A portrait of Henry Tiffany Scott, RN's mentor, early benefactor, and significant participant in RN's ultimate economic collapse. Courtesy San Francisco Public Library.

*RN with his oldest daughter Frances in about 1917.
Courtesy Burgess Family collection.*

*RN, the builder, with plans, riding boots, and his oldest daughter, 1918.
Courtesy Burgess Family collection.*

RN in 1919, the year prior to his bankruptcy, with his two oldest daughters Frances and Suzanne. Courtesy Burgess Family collection.

RN's five children in April, 1923. Left to right: Suzanne, Robert, Jr., Polly, Frances, and Nancy. Courtesy Burgess Family collection.

CHAPTER 15

Behind the Memoirs

RN's descriptions of the circumstances underlying his personal financial collapse, evaluated in the light of additional research, raise questions about his motivations in writing the *Memoirs*. An argument can be made that his own portrayal of the events he described was an effort at writing an exculpatory document for the benefit of his descendants. The unanswered question of his life is what conduct on his part, what errors, either of omission or of commission, was so egregious that it caused almost all of his professional associates to seek to disassociate themselves from anything to do with him. What did he do, or fail to do, that put so many of his peers and seniors in the banking business at such great risk that they felt his banishment was an appropriate remedy?

In his description of the initial meeting with Henry Scott in which they discussed the difficulties that Mercantile Bank, as well as its associated trust bank and his own Western Mortgage & Guaranty Company, were facing, he described extremely serious penalties attaching to illegal renewal of outstanding mortgages (and linked certificates of participation). He said that for each individual illegal renewal, a fine of $5,000 and five years in jail were prescribed by law. Such serious penalties would have certainly gained the attention of officers and directors in the organizations which would have been affected. He attributed these circumstances to a new state law. "A few years ago we were brought under a state law requiring that we do not renew mortgages on hand and any new loans must be appraised by an appraiser approved by both the banking and insurance commissioners who are appointed to appraise all loans."

He further described the problem, writing in the *Memoirs* that, "The confusion and tangle that involved Western Mortgage & Guaranty Company and its directors and others was due to the California legislature passing a law that was retroactive, bringing such companies under the jurisdiction of the Insurance and Bank Commissioners. Western Mortgage had a considerable amount invested in five-year loans, and (it) sold certificates against these to various banks. Unfortunately, they matured at a time when the banks were suffering from the money stringency following World War I."

To more completely understand the events he described, the "retroactive" rules he referred to, and the draconian penalties to which he and his colleagues were potentially subject, a review of the actual legislation he referenced is helpful. The legislation itself was located in the State Law Library in Sacramento and is entitled The Statutes of California and Amendments to the Codes; Passed at the Forty-First Session of the Legislature, 1915. The description of the new law describes it as "An act to revise and amend chapter VIII of title II of part IV of division first of the Civil Code, relative to mortgage insurance." The original legislation amended by this 1915 act was a 1913 statute creating the original chapter VIII, of title II, of part IV of the Civil code. In other words, the legislation to which RN referred was not retroactive, but had been the law of the land since August 10, 1913. Assuming his meeting with Scott on this topic occurred in late 1918 as we have suggested, when RN first brought the matter to Scott's attention, they were discussing laws that had been on the books for five years.

In California, legislation against abusive real estate lending and appraisal practices has a rich history. Unfortunately, less than ethical mortgage lenders and brokers have long preyed upon ordinary citizens who are not familiar with the technical aspects of real estate lending. Consumer complaints about practices involving fraudulent appraisals and predatory lending have periodically resulted in legislation designed to curb such activities. The legislation that RN mentioned in the *Memoirs* was an early example of what has become increasingly common as the state's population has grown and land development has expanded accordingly.

The initial 1913 legislation did, as RN suggested, bring the laws governing mortgage insurance under the joint jurisdiction of the state banking and insurance commissioners. It did much more than that, however. Among other things, it defined mortgage participation certificates, the instruments RN had been using to finance his building activities since 1908. It specified that any certificate that "purports to guarantee the payment of principle, interest or other sums agreed to be paid under the terms of any such note or bond secured by mortgage or trust deed...shall be deemed a policy of mortgage insurance."

The law further specified that "No mortgage insurance company shall guarantee under any mortgage or trust deed a principal amount exceeding sixty per centum of the market value of the real estate taken as security therefor." This limitation is interesting in view of RN's practice, beginning on 1908, of having the trust bank certify that the certificates were issued in amounts no more than 90% of the face value of the underlying mortgages. The new legislation, at sixty per cent of the value of the property, was specifying a substantially more conservative level of coverage than what Western Mortgage & Guaranty had been selling for then five years in 1913.

The legislation required that any firm engaging in the sale of certificates of participation needed a minimum of $250,000 of paid-in capital in its treasury. It specified the kinds of institutions for which such certificates were permitted investments and required a certificate of compliance from the state insurance commissioner prior to engaging in the business.

In a response to what were abuses in practice at the time, the law further required the submission of a quarterly report to the insurance commissioner, verified by the president or vice-president and secretary/treasurer, or any two principle officers of the company so engaged. The contents of the required report were to include a description of the underlying property securing the obligation, the fair market value of the land and improvements securing the loan as demonstrated by appraisal, and the amount of any certificate of participation issued against the mortgage or trust deed. An appraisal was required for each and every parcel of property taken as security. Such appraisal had to be made by an appraiser approved by the insurance commissioner and signed and verified by the appraiser or an officer of the appraising corporation; it had to be accompanied by a certificate, signed and verified by at least three directors of the issuing mortgage insurance company, attesting that the appraisal was correct, did not exceed the market value of the property, and that the principal loaned did not exceed 60 per cent of the fair market value of the property. Finally, and most significantly for RN's version of events, the law specified the penalties associated with violation. Violation was a *misdemeanor* and carried a penalty of $10 per day for each day that failure to comply continued.

The legislation, as amended in 1915, essentially kept the same provisions as the earlier version except it tightened them, increasing the regulatory burden imposed. The earlier requirement of a sixty per cent ratio of certificate to property value was reduced to fifty percent. A new provision required that any company engaging in mortgage guarantees create an annual fund or "surplus" by setting aside ten per cent of net earnings until an amount equal to twenty-five per cent of its paid-in capital had been accrued. Also, the law prohibited paying any dividends that had the effect of reducing either paid-in capital, the newly required surplus fund, or whatever funds were necessary to pay all liabilities for operating expenses, taxes, or losses.

For each property securing a mortgage and accompanying certificate of participation, an appraisal was required every two years with such appraisal certified by a trust bank. It required a statement of the amount of any unpaid principal and a filing with the state superintendent of banking. The original requirement that each appraisal needed to be signed and verified by at least three directors of the mortgage company, stipulating that the appraisal was correct, that the appraised value did not exceed fair market value, that the loan amount was less than fifty per cent of fair market value, and a requirement for demonstrating evidence of clear title or title insurance, did not change in the new law. Nor did the penalties under the amended law. Violations remained a misdemeanor with the same penalties.

The modified 1915 law thus further restricted the operation of mortgage companies engaged in the business of selling certificates of participation, both by tightening the capital requirements under which they were required to operate and by insuring a further margin of protection for investors against declining real estate values. It also left intact the rather modest penalties associated with violation which were obviously a far cry from the severe penalties described by RN in his meeting with Henry Scott, and would scarcely seem to be such that exposure to them would have so angered colleagues and associates that they would have permanently disassociated themselves from RN.

The events described in this and in the preceding chapter happened a century ago and raise many more questions than can be answered with the information contained in the *Memoirs* and in other sources. In trying to understand what actually happened, and what produced the collapse of RN's financial life we must ask what we can know with some certainty, what we can infer or make educated guesses about, and what is unknowable. From RN's words in his *Memoirs*, we know that he was ostracized, rejected, banished, and locked out from his former financial peer group, essentially for life. Recall the meeting at which attorneys for the directors of Western Mortgage & Guarantee had offered him large sums of money if he would go to Mexico for five years, an offer which he disbelieved and rejected. Such sanctions would not have been the result of exposing his colleagues to minor, misdemeanor penalties. Something else was at work, something a good deal more serious.

The millions of dollars of certificates of participation that Mercantile Bank had syndicated to its correspondent banks throughout the country were worthless if the underlying mortgages, upon which the certificates were based, had expired. The correspondent banks were understandably worried about this growing exposure to a weakening housing market and a growing file of expired mortgages. Scott realized that he had to find a way to renew the loans so as to render the certificates operable. RN implied in the *Memoirs* that the mortgages were in fact renewed. He was silent on who actually took the steps to effect such action, but the reader is left with the strong impression that it was done, by some person or persons, pursuant to Scott's direction.

RN shared with Scott that the penalties for each illegal renewal were $5,000 in fines and a five-year jail term. Scott directed RN to develop a plan to renew the mortgages and to advise him what he needed for his own "protection." RN's response was the four conditions listed in Chapter 14, and, interestingly, two of them look as if they might have been verbatim quotes from the actual legislation. From this distance, it looks as if RN was insisting on conditions which had been in the law for five years at that point in a belated effort to get into compliance.

At this point, a biographer is well into the area of educated guesses and inference from what facts he has. A review of the actual legislation has shown that the penalties for violation of the 1913 law, as amended in 1915, were misdemeanor penalties; a nominal fine for each day an offender was not in compliance. The penalties RN shared with Scott were a far cry from these. If the penalties he described were not for a violation of these laws, what laws might they have been the penalty for?

It is this question that suggests a path to understanding what actually happened to RN's reputation and finance career. Two explanations, not mutually exclusive, seem at least plausible.

The first relates to the question of what action was actually taken to renew the mortgages and of how confidential that action was. A literal interpretation of RN's words would suggest a simple extension of the existing maturity date on each expired mortgage. Such action, done unilaterally, without the knowledge and consent of the borrower in each case, would have been fraud (probably under the provisions of the 1909 Bank Act which regulated savings banks, commercial banks, and trust companies) and the penalties would have been for the commission of *felonies*, not *misdemeanors*. Banker Lipman's counsel to RN to keep his knowledge under his hat was doubtless shared by Henry Scott, but in an organization as large as Mercantile, actually getting the needed work done would have contained a very real risk of leakage. When the rumor mill began to be filled with stories of possible jail sentences and fines for officers and directors, a very unpleasant focus would have been placed on RN. Under such a construction, RN's stated penalties of $5,000 in fines and five years in jail for each offense makes sense. If the action taken by Scott and RN exposed the officers and directors of Mercantile Bank, Western Mortgage & Guaranty Company, and the trust bank to such penalties, their desire to distance themselves from RN becomes very understandable.

A second explanation for the heavy penalty to which he was exposed by his peers lies in the possibility that Western had been operating in violation of the very strict and precise Civil Code section regulating mortgage companies and their issuance of certificates of participation for an extended period of time. Ample evidence in the Memoirs suggests that attention to administrative detail was not RN's strongpoint. His comment that the law was "retroactive" suggests a level of ignorance as to its particulars which might have been acceptable as long as economic conditions were robust, but had become increasingly risky within the context of a housing collapse as occurred in 1916-19. Had Western been in violation of these regulations for years, perhaps for the entirety of its existence? Why did he wait until conditions were as bad as they had become before notifying Scott of the regulatory situation? Did his silence on the matter imply ignorance? The answers to these and other questions lie at the core of the rationale for the sanctions imposed on him.

As the man responsible for real estate lending and finance, so long a profitable branch of Mercantile Bank's business, RN was squarely in the bubble when things began to turn down. It is not hard to imagine the bank's directors asking how it was they came to be involved in the mess they found themselves in. On whose watch did all these unacceptable things, things with possible draconian legal penalties, occur? They occurred on Burgess' watch. He brought the business to the bank in the heady days following the earthquake and fire and he grew it dramatically in the intervening years. In the minds of his officer and director colleagues, it was his area of responsibility and expertise, and, by 1918, it was beginning to look as if the difficulties would, appropriately, be laid at his doorstep.

The failure of RN's *Memoirs* to mention the details discussed above suggests, as mentioned, a desire on his part to put the best face possible on a set of circumstances which engulfed him and his colleagues, probably in no small part because of actions for which he was responsible. As the man in charge of real estate lending and of the sale to investors of certificates of participation, he was in a position in which he should have known the consequences on Mercantile Bank's loan book of rapidly declining real estate values and increasing mortgage delinquencies. If these things were not his responsibility, whose were they? In the end, his failure to be on top of changing laws, of changing market values, and of the consequences of these changes, were what ended his first career. He would need to start over, and he did.

CHAPTER 16

Partial Recovery

The second half of RN's life was a pale imitation of his first forty-one years. His bankruptcy in late 1920, coupled with the complete loss of most if not all of his earlier business relationships, left him on the outside looking in at a local commercial world in which it was impossible for him to participate. In the twenty-five years between 1920 and 1945, he was beset by conditions over which, in his younger days, he might have exercised some measure of control and dominance. As a bankrupt, tainted by his role in the mortgage crisis and his associations and responsibilities within Mercantile Bank, he was forced to look elsewhere for opportunities. Throughout the 1920s, he ventured far afield from his prior experiences, engaging in an array of opportunities none of which brought the satisfaction and financial results he hoped for. His credit was bad and, as credit was the life-blood of his field, he was stymied. Toward the end of that decade, he was taking temporary assignments in the east in the banking industry, drawing upon his financial experience and business acumen. His writing in the *Memoirs* suggests that he was away from home at least as much as he was in California. After the market crash in October of 1929, he went home to Walnut Creek, turning his attention to the development of his and Anne's property at the Homestead. When World War II restrictions on building materials crimped his building activity, he built government housing in Alameda and Contra Costa Counties for the duration. At war's end in 1945, at age sixty-seven, he was finally able to resume his chosen field, the financing and building of real estate developments. A notable aspect of his new life after 1920 was that he never lost his lifelong commitment to hard work. His descriptions of the work he did on the Lakewood project during the Depression of the 1930s, as a much older man, echo the hard work he performed as a child on the farm in Danville.

During the most difficult period of RN's business career, at the height of the shipbuilding and real estate finance crises, his domestic life was dominated by the circumstances of a growing family in Diablo. Thanks to his foresight in 1909 when, after the acquisition of the Rice property, he had gifted the Homestead and surrounding acreage to Anne at the time of their marriage, he spared his spouse the worry and anxiety which might have attended his financial misfortunes. The Homestead property was in her name and on it she grew and sold crops from the surrounding land. She thus had some money of her own prior to the death of her mother, Frances Webster Fish, in August of 1923. Anne was her mother's sole heir. Her brother, Irving Fish, had died in an automobile accident the prior summer leaving no heirs. Anne thus inherited a substantial amount leaving the family a level of comfort which would have been impossible had RN been the only provider. As RN described her wealth, much of it was in land in the Central Valley of California, as well as in a portfolio of stocks and bonds. In the late 19th century, her father, Lafayette Fish, had amassed considerable acreage in the Central Valley in connection with his wheat growing and grain exporting business, and Anne inherited much of this acreage. She was thus financially well able to navigate the turbulent period of RN's financial weakness.

The quality of RN's writing in the *Memoirs* reflect the momentous changes that occurred in his life at this time. The chapters covering his first four decades are recorded in a much more organized, systematic, and chronological fashion. Perhaps reflecting his fall from financial security, the later chapters, covering the second half of his life, are much more difficult to follow. Events are often recorded in far reaching parts of the country with very little identification of time or contextual circumstance.

These were not good times professionally for RN and his writing reflects the strain under which he must have been living during that period. The stigma associated with bankruptcy has long been recognized, both in the history of this country as well as in Western Europe. During colonial times in America, bankrupts were perceived as little better than criminals and thieves. The work previously cited by Rafael Efrat describes harsh penalties for bankrupts including imprisonment, flogging, and public shaming. During most of the 19th century bankruptcy stigmas remained, and "much of the Victorian era culture revolved around the humiliation associated with debtor's default." Attitudes began to shift slowly during the 1920s as debtor's prisons were essentially extinct and as bankruptcies began to rise during that decade. RN would not have escaped this social opprobrium in the aftermath of his filing in late 1920, and he was destined to spend almost twenty-five years trying to reassemble his professional life, working against all odds in circumstances unfavorable to his success. [1]

He entered the 1920s with this burden and thus missed out on the economic expansion of the period. The 1930s brought the Great Depression of August 1929 to March of 1933, a forty-two month long economic collapse resulting in 25% unemployment and a 27% decline in GDP. This was followed at decade's end by one of the most severe recessions of the 20th century, between May 1937 and June 1938, during which unemployment climbed back up to 18% and GDP fell by a similar amount. These events made a return to RN's former level of accomplishment impossible and were then followed by World War II which brought severe restrictions on the availability of building materials, confining his activities to the construction of government housing, primarily in Alameda County.

RN and Anne's children all came of age during these difficult years. Their oldest, Robert Noble Burgess, II was born on May 13, 1910. Robin, as he was known, was followed by Frances Webster Burgess on June 21, 1914, by Suzanne Fish Burgess on May 11, 1917, by Nancy Ann Fish Burgess on February 19, 1919, and finally by Polly Holcomb Burgess on July 21, 1921. The family home also changed midway through the 1920s when the Diablo home was sold and the Homestead in Walnut Creek, available after John Scott's vacancy of the property following the conclusion of his

---

[1] Rafael Efrat, Bankruptcy Stigma.

shipbuilding activities in 1922, became their primary residence. Anne's financial capacity was what kept the family afloat, providing private school educations for the children and travel for each upon their graduation from High School including grand European tours for a couple of them, much as she had taken with her own mother in 1905.

During these decades RN was frequently away from home as his activities in pursuit of some business opportunity that he might pursue to financial success took him throughout the United States. His recollections in the *Memoirs* reflect this frustrating period. In the early post-bankruptcy years, the early 1920s, he characterized his frenetic activity as switching from one thing to another, "trying to make a few bucks to keep self and family going." Writing in the late 1920's, just prior to returning from another unsuccessful trip to New York, he said, "My ventures to make worthwhile money had all pooped out. The times were just wrong it seemed to me, but it was probably me too (*sic*)."

Reading about these years in the *Memoirs* produces the sense of a man in his early forties trying desperately to regain what he had lost and leaving no stone unturned in the effort. His engagements were diverse, including financing movies in Los Angeles for Samuel Goldwyn, evaluating an oil drilling opportunity in Texas, consulting on the Palos Verdes subdivision development in Los Angeles, and buying and operating a 100,000-acre sheep ranch near Albuquerque, New Mexico. The details of some of these adventures reflect aspects of RN's character as well as the reality that times had changed for him. His earlier successes were not going to be repeated in a new era where, as a bankrupt in the 1920s he was forced to miss much of the action and as a builder in the 1930s he could never obtain the financing help from large banks that he needed to replicate his past achievements.

One of RN's initial projects after bankruptcy involved being called upon by Edward Gardner Lewis to evaluate a financing project Lewis contemplated in the Southern California community of Palos Verdes. E.G. Lewis was a magazine publisher, a land promoter, and political visionary active in early 1900s. In about 1922, he acquired an option to purchase 16,000 acres of land on the Palos Verdes peninsula then owned by Frank A. Vanderlip, Sr., the president of the National City Bank of New York. Vanderlip had acquired the Palos Verdes property from Jotham Bixby in 1913 and was holding it for resale. Lewis purchased the option with the intent of developing it into an exclusive subdivision. He designed an elaborate financing plan and asked RN to come to Southern California and evaluate it. How RN knew Lewis is not spelled out in the *Memoirs*, but it is probable that the introduction was through Harry Thomas Cory, an engineer of some repute in the development of the Imperial Valley and an associate of faculty members at the University of California. In RN's telling and in some of the literature about him, Lewis was an accomplished and bold promoter and an aggressive fund raiser. RN and Anne went south to meet with him and explore the opportunity.

RN demurred when Lewis tried to convince him to take compensation in the shares of his promoting company, insisting on cash instead. This was arranged and RN agreed to hourly compensation. Anne and RN planned to rent a home in Los Angeles feeling that a change of scenery might do them both good, but her mother's health condition deteriorated and she was forced to return to Northern California to help, leaving RN alone in the southland. [2]

---

[2] RN's role with Lewis' Palos Verdes project was not major and involved reviewing the financing plans which envisioned raising $15,000,000 through the sale of trust indenture notes to investors. RN encouraged Lewis to include the local real estate brokerage community with commissions of 5% on each note sold because each note was the equivalent of one lot in the new development. Lewis succeeded in raising the $15,000,000 over the course of a year, fully subscribing all lots. In RN's reporting, Lewis had abandoned the practice of commissioning the brokerage community, in the process earning himself their enmity. Shortly after full subscription, members of the local banking and real estate communities banded together against him and were able to get all subscriptions rescinded with all funds returned to investors. Lewis brought suit against the group, but to no avail. He lost the project, declared bankruptcy in 1924, and later served time in jail for mail fraud.

While in Los Angeles in 1921 RN also became involved, briefly, in an attempt at financing lower-budget movies known as shorts. He recounted working with Benjamin B. Hampton, an actor and producer of movies in Hollywood during the years between 1900 and 1930, to finance movies for Samuel Goldwyn. Hampton had secured a contract to produce six shorts, to be featured along with major production films. He had the agreement to produce these six at $600,000 each, but needed financing for his project and so hired RN to secure it at a salary of $600 per week.

RN's marketing skills are on stage in this environment as he described his plans for securing the financing. He planned a sales center in the Alexander Hotel in which he planned to present the film offerings. The hotel room was decorated like a stock brokerage office except that in place of a quote board he would have a display of each movie. The display would include its performers and their box office records, and the likely box-office receipts of the film. Since Samuel Goldwyn had agreed to return all principal invested at the end of a five-year term, the investor risk was only on how much each picture might earn. As RN described it, "The fans would be influenced by their favorite stars, the return of their principle (sic) was guaranteed by Mr. Goldman." The Southwest Trust Company was engaged as Trustee, blessing the plan and agreeing to underwrite all six pictures.

RN went home to northern California to resume family life and, as he put it, "to brag a bit." Later that summer of 1921, the silent screen actor Fatty Arbuckle caused the death of a young actress in the St. Francis Hotel in San Francisco at a Labor Day weekend party he hosted. The circumstances of this tragedy and the publicity surrounding it caused a short-term fall-off in demand for Hollywood products and RN's financing plan fell through, with Samuel Goldwyn ultimately providing the financing from his New York offices. RN's movie-financing days were at an end and he turned elsewhere to find money-making opportunities.

For a short time, he entertained the possibility of going to Texas in search of oil-producing properties which might be consolidated into large producing fields. The man offering this opportunity was a local attorney whom RN had known some time earlier who later prospered in the activity. However, RN said he turned it down because he knew trying to commute between Texas and California would ultimately ruin his family life.

***

RN's difficulty in getting traction on almost anything he tried at this stage in his life may have gotten him into situations the nature of which would preclude their inclusion in his autobiography. A search of the Westlaw data base produced two legal cases, in which "RN Burgess" was involved indirectly. These cases, initially tried in 1925, came to the Los Angeles Superior Court on appeal and were decided in 1933. RN Burgess is in quotation marks because definitive proof that the individual is the same as the subject of this book is lacking. Circumstantial evidence, however, points strongly to the likelihood that it is one and the same person. It is known that RN was in Los Angeles at the time of the lower court cases, both in 1925. It is known that real estate finance was his area of special competence. It is known that RN had a propensity to form new corporate entities almost without restraint, and it is known that RN was at a low point in his life during this period. These circumstances suggest a high probability that the subject of this book was the same RN Burgess. There is no evidence in either of the cases that he was ever charged or convicted of any crime; his role in both was ancillary to the activities of both plaintiff and defendant. But his actions as described in the two judgments certainly were such as to raise questions about the propriety of his conduct.

The first case, Holcomb vs. Long Beach Investment Company, involved an exchange of two commercial properties in Southern California. The plaintiffs in the case, the Holcomb sisters, owned a 100-acre property in San Bernardino County known as the Chino Ranch. The market value of the property was $65,000 and it was owned subject to a $25,000 first mortgage. The defendant, Long Beach Investment Company and its President and shareholder,

H. O. Henderson, as well as another shareholder, C.J. Jasper of Oakland, owned the Alta Vista Court apartments in Long Beach. The apartment house had been recently acquired by the defendants for $30,000 and was held subject to a $23,000 first mortgage and a $10,000 second deed of trust. The plaintiffs were elderly ladies, with no knowledge of Long Beach real estate values, who had been friends and members of the same fraternal lodge as the defendant Henderson for many years. Henderson proposed an exchange of the properties to the plaintiffs in early 1925, suggesting that the fair market value of the apartment house was $78,000, notwithstanding his recent purchase of it for $30,000, and that the attendant income was $500 per month. The Holcomb sisters agreed to the transaction.

Henderson's associate, Jasper, then negotiated an exchange agreement with the sisters which was signed by both parties on February 27, 1925, and the sisters took possession of the apartment house in April of that year. When they acquired the apartment house they took it subject to the $23,000 first mortgage and the $10,000 second. The Holcomb sisters thus were persuaded to trade their ranch property, with a value of $65,000, for a $30,000 apartment house, which they had been told was worth $78,000. Their expected equity after the trade would have been that value, less their debt, or $45,000.

Sometime after the closing Henderson began pressing the sisters to repay the $10,000 second mortgage, suggesting that they refinance the existing indebtedness. It was while researching this prospective new financing that the sisters discovered the fraud perpetrated in the exchange. An appraiser from the State Building and Loan Association appraised the Alta Vista Apartments and informed them that it was substantially overvalued and that Henderson's Long Beach Investment Company had recently purchased it for only $30,000 and that the income was between $300 and $400 per month. When they learned this, the sisters were in the process of trying to obtain a loan from the Farm & Home Loan Association. RN Burgess was the President of this firm.

Upon learning of the fraud to which they had been exposed,

the sisters brought suit for damages against Long Beach Investment, Henderson, and Jasper. A jury awarded the plaintiffs $45,000
for each of the two defendants, a $90,000 award. It was from this
judgement that Defendant Henderson and Jasper appealed. The
Appeals Court judgement came down in January of 1933 sustain-
ing the trial court's findings. It was in the appeals court judgement
that the conduct of RN Burgess was described and condemned.

Henderson and Jasper claimed in their appeal that the Holcomb
sisters had waived any claim for damages for fraud and also rati-
fied the exchange agreement because they had signed a written
agreement after they knew of the fraud and were fully informed
concerning the entire transaction.

The sisters had gone to the Farm & Home Loan Association
(Burgess) seeking a refinancing in the fall of 1925. Their loan application reflected a total of $41,000, $23,000 to cover the first mortgage, $10,000 for the second, $5,200 to cover a new third note and
deed of trust, a $1,600 commission to RN Burgess, and $1,200 in
accrued interest. As these negotiations were underway, Burgess
offered to purchase the Alta Vista Apartments himself for $56,000.
Unknown to the sisters, Burgess was acting in consultation with
Henderson and was privy to all the details of the fraudulent exchange. RN's plan was to fund his purchase of the apartment
house by assuming the sisters' $41,000 debt and by issuing $15,000
of "gold bonds." He represented that the bonds were worth their
face value and were secured by property worth three times that
value.

The sisters relied upon these representations and sold to
Burgess accordingly. A condition to the prospective sale was that
they would sign a complete release of all claims and damages
against Henderson and Jasper for fraud in procuring the original
exchange of properties. The release, dated April, 1926, is total and
complete. The sisters acknowledged "the entire transaction on exchange and sale to be satisfactory in every detail… and agree to release and do hereby release H.O. Henderson and the Long Beach
Investment Co. and the Farm & Home Loan Association…from all
claim whatever… in connection with the exchange of said ranch

property for the Alta Vista Court at Long Beach, and hereby state our satisfaction in the above transaction."

The appeals court judge wrote that, "The chief consideration for the execution of this release was the $15,000 in gold bonds. This consideration failed. Burgess never did deliver bonds of the face value of more than $7,000. In lieu of the remaining bonds he delivered four several promissory notes signed by him of the aggregate value of $6,950. Nothing further was ever received on the purchase price of the property. Both the notes and the bonds were worthless. Henderson testified that the bonds were worthless. The Farm & Home Loan was soon thereafter declared to be a bankrupt corporation. The respondents (i.e., the original plaintiffs) were unable to collect any sum whatever from the notes or bonds. There was therefore a total failure of consideration for the execution of the release. It became nudum pactum (i.e., not a legal contract) and void for want of consideration."

The court went on to say that Burgess and Henderson conspired to procure the release of liability fraudulently. They coordinated on the terms of the purchase of the apartment house, and Burgess, as president, knew that his "gold bonds" were without value. In the court's words, "…the respondents (original plaintiffs) were the victim of a double fraud. The very language of the release indicates the conspiracy of Burgess and Henderson to procure the document." Absent this conspiracy, Burgess would have had no motive to insist on the release as consideration for his purchase of the apartment house.

So, in lay terms, Burgess conspired with Henderson in April of 1925 to extract a release from the Holcomb sisters whom Henderson had defrauded in an exchange done in February of the same year. The release was supposed to be a condition for his agreement to purchase the apartment house from the sisters by assuming the $41,000 debt they owed on it and adding $15,000 in worthless "gold bonds."

The second case in which RN appears, again not as a principle, but as a participant in events, is Vaughn et. al. vs. Peoples Mortgage Co. et. al., and the events in the case occurred in April 1925 in Los Angeles County. In this case, RN was a Vice President of Protective Building & Loan Association and agreed to make a loan to Arthur Vaughn, his wife Libby Vaughn, and his sister Jessie. At the trial court, the plaintiff argued, among other claims, that the loan in question was usurious because the fees and other costs exceeded the 12% legal limit. Vaughn intended to use the funds to purchase a vacant lot, and then relocate a 19-room apartment house onto the site. Burgess agreed to loan him $25,000 for six months at 8%, a bonus of 10% to Burgess (to be partially paid via the purchase of stock in one of RN Burgess's companies), and a commission to two loan brokers, Neville and Belcher. The interest was to be paid in advance and, along with the commission, was to be added to the face amount of the loan. As a result of this agreement on terms, Burgess issued a written order to Protective Building & Loan to issue a check to Vaughn in the amount of $4,841.20 which was written as directed and signed by two officers of Protective. Vaughn in turn endorsed the check over to RN Burgess, Trustee, who had an escrow prepared reflecting interest of $1,201.20, a bonus to Burgess of $2,600, commissions to Neville and Belcher of $520 each, $15,000 for the purchase of the lot, and $9,960 payable when the apartment house had been relocated to the lot and was ready for occupancy. A promissory note in the sum of $28,801.20, a deed of trust securing payment thereof, and an application for the purchase of stock by Jessie Vaughn was delivered to Vaughn and signed by her.

Burgess then drew up an agreement stipulating that, as partial consideration for his agreeing to make the loan, the Vaughn's would purchase 26 shares of capital stock, at $200 per share, in one of several companies identified in the contract. These included The Agricultural Credit Corporation, the Protective Building and Loan Association, and the Home Foundation Company (which name was later changed to the Farm Home and Loan Company, Burgess' firm in the previous case). The trial court ruled against the Plaintiff, Vaughn, arguing that the usury claim could not be upheld because RN had acted outside the scope of his agency in making a side deal selling the stock as an additional bonus for himself, unbeknownst to his principal, Protective Building & Loan. The Appeals Court agreed, writing that RN's associates at Protective testified that they, "...did not know Burgess was receiving any of the proceeds of this check, nor that he was purporting to sell any stock..." Further, "the application for the purchase of stock was a mere subterfuge adopted by Burgess to exact a personal bonus for the loan to Jessie Vaughn." In the Appeals Court judgement, "a loan is not rendered usurious by the lender's agent charging the borrower, for his own benefit, a commission or bonus for procuring the loan, in excess of the maximum legal rate of interest, where such charge is made without the lender's knowledge or consent, either express or implied, and is not ratified or shared in by him."

All the companies named in the suit were operated by RN Burgess and were located in the same suite of offices with Protective Building & Loan. The court wrote that, "Although Burgess was only vice president of (Protective), he was apparently the dominating influence therein."

Burgess was not a party in either of these cases and was not called as a witness, but was clearly involved in conduct in both which seems well beyond the margin of propriety. In the Holcomb case, in full awareness of a fraud perpetrated upon the two elderly and naive sisters, he conspired with the defrauding party to extract a full release from the fraud as a condition to his purchase of the property in question. In the second instance, he exceeded the scope of his agency with his principal Protective, by making a side deal for extra compensation without its knowledge.

RN's business was real estate finance, a narrow segment of real estate law that was lightly regulated during the years during which he practiced. This level of state oversight has been substantially increased in the decades following his experience in Los Angeles, and the outcomes of his conduct for him personally would be much more rigorous if the events described took place today. The conduct described suggests a man operating on the legal and ethical edge, cutting corners, taking advantage of naive persons inexperienced in real estate matters or in the financing thereof. It seems likely that in the aftermath of personal financial devastation, RN went into a new area and, being unknown, felt he might cut some corners in his search for success.

In thinking about these cases, one is tempted to judge behavior by contemporary standards. By such standards, RN definitely crossed a line, ethically and legally, with his conduct in 1925 in Los Angeles. But today's standards are not the standards within which RN's business career began. As mentioned earlier, a conflation of the ideas of Charles Darwin and those of Herbert Spencer in the second half of the 19th century resulted in the concept of Social Darwinism and an attempt to apply the Darwinian evolutionary concept of natural selection to human society. Spencer's term "survival of the fittest" seemed an apt description of business practices in this transformation of Darwin's ideas from non-human species to society. Business customs and conventions which would seem sharp and cutthroat by today's standards became the norm.

RN was not immune to these undercurrents within social thought. Numerous quotations from the *Memoirs*, used in these pages to describe his conduct in his business dealings speak to the fact of his pride in outwitting his adversary, often employing what we might characterize today as subterfuge and less than full disclosure. When viewed in the context of an environment in which such behavior was seen as perfectly normal, indeed exemplary and shrewd, his pride in his own actions is understandable. A modern reader cringes at his description of some of the tactics he employed, but in his mind, they were not only justified, but were considered "smart."

***

For some time prior to these legal involvements, RN had begun to explore what would become the grandest of his post-bankruptcy undertakings, sheep ranching. Before he began this totally new business, however, he happened upon a windfall of sorts. Calling on a former lender, the Canadian Bank of Commerce in San Francisco (CBC), on one of his trips home from Los Angeles, he was advised by the Manager of the San Francisco branch that, on the occurrence of his bankruptcy and of his bankruptcy trustee failing to assume his CBC loan and take possession of the collateral, the collateral had been sold out by the bank. The manager agreed to restore his collateral to the level it had been at the earlier date and to make the $5,000 loan, giving RN some seed capital to begin his new venture.

This event stimulated a search of several of his former banking relationships to see if similar outcomes had occurred. His equity interest in multiple California banks, in the form of stock, was held in his California Investment Company. As mentioned, he had interests in WG&M Co, 1st National Bank of Walnut Creek, the Bank of Concord, the Humboldt National Bank, and the Home Savings Bank of Eureka. Various loans to him had been secured by shares of stock in these institutions and he found that, similar to the Canadian Bank in San Francisco, they had sold out his collateral on the occasion of his trustee not assuming the obligations. This meant that these banks, if they were willing, might either exchange the shares of his stock that they held for his payoff of their loan, or, restore his former account to an active basis. Enough of his former lenders did this so that he was able to sell his bank stock, use the proceeds to pay off $100,000 of former loans, and get $20,000 back for his own use.

The capital thus provided enabled RN to contribute to household expenses at home, and to plan and provision an extended driving trip throughout the Southwest. Having determined that sheep-ranching offered the promise of a good return, he planned a trip to search for suitable ranch operations in which to invest. To facilitate this travel, he bought a used Buick automobile in Los Angeles and had it fitted out for camping, attaching a large wooden trunk with drop-down table and legs to the rear end, and purchasing a supply of camping gear in anticipation of many nights on the ground. He also hired a guide, Charles Spencer, who was described by RN as an experienced camper with good knowledge of the country and of potential ranch properties, and who was also an excellent cook. The plan was to take an extended trip, looking at potential investments throughout Arizona and New Mexico, and the provisions they acquired reflected it. They had a large canvas tent which could be attached to the car during camping periods in inclement weather. Each man had an 8x12 foot ground tarp replete with horsehair ropes to encircle it to fend off poisonous snakes and a sleeping bag and air mattress. A large stock of canned goods was packed in the wooden trunk to supplement whatever food they might be able to cadge from local farmers along the way. RN described Spencer's abilities as camp cook in glowing terms, depicting in detail how he could cook delicious biscuits in his Dutch oven and roll up a whole turkey in a ball of clay, let it cook overnight, and serve it at breakfast.

Well provisioned for an extended trip, the two left Los Angeles in late August of 1921 heading to Flagstaff, Arizona. Spencer directed RN to a property he had in mind in the area, but, feeling it was inappropriate for his needs, RN turned it down. They continued on to Gallup, New Mexico, turning north at Shiprock on the way to Durango, Colorado. Finding nothing of interest, they turned south back into New Mexico and then east to Albuquerque where they found the property that would put RN in the sheep-ranching business.

It was an extensive parcel. About 70 miles east of Albuquerque, it comprised some 100,000 acres of land, 33,000 head of sheep, and lease rights to an additional 100 square miles of government-owned desert range for additional grazing land. The range of acreage these sheep covered was immense, including the leased desert range and the highlands near Grants New Mexico for summer pasturage and lambing. On the leased range water was scarce so catchment basins were built to preserve rainfall runoff. Evaporation was a problem, however, so the basins were covered with a half inch of oil to protect the water. RN said that it was common to see both sheep and cattle in the area with black rings around their noses from dipping into these reservoirs.

This was an operating ranch and had all the improvements necessary to conduct the business. As RN described it, "It is some job to sheer 33,000 sheep and get the wool to market as well as to take care of from ten to fifteen thousand lambs too." Whatever complexities he foresaw in operating this ranch, he must have assumed they were manageable because he bought it. The *Memoirs* do not record what he paid for the property, nor how he paid for it. We have seen that he had some capital at this time, 1921, but enough for a down payment on a ranch of this size seems a stretch. And who was going to loan him the difference? RN was clearly a good salesman, and he was well outside of the geographic area that was the site of his undoing, but how he was able to complete such a purchase remains a mystery. The most likely explanation is that he bought it from the seller on a land contract, signing up for a series of payments over a period of time. He was about to learn that financing the purchase was the easiest part of the whole program.

It was never RN's intention to remain in New Mexico nor to relocate his family from California (one could scarcely imagine Anne approving such a relocation), so he needed a local operator. To this end he contracted with Charles Spencer offering him a salary, his Buick, and a profit-sharing arrangement in return for running the day-to-day operations. These details concluded, RN headed back to Northern California and Christmas with his family.

When, shortly after the Christmas Holiday, he returned to Albuquerque, Spencer was gone. Locals reported he was last seen leaving the area in RN's Buick with a redheaded woman at his side. RN never saw him again. After making arrangements for local management, RN continued to own the property for several more years, writing that it returned him between $8,000 and $12,000 of profit per year during that time. He realized that he couldn't make it work, however, especially without local Spanish-speaking help, which he found quite difficult to obtain. Searching for a solution to this dilemma, he became entangled in yet another law suit.

Numa Boone was a successful rancher in the San Ramon Valley who had gone into banking later in life. He was also a former schoolmate of RN's in the Danville school in the early 1890s. In San Francisco one day after another trip to New Mexico to oversee his holdings there, RN ran into Boone on the ferry boat back to Oakland. Upon learning of RN's involvement with sheep-ranching in New Mexico, Boone expressed an interest in investing in RN's operation explaining that he had just sold his interest in the Bank of Concord to the Bank of America and was seeking additional investments. He further elaborated that he was involved with a man named Manuel Monese, a very successful local sheep herder who was also a Spanish linguist. The specific nature of Boone's involvement with Monese would not become clear until much later. RN suggested that for an investment of $50,000 Boone could become a partner in the New Mexico ranch. Boone offered to use some of the proceeds from the sale of his bank and to collaborate with Monese who would also put in some money, $15,000, and relocate to New Mexico to personally operate the ranch. After a visit to Monese's local sheep operation, the men agreed on a deal. Monese, would sell his sheep ranch and use the anticipated proceeds to fund his part of the deal. Seemingly, a solution to RN's management problems had been found.

Boone, however, had no cash. He had accepted ownership in Bank of America shares in exchange for his bank, leaving him unable to pay RN the agreed-upon amount. They agreed on a payout over time, with Boone signing a note agreeing to payments of $10,000 every six months, and the two met shortly thereafter in San Francisco to sign all the necessary papers. The plan was that within 30 days Monese was to arrive in New Mexico with his $15,000 investment and take over the ranch. These arrangements made, RN went back to the ranch to await the sheep-man's arrival.

The time for Monese's arrival came and went and when he failed to arrive at the ranch, RN sent a series of strident cables to Boone inquiring as to the cause of the delay. After some four months of this, RN finally received a wire from Boone indicating he should "Come home. We are in great trouble." RN returned to the Bay Area to learn that he and Boone were defendants in a lawsuit filed by Manuel Monese. Troubled about Boone's evasive manner in discussions they had, RN retained attorney Willard Williamson and appeared in the Superior Court in Martinez at the appointed time before Judge R. H. Latimer. Walking into the Court, both men were greeted by Numa Boone and his counsel, George Rogers of Martinez. After the first day, Williamson filed for dismissal which was granted by the court. This happened two more times after which RN happened to run into the Judge on the commuter train to San Francisco. Telling RN that he had known him and his wife Anne since both were children, he said he would like to see RN let this case go to trial. Indicating that unless new matters came to light he would have to dismiss again, he said the only way RN would get his name cleared would be through a clear verdict in his favor. "There will always be a doubt where you win by having a case dismissed. You can't afford that. Go to trial and win the case - have it clean."

Accordingly, RN sent word to Boone's attorney that they were going to go to trial and the men arranged a conference the following morning. It was at this meeting that the details of what had actually happened were revealed. The nature of RN's relationship with Boone is important in the light it sheds into the ultimate settlement of the case. Boone and RN, in addition to being former schoolmates, were also competitors in the banking business and RN's description of Boone's capacity for this profession was not flattering. In the *Memoirs*, he wrote that his boyhood friend had "grown up to be a big and successful rancher. He was drawn into the San Ramon Valley Bank and became its president. I believe that was unfortunate for him as he was not of banking timbre."

The headquarters of the San Ramon Valley Bank was in Walnut Creek and when RN established the First National Bank of Walnut Creek in 1912, he hired away Boone's Vice President, Hayward Cope, angering Boone in the process. In retribution, Boone opened a branch of his bank in Concord so as to compete with RN's controlling interest in the Bank of Concord. At the time, Concord had two banks, RN's Bank of Concord and the First National Bank of Concord, owned by Foskett and Elworthy, the men who had sold RN the 3,700-acre ranch back in 1908. Both RN's bank and the First National habitually sent their weakest credit customers to Boone's new San Ramon Valley branch, thus insuring its ultimate insolvency. A bank examination revealed that Boone's bank was undercapitalized and laden with bad debts which required corrective action. Boone offered to sell the bank to RN, but was turned down, whereupon he offered to buy RN out of the Bank of Concord at a very good price, which RN accepted.

RN, accordingly, entered his new relationship with Numa Boone equipped with a history and, reading between the lines of the *Memoirs*, it appears to have been somewhat checkered. At the meeting of the disputants before the third trial with RN represented by Williamson and Boone represented by George Rogers, it became apparent that Rogers did not want to play an active role in the proceedings, preferring that Williamson take the lead in the case. Nor did Rogers want his client to be put on the stand, preferring that the conflict be presented as one between Monese and RN. Williamson responded, rejecting that approach and insisting that Boone and Rogers were being less than fully candid. '...we feel the information we have received from Boone and you are half-truths. Come clean if you wish us to make the fight for both." Rogers then advised his client, "We have to tell them everything, or you will be finding yourself facing a jail sentence, perhaps the penitentiary."

At that point, the truth came out. Monese, it turned out, was quite illiterate and had difficulty signing his own name. Some years prior, he had gone to Numa Boone as President of the San Ramon Valley Bank, seeking the banker's services as a trustee. Monese placed $15,000 in trust with Boone. Recently, he had added additional funds to this trust deriving from the sale of his local sheep-ranching operation, roughly $15,000, in anticipation of traveling south to New Mexico and his engagement with Boone and RN on the new ranch. Boone thus held $30,000 of Monese's funds in trust and it was gone, with Boone unable to account for it. RN felt that Monese's illiteracy had resulted in a jumbled story to his attorney, deflecting the thrust of the lawsuit to RN rather than against Boone.

When the facts were disclosed, it was shown that Monese's money had been lost to his wife in a divorce settlement in which she was awarded all of his assets. Boone's intention had been to fund his purchase of a partial share of the New Mexico ranch with this $30,000 and $20,000 of his other funds, not the proceeds of the sale of his bank to the Bank of America. How he would have dealt with his violation of his fiduciary obligation to Monese is not made clear, but, in the end, the case went to trial and was dismissed. Boone subsequently settled with Monese and was never charged. The prospective partnership with Numa Boone on the New Mexico ranch was thus never consummated and RN would need to continue alone. The episode left bad feelings, however, as RN commented that, "I believe his (Boone's) explanation of the matter to his friends in the San Ramon Valley did me great harm, though I did not know about it until years later."

Unable to secure a bi-lingual partner to run operations on the ranch, RN returned to New Mexico to find 3,500 sheep missing and an $8,000 deficit for the year just ended. In yet another example of a staged social event with a very specific agenda, RN invited all the stakeholders in the ranch enterprise to a dinner. Present were the man from whom he was buying the ranch and livestock, his local banker, and the buyers of both sheep and wool. In anticipation of gaining some alcohol-induced insight into his situation, he had gone to his cellar at home and taken out four bottles of Perfection Scotch, each worth $20 a bottle during those Prohibition times, thinking it might make the participants talkative enough to reveal what was going on. His strategy appeared to have failed, when, by the end of the dinner, no one had volunteered anything of value. But then the sheep buyer, a young man, unexpectedly began to talk. Announcing against the opposition of his peers that he was going to reveal the facts about the operation that RN had purchased, he explained that New Mexico ranchers did not want non-resident cattle or sheep men operating in what they saw as their territory. If the outsiders persisted, their stock was stolen until such time as they finally saw the light and sold out. "Burgess, you are facing the men who caused your loss and the only way you can put an end to it is to move here with your family and be one of us. If you do this, the stealing will stop at once."

His eyes thus opened to the reality of being a non-local sheep rancher in New Mexico, RN wasted no time in extricating himself from the deal. He went into Albuquerque the next morning and borrowed $10,000 from the banker, another $10,000 from the wool buyer, and a similar amount from the sheep buyer. These funds allowed him to pay all his ranch bills and get current on his obligations. He then drafted a letter to the seller of the ranch indicating that, "The bank, wool and lamb buyers have purchased the ranch. They can work it out to suit themselves." He wrote that, "After what I was told at the dinner party which he (the seller) had attended, I felt perfectly justified in stepping out of the deal and from under the obligations. These men accepted the situation. I never heard from them again. I believe they got a Spanish-speaking sheep foreman from that area and came out very well."

In recounting this experience in the Memoirs, RN wrote that "in a few years, the United States Government took over Inscription Cliffs with an acreage for their historic value...It is now a National Park and it lies within the ranch." Additional research suggests, however, that the U.S. Government acquisition occurred on December 8, 1906, long before RN bought the acreage, and that it is now known as the El Morro National Monument. RN's New Mexico adventure was over. Without knowing many more details than he provided it is impossible to render a financial judgment on this chapter of his life. He seems to have made a modest profit for several years and then had a bad year with lost stock and a deficit operation. His narrative about how he extricated himself from the deal would have benefited from more clarity, but is interesting and reflects again his creativity in arranging events with multiple parties in a fashion which produced the results he sought.

His decision to involve himself in this undertaking involved a level of risk above and beyond anything he had engaged in earlier in his life. Buying a 100,000-acre sheep ranch in New Mexico far from home and far from his contacts and relationships and in a completely new business, speaks to the depth of his mid-life financial collapse and, implicitly, to the extent he was ostracized in his former peer group. Feeling that he needed "to get new surroundings," he removed himself completely from his former associates and friends, striking out on his own in a business and location foreign to anything he had encountered to date. One wonders what Anne thought of this adventure or even if she might have supported it financially to some extent, though that seems doubtful given the earlier separation of their financial lives. How, and through whom, did he get involved with Charles Spencer, the "guide," who first presented him the ranch and then ran off with his car and a "redhead?" These questions suggest a man who was searching far and wide for a path out of the financial difficulties and social stigma encountered after the collapse of his businesses back in the Bay Area.

The *Memoirs* contain anecdotes about additional forays into various business activities, none of which panned out. He spent a short time working on a project to create a railroad between Durango, CO, and Gallup, New Mexico. He was recommended by H.T. Cory to the sponsors of this project, Harry Chandler and Harrison Gray Otis, as a consultant to explore the purchase of railway rights-of-way over the proposed route. A Northern California firm led by C.A. Cooper, his nemesis in the Moraga Land purchase of a decade earlier, was able to secure the contract first, however, and the opportunity was lost.

He spent time attending a few meetings on a project, also with H.T. Cory, to finance small farms for returning veterans. This plan, embodied in a bill making its way through Congress (Bill S-3477), was to create a private fund of $20,000,000 seeded by wealthy private investors to acquire farm properties, equip them with all necessary accoutrements, and then make them available to veterans at very attractive financing terms. The bill never made it out of Congress.

As the 1920s wore on RN turned his attention to opportunities more closely aligned to his financial expertise. He took assignments from financial institutions in the area of credit evaluation. In 1929, he was employed by a bank holding company (an institution that owns shares in one or more banks for investment purposes) known as the All-American Company. The firm was engaged in due-diligence for the proposed acquisition of a twenty-bank portfolio throughout the country and had hired RN to visit a number of the banks in the east, interviewing officers and inspecting the receivables of each bank. This assignment had a curious ending, a rebuke of RN's conduct by his client. The background was that one of the banks under due-diligence had in its loan portfolio a $5,000,000 loan to the Singer Sewing Machine company. RN reported that on his way to that bank, on the train out of New York, he happened to sit immediately behind a man engaged in conversation with a colleague. One of the men was a Sales Manager with Singer according to RN's account. Eavesdropping on their conversation, RN learned that, in the opinion of the Sales Manager, who had resigned and was returning to his home, the company was dangerously extended by having borrowed several million to finance warehouses to house machines, manufactured but not selling. Eager to report this intelligence to his client, RN returned to New York and told his story. As he put it, "I got my ears slapped down and was given other work to do, but felt for some reason they were not happy." Was his gathering of business intelligence in this fashion somehow bad form? RN doesn't elaborate, but, again, something in the way he went about his business had alienated his client.

Another episode in New York brought him back in touch with the Mercantile National Bank of San Francisco and was probably recorded by him because his intuition about another man proved correct, contrary to the expectation of his client. The All-American Company, was engaged in ether an initial or follow-on offering of their common stock, probably in anticipation of the bank portfolio acquisition. The offering was for $10,000,000 but only $6,000,000 had been subscribed. In RN's description, "There were some very rich and well-known men on the Board of Directors and the failure of the issue to be oversubscribed as they expected panicked them. They did not foresee the coming crash."

Instructed by his client to take the issue to Goldman Sachs to a Mr. Wineman, RN responded that "You warned me not to interview any Jewish gentlemen." He was assured that these men were different and would make good partners. Wineman met with RN, listened to his pitch, and immediately agreed, saying that he liked the plan and would add (to the prospective twenty-bank holding company portfolio) the Mercantile National Bank of San Francisco as well as its trust company. Returning to his client with this report, RN, on being told he had been played for a fool by Wineman, said "I have a strong feeling that Mr. Wineman means just what he said."

Then, as he was walking back to his hotel, he ran into John Drum, the President of the Mercantile National Bank of San Francisco. RN recalled Drum walking in a very stooped and depressed fashion, but did not speak with him. Later he learned that Goldman Sachs had, just that morning, taken Drum's collateral on his defaulted personnel note which consisted of his controlling shares of the bank. Goldman, thus in control of the bank, was in a position to add it to the All-American offering. Wineman had meant what he said and performed as promised.

On these frequent business trips east, RN supplemented his working schedule with plenty of time for relaxation. In the *Memoirs*, he mentioned being invited to a horse-racing derby in St. Louis by Mr. Alley, General Counsel of the All-American Company. They were to be guests of the Governor of Missouri and would be seated in a private box. He declined this invitation out of fear of embarrassment at being unable to place big bets as he expected the other guests to do. He also developed a relationship with Francis Irenee Dupont, the manager of the E.I. du Pont de Nemours Company, and great grandson of its founder, and a man-about-town in New York in the 1920s. His remarks from the *Memoirs* are suggestive of a position in society he must have yearned for. "He told me much about the gaieties of New York. He said the yachting parties were scandalous. He told me he would get me invited, and if I wished to be popular I would have to think of something more sensational than having the ladies go in swimming naked...he used to send me a bottle of Scotch each week. He said 'don't buy from the bootleggers.'"

By the mid-1920s the strain of RN's peripatetic lifestyle must have begun to wear on Anne as she wrote him in 1927 that she was not well, needed surgery, and hoped that he might sell his then current business interest and come home to his family. This he did and Anne's surgery went well enough that she was able to embark on a European tour with their oldest child, Robin in the summer of 1928. While Anne was abroad, RN spent time with the other children, taking a camping trip that summer throughout northern California with Fran, his oldest daughter. His camping trips with his children seemed to echo his New Mexico experiences with lots of outdoor cooking of game shot along the way and similar adventures.

In 1929, still splitting his time between New York and home, he went camping again, this time with the other children. That summer he took Polly and Sue on a trip up into the Sierra Nevada mountains, stopping in Sonora to pick up his nephew Peter Burgess and heading for an ideal fishing spot he knew of in an isolated valley east of Pinecrest, CA. On arrival home, the girls were the proud owners of six chipmunks and a cage, courtesy of a friend of RN's who happened to be camping in the valley at the same time.

Anne's health had been an issue for the family from the beginning, with recurring bouts of intestinal flu and chronic high blood pressure. As a child, she had made a globe-encircling grand tour with her mother and brother Irvine in 1905. Anne's written record of this trip is an interesting travelogue, describing conditions in locations both primitive and advanced and providing social commentary as a backdrop to her descriptions. Anne had inherited her Mother's love of adventurous travel and planned similar excursions with her own children. RN's description of this activity is interesting for what it says about his own assessment of his character. "Anne loved to travel and did a lot of it. We planned to have efficient help to ease her daily life, and for vacations and travel she planned to take each child, as they graduated, to Europe. I could not go as I did not have the means and would not travel at her expense. I was touchy that way. From the time I left home at seventeen I had always been helping others – Father, Mother, brothers and sisters, and Aunt Hattie and her three children. To me it was not a chore or something I begrudged, but my way of life. I did it as a necessary duty, and my sister Marie, was the same way. She dedicated her life to helping others in need, without even knowing it."

As RN struggled through the 1920s, looking for opportunities in disparate venues and taking temporary assignments in the financial arena throughout the country, the nation was enjoying an economic boom, dubbed the Roaring Twenties. The Twenties were a release of the energy which had been bottled up by the War that ended in 1918. The period involved great technological advances with automobiles, airplane travel, and home appliances becoming widespread throughout the population. The motion-picture industry expanded and produced "talkies" late in the decade. It was a time of great cultural movement, with old values brought into question and then replaced by newer, more relaxed standards. These cultural shifts began in the major metropolitan centers of Western Europe and the United States and spread gradually into the smaller communities and districts. RN's reports of his experiences in New York reflect these changing cultural mores, and must have clashed with his Puritanical instincts.

Aside from two short and shallow recessions in 1923-24 and again in 1926-27, the boom that began with the end of the post War depression in July of 1921 continued almost unabated throughout the decade. But when the balloon burst, it burst in a big way. The stock market crash of the fall of 1929 was a key precipitating event exacerbated by a domestic banking collapse in 1931-32 and, later, by protective tariffs which produced a collapse of world trade. A decline in economic activity of 27% and unemployment of almost 25% characterized this unprecedented setback. In just a little over four years following the recovery of March 1933 a new recession followed. Triggered by tight fiscal policy (a desire by Congress to balance a budget swollen by New Deal spending), similarly tight monetary policy on the part of the Federal Reserve Bank, and declining profits in the corporate sector, this recession was one of the worst of the 20th century.

In the fall of 1929, RN was in New York under assignment with the All-American Company. On Black Thursday, October 24, 1929, he was in his office when his client called him in and told him he was no longer needed. As he put it, I "was called in and put on vacation, and I have been on that vacation ever since." The Dow lost only 7 points that day because Wall Street leaders, in imitation of the reaction to the Panic of 1907, began to buy heavily and headed off a panic. The following day, it recovered slightly more as it did on the following Monday. The next day, however, Black Tuesday, in a record 16 million-share trading day, the index lost another 30 points. The market highs of the preceding September were not seen again until November 1954.

The market crash of 1929, and the ensuing Great Depression of the 1930s ended RN's career as a financial consultant and his life thereafter turned to undertakings closer to home. His financial collapse in 1919 had been followed by a decade of slowly getting back on his feet and rebuilding his credit, largely in areas far removed from the site of his earlier accomplishments. He now returned to that area, but to engagements in projects much smaller in scope and potential than those in which he had engaged in his younger years. As the 1930s began, he was back in Walnut Creek beginning to concentrate on what would finally become his signature development.

CHAPTER 17

Depression, War, and a Lost Career

The great depression that followed the market crash of October 1929 came as RN was entering his early 50's. No longer the brash young real estate and finance man he was in his prime years, he was now well into middle age, returning to Walnut Creek from his engagements in the east with very little to show for his effort. His physical energy may have been declining, though the amount of hard work he was about to invest in his Walnut Creek subdivision, Lakewood, certainly did not reflect it. On periodic visits to the Homestead during the late 1920s he had begun work on what would become his later-life work, the project that would occupy him until the early 1950s.

RN had purchased the 1,750-acre Rice Ranch in the spring of 1908. In 1909, upon his marriage to Anne, he had gifted 155 acres of that land to her as her sole property. After his discharge from bankruptcy, they had only her portion of the property left. They had used the Homestead house as a weekend place from its initial acquisition until the mid-20s. At that point, they sold the home he had built for Anne at Diablo and established their permanent residence at the Homestead in Walnut Creek. That site and home, still occupied, reflects the numerous changes occurring since its origin as the one-story Ygnacio Sibrian adobe, and the later Rice home. After RN's purchase of the property in 1908, he continued improvements to the home and its surrounding land. He built two dams at the head of the two canyons which open on the east side of the house, the larger of the two completed in 1909. These dams were originally designed as catchments to hold and retain winter rains in support of orchard and crop irrigation. Following his marriage to Anne, he had the house remodeled. It was remodeled again in subsequent years by George Applegarth, the architect of several of RN's San Francisco buildings, his home at Diablo, and of the Diablo Country Club.

By 1928 Anne had been managing her portion of the land in a for-profit farming operation for a number of years. She had done well, selling walnuts and other vegetables, but a collapse in walnut prices in late decade, and a deficit operation, caused her to want to revisit their arrangement and she suggested that RN take the property back. RN agreed and asked her to calculate her losses in interest and unreimbursed operating costs over the years of her ownership to arrive at a fair price at which to sell him back her land. To this she added her costs for various other improvements to the property including the remodeling of the main house, the new barn, the swimming pool, and the tennis court, arriving at a figure of $112,500. After agreeing on this price, RN asked her to select the parcel that she wanted for her home. She wanted the house and fifteen acres immediately surrounding it which they valued at $30,000, leaving a value of $82,500 for the balance of the property. Her parcel was encumbered with a $10,000 mortgage which RN paid off, so that she owned the property free and clear. He wanted Anne to own her property outright and have no part in the 140-acre prospective subdivision property, which she deeded to him, so as to protect her from any liability under the debts he knew he would incur. The obligation thus created was memorialized by his note to Anne for $82,500, at 6% interest, later reduced at the suggestion of her attorney, Allen Chickering, to 1%.

This domestic transaction set RN up to begin his Lakewood development. The depression was in full swing, however, and he lacked capital. He encountered Fred Lipman, his acquaintance since childhood, now President of Wells Fargo Bank, and asked him to consider a $15,000 loan to fund his subdivision work. Lipman was not interested, "That is something I can't possibly help you with, so don't come to our bank." But he went on to suggest that RN still had good relationships with many in "country banks" who thought well enough of him to agree to a loan. Lipman then lectured RN on how to approach one of these banks, the St Helena

National Bank in Napa, instructing him to "go with confidence that you will get the loan, and don't come away without it." Following Lipman's instructions, he obtained a $15,000 loan from the bank and was able to begin work on Lakewood. Lipman's unequivocal rejection of a loan from his own bank speaks to the extent to which RN's economic standing had fallen within his former peer group. More than a decade after his bankruptcy, his name was still not welcome and he was directed to a bank far from the seat of his former home area.

The family situation changed again during these years, precipitated by an automobile accident in Berkeley. All four of the Burgess daughters had been enrolled in the Anna Head's School in that city and Anne had purchased a car for their commute. One morning early in the school term, a truck coming down a hill collided with the car containing all the girls, tipping it over and causing some minor injuries. Feeling that the incident might well have been much worse, both parents decided to rent a house in Berkeley for the duration of the girl's school experience. Anne found a furnished house on Claremont Avenue and moved in with all four girls and Robin, who was by this time working in a local gas station. Sometime thereafter, another location, at 6425 Chabot Ave. in Oakland became their home, again temporarily. Feeling that he could not afford the time of a daily commute, RN chose to remain alone at the Homestead.

His walnut crop had to be managed, but as a sole operator now, with no capital and no payroll, there was no one to perform the labor but him. In the *Memoirs*, he paints a sad picture of a fallen financier, alone in his kitchen after a hard day's work on his subdivision, shucking walnuts by hand far into the night, preparing to drive them to the confectionary market in Berkeley in the morning. His payroll in this new undertaking consisted of only one man, Robert Green. Known to the family, and all the children, as "Mr. Green," Bob Green began working with RN in 1928 and stayed with him for 25 years as his loyal, hard-working foreman and right-hand man. Green's salary in these initial Lakewood years: $1.00 per day.

One of the earliest jobs the two of them undertook, with the help of some Puerto Rican laborers hired from the union hall, was the expansion of the lake above the larger of the two dams' RN had built in 1909. After securing the loan from the St. Helena National Bank, he hired a steam shovel and tractor with the idea of dredging, smoothing, and enlarging the lake. Digging a small depression for the storage of fish, he proceeded to deepen and square off the sides. He also began construction on the roads that would eventually surround the lake and provide access to the Highlands of Upper Lakewood. The winter of 1929 and 1930 yielded significant rainfall on the heels of the two dry years preceding and this rain produced a desire for urgency on the lake job in the fall of 1930. In responding to this urgency, an accident occurred which had the effect of taking RN out of action for several months. Riding on a tractor-towed V-frame on the lake bottom, RN's leg was broken when the frame hit a submerged log and flipped over. A second flip caused the frame to hit RN just above his right ankle, producing a clean break and twisting movement such that he could look down and see the sole of his boot.

RN's description of this event, and the resulting circumstances, reflect characteristic drama. Immediately following the incident, he recounted that he had Mr. Green and the tractor driver straighten his leg, and, "then I gave orders." He instructed Green to get to a telephone and call Anne at the rented house in Berkeley advising her of the emergency and asking her to reserve a room for him at Merritt Hospital with a physician to set the broken leg. He then asked the laborers to remove their neckties, leave them with him and walk up the lakebed to the location of a small cabin. He instructed them to remove the door of the cabin and bring it back to serve as a stretcher. He instructed another laborer to locate some fence boards and cut two of them to specified lengths for splints. When these items were on hand, he asked the laborers to help him straighten out the damaged leg, which they did, leaving him free to fasten the fence boards to his leg with the neckties. With his leg thus straightened and splinted, he was ready when Green returned with a fire truck from the Walnut Creek fire department.

Four men then carried him up the hill to the fire truck and took him into Walnut Creek.

Arriving at the office of Dr. Beede, he was asked if he wanted something for his pain. Replying that it was a good idea to get the leg set before administering pain relief, he said he'd hold off until he got to the hospital. The Doctor responded that he was correct, provided he could stand the pain. He felt he could, so they left, siren blaring on a firetruck, and headed for the hospital 20 miles west in Berkeley. At the hospital under the care of Dr. Hitchcock, RN was advised that the break was a clean one and that the Doctor wanted to pull his leg out straight and position it for casting. He said it would be painful, but that he didn't want to administer morphine as he needed a muscular reaction to set the break correctly and morphine would preclude that. Asked if he could stand the pain, RN responded "Yes, when you are through I will have the morphine." The leg was set and placed in a cast and RN was moved to the Claremont Avenue house to recuperate.

One of his first visitors in the upstairs porch which was his assigned quarters was Jim Irvine. RN's description of the interchange between the two of them about Irvine's prospective marriage to Katherine Brown White is interesting for what it suggests about their relationship ten years after his bankruptcy. RN described Irvine being uncharacteristically tongue-tied initially and challenged the older man (Irvine was about 64, RN 53), saying "Out with it, Jim...don't be back-ward. It is about a girl, isn't it?" Irvine then sought information about White from RN, indicating he had been seeing a lot of her and was quite fond of her. He had heard stories, however, that disturbed him and that would preclude the marriage if they proved true. When he equivocated at RN's question about his love for her, RN exploded, "Jim, you are a damned old ostrich. Don't you know it...if you love the girl, marry her, give her a million dollars so she will never have to ask for money, and have Guy draw up an agreement as to your separate property rights. Because you have your head in the sand you can't see that anyone knows about it, but it is general knowledge." Irvine, angry at RN's bluntness withdrew to go downstairs to dine with the rest of the family, later calling up his goodbye. A wire arrived from Eugene, Oregon several days later with an announcement by Irvine that he and White were married. It was July of 1931.

RN's convalescence proceeded and he was soon walking with the aid of crutches. Another episode with Jim Irvine followed and provided more insight into their relationship. At a luncheon appointment at the Palace Hotel in San Francisco, RN presented a prospective $25,000 investment, which Irvine decided was not worthy. RN did not describe the investment in his recounting of the luncheon, but it apparently stimulated Irvine to evaluate for RN's benefit the excellent returns he had achieved on his asparagus crop the previous season. Asparagus was Jim Irvine's favorite lunch according to RN, in this case served cold with a half of an avocado, lemon juice, and coffee, at a price of $1.00. Irvine then busied himself calculating what his crop would have yielded at the retail prices charged in the restaurant.

On the street after lunch, Irvine suggested to RN that he hadn't seemed to enjoy his lunch. RN responded, "No, Jim, I did not. I feel it is a compliment when you invite me to lunch, but not so when you spend the entire time griping about a $160,000 asparagus return." RN's description of Irvine's response is characteristically self-serving: "Bob, the reason I like you so much is because you are about the only one that helps me by speaking out your opinion. There are so many who toady to me, and I shun them as much as I can."

Back in his office, RN was surprised to see a messenger from Irvine. The messenger was carrying an envelope containing $25,000. RN telephoned Irvine, indicating that he was convinced Irvine's analysis had been correct and that they should not make the investment. Irvine objected, saying, "Go ahead and invest it as we intended. We may not lose it, and if we win, it will be a nice profit. Should the money be lost all I want from you is a statement showing I made the loss so I can deduct it from my income tax." RN reported that they made the investment and indeed lost the entire investment.

RN's personal financial picture during these depression years was always marginal. The family had money and could live a life reflective of that capacity thanks to Anne's inheritance after the death of Frances Webster Fish in July of 1923. The private schools, the European tours, the elaborate improvements to the Homestead could scarcely have been afforded on RN's income alone. His writing about this fact in the *Memoirs* reflects his feelings and suggests an understandable reticence about becoming involved in her financial affairs. When she solicited his advice and counsel he responded, however, recalling what he remembered as successful advice.

Anne's inheritance consisted of a securities portfolio as well as a portfolio of mortgages on Central Valley land, the product of her father's considerable holdings there during the late 19th century. During the Depression years, Anne sold much of the land she inherited pursuant to land-contracts (under which she held title until the buyer's payment obligations were completed) on which she found it necessary to foreclose when farmers could not make their payments. All this she seems to have managed herself, without much assistance from RN, perhaps demonstrating aptitude inherited from Lafayette Fish.

RN records one anecdote about Anne's investing approach and his contribution to the effort. One day in the first half of 1928, Anne advised him that she had invested $10,000 in Transamerica stock with expectation of making enough to fund her then prospective trip through Europe with Robin. He commented that, "Her investments were not any of my business - it was her money, but when asked I expressed my opinions." RN's business contacts had led him to believe that Transamerica, which was the bank holding company for numerous banks acquired by the Bank of Italy in the 1920s, had been the repository for poor credits acquired during the bank's expansion and was therefore too risky for her portfolio. She disagreed and the two had words over the matter. Frustrated, RN left the meeting and went out into his orchards. Not long afterwards, Anne advised him that she had sold half her stock, retrieving her initial investment, and planned to speculate with those funds. RN said he commended her on her approach, but advised her to keep an eye on the Transamerica stock as he still expected the firm to decline in value. His judgement soon proved to be correct and her initial investment in the company declined to a value of a few hundred dollars and was liquidated. Nonetheless, he commented that, "On the whole, I feel Anne did remarkably well with her investments."

In another instance of Anne seeking his advice, she asked him what he thought of the prospective combination of the Best and Holt Tractor Companies to form the Caterpillar Tractor Company. She had an $8,500 position in Holt preferred stock, acquired years earlier by her father. RN responded that, while he thought the company's idea of building track-laying tractors for marsh lands was a good thing, he knew nothing about the business and the management of either firm. He urged her to go to San Francisco and discuss the matter with attorney Allen Chickering as he was a director on Holt's board. Chickering advised Anne to hold the stock which she did, RN reporting that she "pulled out $200,000 in dividends and splits and had many times the original investment on hand." RN estimated that this investment alone amounted to almost half of her holdings and allowed her considerable financial freedom which otherwise would have been unavailable.

RN's resources suffered by comparison. Shortly after his accident in the lakebed, he was contacted by the State Department of Labor in the matter of a claim for $140 on the part of the Puerto Rican laborers he had hired to assist on the job. Responding to the complaint, he visited the Deputy Labor Commissioner's office and stated that the amount of the claim was at least double the rightful amount. The Commissioner responded that if the claim were to be pursued and went to a hearing, the charge would be much larger. RN acceded, telling the Commissioner he would return shortly. Leaving the office, he went to a lender and placed a mortgage on his automobile, the proceeds from which he used to pay the claim.

Perhaps it is not surprising that RN's post-bankruptcy life left him inclined to undertake higher-risk schemes that had the promise of making a quick hit. The contrast between what he had achieved in his earlier life and the standard of living it produced with his existence during the 1920s and early 1930s is striking. Also, the fact of his wife's financial independence must have grated on him, occasionally driving him into promotional activities that seemed to promise a fast return. One such occasion, in the early 1930's, is described in the *Memoirs*. As he described it in his own words, it was, "A big bubble. At some point... I had to try my hand at quick money." He was approached by a promoter seeking financing for an unusual project. Some of the largest public utility companies in the country sought to finance a project to write and publish a history of public electricity projects in the United States. According to RN, the would-be sponsors of this project had collected five tons of records and were storing them in a fire-proof vault in anticipation of finding an independent publisher willing to take on the job. It was critical to this project that it be seen as independent, not in any way connected to the utility firms because of political friction between the industry and the United States Congress. An independent publisher, with the assistance of fifty editors, would undertake to publish 5,000 high quality copies of the book for distribution to every high-school, college, and public library in the country.

RN was interested and located a couple of partners, giving each a quarter interest in the scheme, taking half for himself. Identifying the fifty editors was comparatively easy; the willingness among academics and others to engage in a project of such historical significance was high. A publisher in Chicago, specializing in financial circulars, was identified and everything seemed to check out. RN's description of this opportunity is not clear, but it sounds as if he and his two partners were going to invest a total of $700,000 in the Chicago publisher (unnamed in the *Memoirs*) and had expectations of an excellent return. In the end, it collapsed the day before he was preparing to make his initial $100,000 payment because his attorneys in New York, Simpson Thatcher and Bartlett, found out that the prospective publisher had a secret partner in the utility business after all. Such a partner, if revealed after the publication of the books, would have shown the undertaking to be the blatant advocacy on the part of the utility company association that it was.

RN's total loss on this speculation was $3,500. It might have been much worse. He summarized his unsuccessful efforts to make a quick killing by saying, "I have been very unfortunate in trying to make a fast buck, but I didn't lay it down to being fiddle-footed. It was solely my trying to meet responsibilities. This was my last promotion. Don't count your profits until you have them in hand, even on your attorney's say-so."

In a philosophical mood, writing these words in the twilight of his life he remarked of his earlier attempts to make quick hits that, "The slow, so-slow way proved best in the end. I settled down to developing Lakewood after the crash of 1929, and slaved through all the depressed thirties."

His efforts in that development were nothing if not prodigious. RN was 52 when that decade began and throughout the next fifteen years he worked, initially with a staff of one, Robert Green, and later with a small payroll of only several men to place subdivision maps on both the highlands portion of the property, which he termed the Uplands, and the lower portion at the foot of Lakewood Road. Much of the work was hard manual labor expended in planting hundreds of trees, then hand-watering them through two particularly dry years. Obtaining a list of forty trees from the University of California, RN and Bob Green raised them from seed stock in his nursery, producing an inventory of trees still in evidence throughout the subdivision. These included Eucalyptus, Monterey and Japanese Black Pine, Arizona Ash, Black Locust, Catalpa, and Juniper. In total, 100 acres were planted, all of which needed to be hand watered during the early years of their lives. One year, an infestation of mice cost them 30% of their crop. After maturity, the trees were watered by septic systems installed with the new homes.

Another wet winter, probably 1931, saw the overflowing of the dam and the threat of a 100,000,000-gallon flood onto the homes in the Lowlands. In consequence, a new overflow system was built, which included the deepening of an existing spillway at the south end of the dam. The rocks pulled from the dredging of the lake became the base of the road system throughout the new development.

As the decade of the thirties passed, RN decided to enter another business, adobe bricks. To this end he created a brick yard in the Lowlands southwest of the Homestead. He mixed the adobe, quarried from an adjacent hillside, with bitumen and straw creating water-repellant bricks 4"X12"X18" in size that were used in a number of homes in both sections of Lakewood. These bricks were more expensive than the standard wood construction employed but provided much better insulating properties.

True to his lifelong pattern, RN continued to work hard, engaging in strenuous physical labor and carpentry throughout the decade of the 1930s. In describing how he and Bob Green divided the work of building the adobe homes he said, "In these original houses I made the window and door frames and set them in position. Mr. Green installed the adobe walls, electric wiring and the plumbing, and plastered the ceilings."

By mid-decade in the thirties, the social scene around Homestead changed as the oldest of the five children began to enter adulthood. As RN described the situation, "The young folks began to bring life and youthful merriment into Homestead." With a swimming pool up the canyon from the large house and a lake just beyond it over the dam, there were ample opportunities for recreation around the Burgess property. A barbecue and long guest table facilitated lots of entertainment, often with as many as sixty or seventy guests in attendance. RN described thick steaks from the Lawrence Meat Market, a long-standing local enterprise, baked potatoes, and corn on the cob, all prepared by himself, as he and Anne hosted events for their various children.

In mid-decade, the first of the Burgess children was married as Frances, the oldest daughter, married James Rolph Moore, a member of the family that RN had worked with in his shipbuilding days. The wedding was on the lawn at Homestead on April 28, 1935. Six years would pass before the next daughter, Nancy, married Gerrit Keane, also on the lawn at Homestead, on July 12, 1941. With the war looming, the remaining Burgess children married rapidly. Another lawn wedding followed on September 6, 1941 as Suzanne married Edward Lee Soule. That November, Robert

Noble Burgess II married Elizabeth Huie at her women's club in Oakland. And finally, Polly Burgess, the youngest, married Thomas H. Carroll in the large living room at the Homestead on December 13, just six days after Pearl Harbor.

RN's sentiments about these changes in his and Anne's domestic life are captured in his comments. "Anne and I were feeling the letdown after five big weddings within a period of fifty-six months, the last four within six months. The family was reduced to the two of us, and we were left to rattle around in a twenty-room house. We had enjoyed the "sparkling" while it lasted, and were happy to have the children all launched happily."

By late in the decade, RN was increasingly active in the building business in both Lakewood and in other East Bay communities. The Japanese strike on Pearl Harbor brought an end to that activity, however. After the United States entry into the war in December of 1941, the availability of building materials was limited to only Richmond in Contra Costa County. Once again in a financial pinch and threatened with foreclosure with real estate taxes and interest on his debt due as well as the cost of carrying his overhead expenses, RN turned to the government in search of work. He declared himself available to build government housing anywhere in California, Nevada, or Arizona and was asked to bid on a 100-house contract in Richmond.

Demand for housing in Richmond, where shipyard work was ramping up furiously in response to the war effort, was quite high. The United States government sought smaller houses that could be built quickly and leased to tenants at a maximum profit to the builder of 10%. Financing soon became an issue for the formerly bankrupt builder. He had thirty lots ready for construction with plans approved by the government. His former bank, the Central Bank of Oakland, would not make such loans and turned him down. He then went to the government housing office and asked them to provide the necessary financing. His initial requirement was for ten houses, a total of $35,000 in required construction financing. The housing office approached the Berkeley office of the Mercantile National Bank in RN's behalf and a loan was closed within several days. Because of his history with the Mercantile Bank, however, he was advised after the initial loan by the Berkeley Branch that there would be no further financing available to him from that bank. Twenty-three years after his bankruptcy and attendant problems with Mercantile Bank, he was still persona non-grata with the institution. Fortunately, his next lot of houses and all subsequent lots were financed without issue by the Central Bank of Oakland, which had changed its position about making these loans.

Early on in this government project in Richmond, RN could see problems developing the nature of which he was all too familiar with because of his past experience. By war's end, he could anticipate having all his capital tied up in rented housing, or, as he put it, he would be "land poor," with so many encumbered properties and insufficient capital available to develop them. He reasoned that taking this risk with only a 10% return was foolish. Accordingly, he modified his agreement with the government, offering lease terms on the houses that incorporated a provision that the first three months' rent would be due on signing of the lease and then applied to the final three months of the term. He also inserted an option to purchase, at the price stipulated by the government, to the lessee. In addition, any alterations or additions to the premises would be negotiated and added to the lease, at a rate which reflected a 25% margin to the builder. In consequence of these changes and the fact that 100% of the tenants exercised their options to purchase, RN's return on the project was much better than initially expected. Once again, the financier was at work, this time in the context of a government contract.

Early in World War II, housing was in such shortage in the Bay Area that alterations and conversions of existing commercial and larger residential structures to apartments were undertaken as a method of increasing housing stock. The work was riskier, because of the likelihood of uncovering unanticipated problems after construction had begun, and a builder often required a guaranteed number of such assignments prior to taking on such work. No exception, RN, when presented with such an opportunity, declined unless he could get a minimum of twenty jobs over which to average out higher-than-average cost problems. This the government would not guarantee, although he susequently agreed to take on the work after assurances that in all probability he would get more than his minimum number of assignments.

RN's portfolio soon grew and he found he could handle about fifty jobs at one time throughout the East Bay. Working from office space in the Builders Exchange and with the assistance of his office administrator, Mrs. E.M. Daily, RN did all of his own estimating for these jobs and, was soon building apartments over existing theaters and adding them above furniture stores, factories, and other commercial buildings. He would spend his mornings in his office, reviewing estimates with Mrs. Daily, and then go out in the field all afternoon visiting jobs in Berkeley, Richmond, Alameda, and East Oakland. The economic results of all this activity gradually improved his situation out at the Homestead. "I was making considerable money, mostly through economical overhead, which went a long way towards balancing losses in Lakewood. At least, I saved Homestead from threatened foreclosure and left myself in shape to work out the subdivision and building there to advantage."

On September 2, 1945, with the unconditional surrender of Japan, World War II officially ended and, within a year of that date, conditions in the building industry were such that RN was able to resume his Lakewood development.

RN and Anne at Berkeley home in 1934.
Courtesy Burgess Family collection.

RN and Anne in 1937. He was fifty-nine, Anne fifty-one.
Courtesy Burgess Family collection.

RN at the barbeque at Homestead, July, 1937.
Courtesy Burgess Family collection.

CHAPTER 18

Fulfilling the Dream of Lakewood

R N's earlier dream of developing Diablo, marketing peaceful country living to urban Bay Area dwellers, had been spoiled by World War I and its attendant economic convulsions, and he had long harbored a dream of creating a smaller suburban neighborhood situated around a placid country lake in Walnut Creek. He felt that a growing network of roads, supplemented by rail access, might provide city workers relatively easy access to residential sanctuaries outside the bustle, noise, and pressure of their places of daily work in Oakland and San Francisco. With the war's end, he at last had the opportunity to pursue this dream and to do so amid the conditions of high housing demand spawned by returning veterans.

He had sold lots and built a number of homes in the Uplands (the portion of Lakewood that lies on the high ground to the east of Homestead Avenue), beginning in 1931, but he was scratching the surface relative to what the property would eventually absorb. Between 1931 and the date of US entry into World War II in December 1941, he had sold forty-two parcels. During the war years eleven additional deeds were recorded resulting in fifty-three lot commitments by war's end. With the end of hostilities, materials available, improved credit, and a growing labor supply represented by returning veterans, he was ready to begin.

He started by getting the Lakewood properties surveyed and recording subdivision maps. He installed five water wells and associated pumping capacity. He installed two 100,000-gallon water tanks to handle the pumping discharge in excess of demand. The water system he installed in Lakewood remained in service until the city of Walnut Creek annexed the subdivision.

Helped by strong post-war demand for housing, RN's financial situation began to improve. The competition for Lakewood lots was so strong that some would-be buyers went to the Homestead and called on RN early in the morning, trying to get their lot offers in before competing buyers. Building into this kind of demand was an experience RN had not had since his early post-earthquake days forty years earlier and the impact on his finances was not long in coming.

Turulu Brady, in her excellent book, *Lakewood, a History of Walnut Creek's Unique Neighborhood*, reported that RN mapped subdivisions on three major parcels in the Lowlands, one in 1940 in the area of West Holly Street known as Lakewood Village and the other two, after the war's end, in the Summit Road area known as Lakewood Ranch, units one and two. He recalled that the Lowlands lots all sold quickly in the context of the buyer's panic. These sales helped his cash flow and he was able to stay current with his primary construction financing source at the time, Golden West Savings and Loan, and to continue paying on the now reduced balance of his $82,500 loan from Anne on her Homestead property. [1]

After signing a contract for fifty Federal Housing Authority-financed houses, he found that strong post-war demand presented him with a new problem: a serious materials shortage caused work to slow down dramatically and he was forced to seek alternative sources of supplies of lumber, re-bar, and nails. He found overpriced nails and re-bar through sources in the San Joaquin Valley but could not locate adequate lumber supplies. He decided to travel north, with Anne, to explore lumber availability in Northern California and Oregon.

As a former owner of the Humboldt National Bank, RN knew some of the members of its Board of Directors, one of whom, identified by RN as M. Devoe, owned considerable redwood acreage along the corridor the State of California was then developing as the Redwood Highway Park. RN met with him and learned that

---

[1] Turalu Reed Brady, *Lakewood, a History of Walnut Creek's Unique Neighborhood*, (Turalu Reed Brady, Copyright 2004, Walnut Creek, Ca).

he had 300,000,000 board feet of timber left to sell. Continuing on their journey, RN and Anne went north to Crescent City, ultimately staying in Eugene, Oregon. They bought no timber on this trip, returning home by way of Redding and Weaverville CA, evaluating additional timber-buying opportunities on the way.

Shortly after coming home, RN returned to Eureka and contracted to buy the 300,000,000 board-feet from Devoe. In addition, he located and purchased additional footage in Weott (20,000,000 feet), and a final 10,000,000-foot parcel west of Ukiah, California. Characteristically, he had gone into the lumber business in a big way. The *Memoirs* are silent as to how he managed to arrange these purchases. Presumably, some lender, perhaps in Eureka and with the high post-War demand for housing in mind, agreed to finance him. Based on his experiences obtaining financing early in the war when he was doing government contract work, it is doubtful that any of his old Bay Area banking connections would have been forthcoming.

He related an entertaining anecdote from his first lumber-buying trip to Eureka with Anne. In Eugene, Oregon, arriving after a day of driving, they obtained a corner room of one of the local hotels. The room had a bath adjoining with access to another room. Shortly after their arrival, RN locked the door to the other bedroom and was surprised to hear someone trying to get into the bathroom. The person was swearing and kicking the door in his attempt to gain entry. On being advised by RN that he had engaged both the room and the bath, the other person yelled, "Unlock that door or I will kick it down." Realizing that the man was part of a group and was obviously drunk, RN instructed Anne to advise the front desk that an intruder was trying to gain entry and that he had already broken a portion of the door. As she complied with this instruction, RN fetched his ".38 automatic and went into the bath and told the drunk to go ahead and kick the panel out, and 'as soon as your foot shows I will shoot and break your leg.'" At the last minute, the management showed up and removed the man from the room. Apparently, he had been part of a group of four engaged in a well-lubricated game of cards all afternoon and became upset when he found that the previously available bathroom was now off limits. RN never lost his fondness for carrying weapons with him. At almost seventy years of age, he was still packing and acting as if he were quite ready to use the gun if sufficiently prodded.

He solved his immediate lumber shortage by having the two smaller parcels harvested at once and shipped to his lumber yard at Homestead. The larger parcel required a local sawmill and he soon contracted with several men from San Rafael to build one and commence cutting and finishing the lumber. After incorporating as the Redwood Highway Lumber Company, RN soon found that the San Rafael men did not have sufficient funds to complete the job and he found it necessary to loan them money, $50,000 in all. He reported that he was pleased with their work, however, as they quickly built the mill, began harvesting timber, and ultimately paid him back. He also entered a collaboration with four other home builders from the contractor's association for the larger timber parcel, forming the G. C. Lumber Company, in which each partner had an equal share.

The post-war lumber shortage soon expanded into a shortage of competent carpenters and foremen and turnover in both positions was a constant problem in the home-building operation. Another anecdote about a court appearance is recounted by RN in the *Memoirs* as he recalled his rescue of a foreman from the San Leandro jail. The offender was scheduled for a hearing in Judge Harris' court and RN went to court to try to extricate him. It developed that RN had appeared before this judge before, decades earlier when Judge Harris had served as police judge in Oakland. Realizing this, he went up to the bench and asked if he could see the judge in chambers, indicating that he had appeared in his police court years earlier and that it was critical that he get his foreman back to work. The judge rebuffed him, saying that, "This court does not operate behind closed doors. I will hear you here when we get around to it." Within a short time, however, the judge motioned for RN to follow him into chambers and asked him about the earlier matter.

RN then related a story about his long-ago experience in Judge

Harris' police court. The story involved a man, a "colored man," to whom RN had lent a team of horses and wagon to facilitate the man's transporting some household goods. When the police department later called RN, and advised him that they had the man in custody, he went to court to obtain his release. The result of the proceedings was a judgement for the plaintiff of $8, which RN promptly paid off, getting his team back and his man freed. Judge Harris, amused by RN's recounting of the story, asked him what the charge was this time. It was drinking, and the judge promptly reconvened his court and rendered judgement of a $3 fine for the offense, which RN paid and thus retrieved his foreman.

For reasons not made clear in the *Memoirs*, RN became embroiled in a dispute with his partners in the G.C. Lumber Company venture. As he explained the formation of the deal, he was one of five builders (all members of the associated contractor's association) who had come together to share the investment in, and the lumber extracted from, the newly purchased Devoe property. Each had a twenty percent share in the company and, with lumber demand as strong as it was in the post-war period, the group should have done well, but, as RN put it, "I was not getting along with my associates." In reading his description of what happened, it sounds as if communication was at the root of the problem. He had proposed at a directors' meeting that he would offer his fellow directors shares of preferred stock held in the treasury of another company he controlled, Lumber Factors, Inc. His proposal was that if they would put their shares of G.C. Lumber Company stock in Lumber Factors, he would issue each of them shares of the 6% preferred stock in return. In other words, as a mechanism to buy out his partners, he was offering his Lumber Factors preferred shares for their G.C. shares. No one agreed to this offer at the time, but shortly thereafter he received calls from two of the associates who accepted the deal and traded in their shares. This put RN in control of G.C. Lumber with 60% of the shares and, when the other two who had not accepted his initial offer heard the news, they were not happy.

While this was taking place, a $15,000 note to the Bank of

America with the endorsement of all the G.C. partners came due and the bank demanded payment. When RN visited the bank manager and told him he would have the funds in a few days from proceeds of a prospective lumber sale, the manager advised him that he would not extend the obligation for any additional time and expected the payment immediately. Further, he informed RN that the four other directors had come to his office indicating they would assume the note and that the bank should send it to their Richmond office for payment. Incredulous that the bank would take these steps without notifying him, RN pushed back, only to be told that the same four directors had attached the Company account and, one day later, all the lumber in the yard.

RN fought back. Writing that, "They thought they had me over a barrel," he soon noticed that the four partners had overlooked all the lumber in transit and the accounts receivable. Also, Lumber Factors, Inc - of which RN was sole owner - had been hired to do the Marketing for G.C. by virtue of which some $35,000 in cash was free of the liens placed by the other four partners, which allowed RN to access enough cash to pay off G.C.'s outstanding bills and other monies due him.

He was soon contacted by counsel for the other four partners, Tinning & DeLap of Richmond, a firm with whom RN had done business years earlier. They urged a settlement instead of a lawsuit and RN agreed, stating as his terms, a sale of his stock to the other partners for $26,000, his cost. The offer was accepted, and the matter finished.

This was the last major dispute described by RN in his *Memoirs*, and, like so many other stories, it leaves a reader with questions as to what really went wrong between the partners. Inasmuch as the other four seem to have stayed allied against RN, one wonders if it was conduct on his part that precipitated the crisis. Recalling his self-acknowledged tendency to operate alone and often to be less than thorough in his communications, it seems reasonable to conclude that the partners grew tired of his style and approach and decided to challenge him. Also, his failure to notify the two non-accepting partners that two of their colleagues had changed their minds and accepted his offer of the exchange for the Lumber Factors preferred shares, certainly might have been the last straw, inciting them to collaborate against him. This is speculation and it is offered solely as a means of trying to understand RN's character and business style. He never identified a date of the foregoing events, but it is likely they occurred in the late 1940s at which point he was 70 or a little older. He was also very tired and doubtless suffering the effects of a lifetime of hard work. As he put it, "I was over-worked and tired and all at once felt like lightening my business load, and sold out all scattered holdings except what was left in Lakewood."

Turning his attention to Lakewood, he proceeded to finish as much of the project as he could, given the significant labor shortages then weighing on the business. He kept building but gradually began to change his modus operandi, as he put it, "from builder to banker." He began to sell his lots to other builders and then took second deeds of trust to help them close the gap between their FHA financing and their own capital. He did the same with his son Bob selling him twenty lots in Lakewood, all of which were built out. What had begun as a building opportunity ultimately became a loan servicing and collection operation, a development not inconsistent with his age and with challenges developing on the home front.

The conclusion of the decade of the 1940s brought increasing problems in Anne's health. Never possessed of a robust constitution, she had long suffered from intestinal issues and RN described numerous times in their life together when her condition weakened and she needed rest to regain strength. In early 1950, she was denied the renewal of her driving license, an event producing depression inasmuch as one of her primary sources of joy was driving in her automobile throughout the local countryside. From her earliest days as RN's intended, when she had so enjoyed driving her "Stanhope with two blacks" through the Berkley and Oakland hills, Anne valued her independence and losing it was devastating. RN tried unsuccessfully to intercede on her behalf, but her Doctor and the family were unanimous in their opposition. So, the driving ended, and, in RNs opinion, "this episode was the beginning of Anne's final failure of health." He described that she lost her "walking poise," and, on her walks throughout the Homestead grounds, would suddenly decline in a crossed-legged position to the ground, remaining there until RN found her, unable on her own to regain her feet. It became necessary to turn her financial affairs over to her daughter, Nancy, with Anne granting her power of attorney to manage her investments and business interests. When the job became too difficult for Nancy, RN assumed responsibility for her affairs.

During this period, RN was having health difficulties of his own. Sometime in the early fifties, he was diagnosed with trigeminal neuralgia, also known as tic douloureux. This condition is characterized by severe, stabbing pain to one side of the face, the cause of which is unknown, but is theorized to be compression of the trigeminal nerve. The episodes of pain can be brief or last for a few minutes with clusters of attacks arriving repeatedly for a few days to a period of months. The primary treatment consists of medications to control the pain and or surgery.

One of his worst attacks occurred in June of 1952 on a visit to the ranch of his friend Jack Fugette in Verdi, Nevada. Jack was a Texan, a flamboyant character as described by RN, who sat at the head of a table of hand-picked guests at his ranch, presiding over the evening's festivities dressed in full cowboy regalia. On the morning after his first evening at the ranch, the condition hit RN as he was getting out of bed, knocking him out, as he put it. The origin of the pain was in the roof of his mouth, preventing him from speaking, so he had to write out the names and addresses of the doctors who were treating his condition back in the Bay Area. In addition, his host obtained a local doctor who arrived and gave RN a shot, rendering him unconscious for the rest of the day.

Returning to the Bay Area for treatment was out of the question as the airlines would not accept him for travel, so a local neurosurgeon was located in Reno who conducted a successful operation the following day. The nature of the surgery was such that the offending nerve was cut to relieve the cause, but RN was left with the possibility that the nerve would reconnect in future years. Indeed, he did write of additional troubles when living in Santa Barbara, though not as severe as what he experienced in Reno.

After returning from his painful excursion, he reported that Anne was doing relatively well. Though not driving, she was deriving considerable enjoyment from entertaining her friends at lunch at the Homestead or being driven to their homes on reciprocal visits. She also regularly entertained her local children and their spouses at dinners, the last of which he reported she hosted on January 26, 1953. On the evening of Sunday, February 8, Anne suffered a fall in the living room during their regular cocktail hour. RN speculated that she also suffered a stroke at the same time. Helping her to her feet, he guided her to her three-quarter couch in the small room off their bedroom while he went to get her a cup of tea. On his return, she was on the floor again. Having gained considerable weight, she was difficult for RN to lift, but he finally managed to get her into bed after which he called the doctor who came and administered a sedative allowing her to sleep the rest of the night.

Anne was in obvious need of home nursing care and RN and Nancy worked diligently to locate one but with no success. A severe shortage of in-home nursing help required putting Anne in a local nursing home, an unavoidable violation of RN's pledge to her that she would have her final days in her own home. Uneasy about this, he engaged Nancy's help in again searching for an in-home nurse, finally locating one in Berkeley. By February 25th, they were successful in getting her home again and in a rented hospital bed to accommodate her lack of mobility. Even back in her own home, however, Anne was not improving and grew weaker each day. A new doctor was unable to stop her decline and on March 8th she went into a coma. Two days later she was given a transfusion and at 10:30 pm on March 10, 1953, RN lost his wife of forty-four years. Anne was sixty-seven years of age when she died; RN was seventy-five. A small family service was held two days later at Homestead and she was buried in the family plot at Mountain View Cemetery in Oakland adjacent to her mother, Frances

Webster Fish. RN's feelings after her loss are apparent as he wrote, "Life has to go on, but I can tell you it is an empty life, so very full of memories of pleasant times that are no more, depressing and unfair to those who have gone on before, because they would not wish those left behind to suffer such sadness."

Traveling south to Los Angeles, RN visited Anne's cousins who offered to come north to help with his adjustment, but he declined their invitation. On his way back north, he stopped in Santa Barbara and made a deposit on a new home there, at 808 San Ysidro Lane, which he later dubbed Ten Gables. RN explained his quick decision to relocate to Santa Barbara, distant from all his Bay Area-based children, by suggesting that his tic douloureux problem was at the root. His doctors had advised him that with his liability to attacks, he was better off in a warmer climate and in a locale with good medical help available. Earlier vacations with Anne at Montecito had familiarized him with the area and he decided to make it his permanent home.

Before he could relocate, however, he had matters to wind up back in Walnut Creek. Initially, he had to settle Anne's estate and to make arrangements for the wrapping up of his own businesses. In the *Memoirs*, he mentioned that he was surprised to find that his separate property now exceeded Anne's in value, the result of his successes in the Lakewood development during the previous few years. He reported that Anne had left her entire estate to him. He said that, by the time of the writing of the *Memoirs*, he had given almost all that she left him to their children in an effort to reduce the value of his own estate with estate taxes in mind.

He next turned his attention to the distribution of those contents of Homestead which he did not intend to take with him to Santa Barbara. In looking through the house, he came across a leather trunk filled with letters he had earlier mailed to Anne as well as a few from other friends. He had not anticipated this as they had agreed, at her request, to burn each other's correspondence a few years prior. He also found another trunk filled with the letters of her Mother and others, concluding that, "she had saved every letter she had ever received from male friends. I read very few, but enough to get the drift. She was a sincere, devoted woman."

He asked two of his daughters to help with the cleaning out of various personal effects, but neither stayed at the job for long; it was too sad for them and for him. "I was too emotional. I found it all I could stand - elegant clothes that Anne wore from when I was courting her, to date." Displaying all the items on long tables in the large playroom, he invited all his children to come and select whatever they wanted, giving the rest to charity.

RN and Anne had a 4,600-book library in the large living room at the Homestead. It had been inventoried several years earlier by cousin Liela Webster Sundin of Los Angeles on one of her Christmas visits. This proved of great help to RN as he made copies of the list and sent them to his son and daughters, asking them to make a selection of whatever interested them. Then, at a family assembly on a Sunday morning, he supervised the distribution of the library, giving each one of his four children present about 900 volumes. Polly Burgess Carroll was at her home in the east and could not participate; RN selected for her, from her preference list, and shipped them, with some furniture, to her home in North Carolina.

By late September of 1953, his business and personal affairs essentially concluded, RN was ready to leave his home of 28 years and move to Santa Barbara. On October 1, a moving van left with his household goods and he followed in a car driven by a hired driver. His life in Northern California was over. He would return from time to time to attend to a few remaining business affairs, including some in the Lakewood subdivision, but his residence and the social center of his life for his remaining years would be in Santa Barbara at Ten Gables on San Ysidro Lane.

The guest-house at Lakewood; RN's marketing center for the Lakewood development and the author's childhood home. Courtesy Burgess Family collection.

*An early adobe home in Lakewood.
Courtesy Burgess Family collection.*

RN's Lakewood Lake in 1939.
Courtesy Burgess Family collection

CHAPTER 19

Santa Barbara — The Final Years

RN Burgess retired to Santa Barbara, at age 75, in the fall of 1953 but, like many men who have worked at a sustained pace for so many years, he never really retired. It was probably constitutionally impossible for him to completely relax. Even the process of moving in to a new home in Santa Barbara was an exercise characterized by the devotion to organization and detail that marked his entire life. He recalled tagging every piece of furniture in the moving van and sitting at the doorway directing the movers to each room according to a color-coded tag. His description in the *Memoirs* of this period of his life hints at his desire to be remembered as a man of the world, a man of wealth, a man well-traveled, and a man full of the savoir-faire and sophistication one would expect from a man who had spent a lifetime in business and finance.

His last eleven years were a mixture of health issues emblematic of his time in life and of travel adventures encountered on his numerous driving trips and during his overseas travel. On arrival at San Ysidro Lane, he went to work making modifications to the house, decorating and arranging it to his tastes and plans. After a lifetime of building he knew what he wanted and knew how to create it. He bought and installed new appliances, installed a large, heavy safe, resurfaced floors and walls, repainted large areas, and installed a new barbecue.

To help him with his day-to-day needs, to drive him on errands, to prepare his meals and otherwise assist him, RN hired a companion soon after his arrival in Santa Barbara. This man, Edoli - no last name is offered in the *Memoirs* - remained with RN throughout the remainder of his life, accompanied him on his world and local travels, and was with him on the occasion of his death.

The improvements to his new accommodations complete, he turned his attention to his health, to some conditions which had long needed attention, and to travel. The *Memoirs* make reference to two major trips during his eleven years in Santa Barbara. In late 1957, he sailed to Hawaii for an extended visit and in March of 1961 he departed on a globe-encircling adventure that lasted until July of that year at which point he returned home early on advice of an acquaintance who thought he did not look up to continuing the trip. In addition to these, RN also took numerous driving tours throughout this period. Most of these were through various parts of California and the southwest, often with Edoli.

He described long motor trips south through Los Angeles, the Imperial Valley, and to Arizona, staying at the Camelback Inn and in other resorts in the area. On these trips, he often stayed overnight with old friends of his and Anne's with whom he had maintained contact. His trips north took him up to San Francisco, always for lunch or dinner with his sister Marie Burgess, usually at the Clift Hotel in the Redwood Room, his favorite. Often, he hosted luncheons at the St Francis Hotel for his children and whichever grandchildren were available. On one particularly long trip he traveled north to San Francisco and then on to Eureka, Crescent City, Eugene, Crater Lake, Alturas, Susanville, and into Reno, where he stayed at the Riverside Hotel for a few days. Then, it was home via Route 395 south to Lone Pine, Mojave, Palmdale, and ultimately to Santa Barbara. He often travelled with Edoli east on Route 66 to Victorville and Apple Valley, then to Twenty-Nine Palms and Palm Springs. He also loved the Riverside Mission Inn in Riverside, as it recalled to mind the many pleasant vacations he had shared there with Anne during their life together, as well as his relationship with Arthur Benton, architect of the Inn, who designed the Chalet at Diablo for RN back in 1916.

In one rather wistful paragraph late in the *Memoirs*, he wrote that he often relived in his mind many of his trips with Anne in their younger days, enjoying the memories of long ago times. He described a trip through Death Valley, a visit with Death Valley

Scotty, and a sojourn at the famous Furnace Creek Inn. There were also trips to Hoover Dam and the Panama Canal. It was, he wrote, "the last view of the Hoover Dam before the water was turned in (*sic*) and the officers gave a banquet for us." They had had an earlier, similar experience while sailing on the German boat *Empress Marie*, during which they visited the Panama Canal and rode on the bottom of the new canal on a narrow-gauge railroad just prior to the water being turned on. These trips, occurring at the time of the openings of both projects, took place in 1914 in the case of the Canal and in 1936 for the opening of Hoover Dam. The 1914 Panama Canal trip was characterized by a level of luxury consistent with his earlier life, at a time when RN was at the apogee of his career and his recollection of how it ended is consistent with that fact. After visits to the waterways of South Florida and St. Augustine, "Anne and I went on our own from there and headed for New York and the Waldorf and the theaters."

In the late summer of 1957, the year of his eightieth birthday, RN hosted an elaborate two-day party for his family. Calling it a festival, he spared no effort to put on a show for his children, grandchildren, and a few friends at his home on San Ysidro Lane. All of his children attended and all the grandchildren, save one who was traveling that summer. Anne's two cousins, Leila and Lessie from Los Angeles, also attended. Most of the guests were accommodated in cottages at the Hotel Miramar in Santa Barbara, while a few stayed with RN in his home. He hired a mariachi band and a magician to entertain all the children. His pride in this event is evident in his recollections of it, and, for some of his descendants, the occasion was their last memory of RN.

Late in that year, his family festival behind him, and in an effort to get relief from gall-bladder trouble without undergoing surgery, he sailed for Honolulu. RN's description of all of his trips includes mention of many names of people he encountered, many of them friends of his and Anne's from their life together. He mentioned the names in the same way he did throughout the *Memoirs*, as if the reader is personally acquainted with each person. Thus, "The next morning at breakfast at the Royal Hawaiian a couple of tables ahead was Madge Thatcher." Who Madge was, or how he knew her, is never explained, but she apparently was a frequent visitor, quite knowledgeable about the area, and served as a very competent guide for a tour of Oahu that day. The driver hired was an old Hawaii hand and knew a number of RN's former friends and acquaintances from his sugar beet-growing days in Contra Costa County sixty years earlier. He had worked as a young man for the Spaulding family, one of the large sugar planters (along with the Baldwins, the Irwins, and the Alexanders), and said he knew many of the members of the families, encouraging RN to visit them and reestablish old acquaintances. He volunteered to drive RN to all their homes, but RN declined the suggestion, feeling he would be imposing after so many years. He wrote, "I had entertained them in groups and singly many times at my home when I was manager of the Sugar Company's Hookston Ranch. Then along came the earthquake and fire and we each went our separate ways. I really would have enjoyed meeting them again, but after I left the Sugar Company I lost contact."

Arriving home from the Hawaiian trip, RN made arrangements for the long-delayed surgery on his gall bladder. The procedure itself was conducted successfully, but complications developed shortly thereafter when the surgeon "injected ether in the drainage tube." Suffering excruciating pain, RN told the doctor that he did not want a repeat of that procedure, whatever it was. However, one week later the same thing happened, once again leaving him in severe pain. Leaving the surgeon's office, he went to the offices of his primary doctor, Dr. Schwalenberg. He announced to the receptionist, who had informed him that the doctor was unavailable without an appointment, "Well, I am about to pass out, and if you prefer it to happen here before all these patients it will have to be so." This produced the desired response and the doctor was soon attending to RN. The pain persisted into that evening and RN instructed Edoli to telephone Dr. Schwalenberg and request a house call. On seeing his patient, the doctor called the operating surgeon and asked him to also come to RN's home. RN spent the night in a drug-induced sleep and had his breakfast the following morning with Dr. Schwalenberg at his side. The doctor visited every morning for the next week, so uncertain was RN's condition and so painful was eating. Whatever was wrong with him, it took the better part of the next year to improve. He described taking forty-six different types of medications and finally solved his problem by systematically recording every bite of food he put in his mouth, noting the attendant reaction, and eliminating items one by one until he had arrived at a diet that did not give him pain. The resulting diet served him for the rest of his life. Shortly thereafter, he needed a hernia operation and checked into the hospital for that procedure. That was the last major operation he needed and he reported that he had "gotten along nicely since, but have a rather limited life. I am no longer a good house guest."

Late in 1960, as he put it in his diary of the trip, "I was so restless that I thought an ocean voyage indicated." He planned a round-the-world tour accordingly. At 83 years of age, he was far from the robust man he had been even a few years earlier, but he was determined to travel again and so arranged for the trip. He asked his daughter Fran to plan an elaborate bon voyage party at the Clift Hotel in San Francisco for all of his children and grandchildren. This she did and on Friday night March 17, 1961 most of the family convened at the Clift for a dinner of toasts and conviviality, sending RN on his way the following afternoon aboard the Orient Line's SS Orsova.

In his *Memoirs* RN mentioned only the goodbye party and a brief description of his trip, including a few anecdotes about people he met and socialized with during the voyage. A more detailed 41-page diary contains substantial information about a routing that took him west to Japan, Hong Kong, Singapore, Bombay, India, the Middle East and through the Suez Canal into the Mediterranean, finally disembarking at Naples. Obtaining a passport for this, his first overseas trip, proved problematic. On application, he was informed there was no record of his existence at the Passport Agency and that he would need to provide supporting documentation for his request. He provided as much as he could, including records of land ownership, service on the Contra Costa County

Grand Jury in 1900, and tax records, all to no avail. The government wanted a birth certificate. Born in Carlton, Nova Scotia at a time when births were not registered, he had no such document. A letter from his sister Marie was helpful, but they needed further corroboration.

Trying to think of anyone else who might remember him from the old days who might provide an affidavit, he finally thought of the widow of his old nemesis, Numa Boone. Nina Boone was still alive, well into her nineties at the time, but she readily agreed to provide the necessary documentation, corroborating Marie Burgess. She indicated that she had known The Reverend Joshua Chase Burgess, the dates of his immigration, his role in the Presbyterian church, the names the members of his immediate family, and the fact that Reverend Burgess had conducted her wedding ceremony. That did the trick and RN was soon in possession of his passport and ready to begin his voyage.

RN's detailed journal of this trip follows the same general pattern of much of his writing about his interactions with the people he encountered during his travels, either by chance or through prior arrangement. His writing expresses a pride in the names he identifies and an assumption that his reader will recognize the people. Many were prominent and his writing reveals his pride in the relationships. Early in the trip, he was interrupted in his morning shave by a knock on his stateroom door. Thinking it was Edoli, up from his quarters in tourist accommodations below, he answered with his face lathered in shaving cream. The lady standing at his door introduced herself saying, "'Yesterday, before the boat left, your good-looking daughter, Fran, introduced herself and said her father had the State Room (*sic*) across the passage and asked if I would kind of look out for you.'…It was Lady Milne; she and her husband Sir John Milne were very kind and thoughtful throughout the voyage. Sir John was on the English War Committee and spent much time in Washington D.C.; so he knew many events and men that I knew from my visits to Washington, Philadelphia and New York during World War I, as President of Pacific Ship Building Company (*sic*)."

An entry from the trip diary expresses the mood and tenor of this trip: "April 24, 1961: Mrs. Barker and Mrs. McGregor gave a lunch in the grill; guests Sir John and Lady Milne and myself; very enjoyable. I just mention some of the social events so you can judge how life on shipboard moves on." In spite of this atmosphere, he reported feeling increasingly depressed beginning about mid-April. He was also suffering from a cold and visited a doctor in Naples who took his blood pressure, reporting it as 220/120. He indicated it should come down and provided some medicine accordingly. He also instructed RN to go to a specific hospital when he reached Rome in the following week, suggesting that English-speaking doctors at the facility would be helpful.

RN's mood at this time seems curiously fatalistic and downbeat for a man who had spent so much of his life as an optimistic builder and achiever. "One thing impressed me. Nothing stops the world from going on. Civilization rises and falls. Nothing does more than delay for a period, and so it will be if we have World War III." His mood apparently changed, though, because on May 8th he wrote of his visit to Rome, "Reserved table for three at 9 p.m. at Hosteria Del Orjo and have invited Harold and Mary Margaret to join me. We had a most enjoyable evening. I told Mary Margaret in Santa Barbara that I would take them to the best restaurant in Rome. I understand this is it, but unless you are along with the money, don't eat on the first floor. I have been told it is gold service, with golden prices. Same food and service and atmosphere on the second floor."

By mid-May, his age appeared to be catching up to him. "Slept fitfully 'til noon and had breakfast and lunch at the same time. Tomorrow will check with the doctor at the British American Hospital. I am not, and have not, been real sick - just damned miserable, and sometimes lightheaded. Do not like missing so much that I would enjoy." Leaving Rome, his route took him by train to Nice and the French Riviera and from there to Paris by car with a hired driver. Rooms in Paris were difficult to get because of a visit of President and Mrs. Kennedy, but Edoli arrived from his home in Venice in time to locate one and RN settled in for his visit.

He found no difficulty in meeting people while traveling. He was garrulous enough to strike up conversations with guests at nearby tables in hotel restaurants and soon be in the process of exchanging telephone numbers and addresses. Never shy in social situations, he would quickly introduce himself and encourage a relationship; "When you like them, get their telephone number." In Paris, he met General Sam Edge Dockrell and his wife Fern Andra. She was an American actress of some repute in the 1920s and 1930s. He was not an actual general, rather a commandant of the Hartford, Connecticut-based Putnam Phalanx, a social group of quasi military stature founded to honor the memories and traditions of the Revolutionary War. They were staying in Bern, Switzerland and invited RN to come and spend a month with them. "They had their own car and said they knew a very attractive Duchess who would join us and make a party of four. She knew the highways and byways of Europe ... and said we would have a grand time. Of course, I accepted."

From Paris, RN went to London, staying at Claridge's for an extended time during which he used hired cars to tour the south of England. While in London, he visited the Balfour Williamson Company, the firm that made his early start in the insurance business in Contra Costa County in the mid-1890s possible. His flair for the dramatic didn't fail him in his eighties. "I knew the only way to make headway was to intrigue the receptionist. He was a man, very pleasant; I asked him to see one of the other older partners who was there in 1895. He took a second look and asked me if I was serious. I said I was." RN explained how he had been one of the firm's suppliers back in San Francisco in the mid-90s and had shipped them many cars of dried fruit, nuts, and grain from Port Costa, California. He was soon meeting with three of the partners of the firm. Picking up a copy of the history of the firm, the managing partner proceeded to ask RN if he knew who the officers of the firm were back in San Francisco at that time. Responding with a list of all the key names from memory, RN soon convinced them that he was who he said he was. He then asked them which one was a Balfour, explaining that Lord Balfour was responsible for

Joshua Chase Burgess coming to San Francisco in 1884 and accepting the call to be pastor of the First Presbyterian Church.

RN was advised that there were three Lord Balfour's and felt that they were purposely misleading him out of a fear that he might attempt to visit his old mentor, who was still alive, nearing 100 years of age. He did not do so, but found the visit with the younger members of the firm quite interesting, particularly the discussion of how business was conducted in San Francisco in the late 19th century. There was no one at the office who knew any of the men he had known or done business with in that era, but those there seemed interested to hear his description of his experiences. "I told them the insurance companies I represented for them were the Caledonian of Scotland (and the) Manchester of England, that I wrote the policies and I was authorized to sign them. They sent such orders for commodities as this one: 300 mules, 300 bicycles for Sidney. 50,000 sacks of white milling wheat for London, and place $300,000 on a Good Ranch Loan at 4%. I have occasion to remember that particular order."

RN was offered an opportunity to visit his new traveling companions from the SS Orsova, the Milnes, but declined the invitation as they lived in the south of England in the Channel Islands and, as he phrased it, "So many things I wish to do but after a trip like this, I have to take it easy for a couple of days. That is the joy of living - I have been on the drive so much of my life that resting comes easy."

Heading north to Scotland and the Gleneagles Resort, he visited Warwick Castle which he recalled as "Anne's favorite." While staying at Gleneagles, he met Hosmer Rolph, a relative through the marriage of his daughter Fran into the Moore family of his ship-building days, and they acknowledged mutual friends from that time. By coincidence, they were both scheduled to have lunch with the Edinburgh branch of the Moore clan, and with RN's son-in-law Tom Carroll, who was traveling in Scotland at the same time.

RN's description of this trip may have encouraged him to undertake the writing of his memoirs a year or so later. The tone of the two pieces is similar in the good descriptions of those aspects of his travel that interested him and in which he had experience, such as farming in Scotland, and both are consistent in his tendency to dwell on the names and circumstances of traveling companions and friends he met along the way.

On his return to London from Scotland he made an important decision. His travel agent at American Express expressed reservations about his ambitious plans to tour the continent visiting new shipboard friends and other, older friends from home. He explained to RN that he had been witness to too many elderly travelers overdoing it and exceeding their capacity with unpleasant results and suggested to RN the he cut short the balance of his trip and return to New York. Indeed, so confident was the man of his recommendation that he had booked passage on RN's behalf on the Queen Elizabeth scheduled to depart at the end of the month. RN wisely accepted this counsel and, with Edoli, embarked on June 30, 1961, arriving in New York five days later on June 5th. After a brief visit with his daughter Polly in New York, they left on a Pan American jet for Los Angeles. Two days later he was back in his home in Santa Barbara complaining of an office full of unanswered mail and various investment problems that required his attention.

His last years in Santa Barbara were quiet ones reflecting advancing age and declining energy. The *Memoirs* record that "Since returning from abroad in 1961 I have had to take stock of myself. As Dr. Lomis said, 'it may be later than you think.' These days I try to limit myself to two hours in my office in the morning and two hours in the afternoon. Sometimes I take one of these shifts in the vegetable garden. The rest of the wakeful hours I put in reading or writing to our children and friends." In his more reflective moments he seemed aware of the blessings he had received in life and deeply appreciative of them. "If Anne were here, I know she, too, would feel wonderfully blessed having five children and sixteen grandchildren. All of them are normal, well and without blemish. They will carry on ably through the future. A wonderful heritage for parents and grandparents."

Characteristically, RN finished his *Memoirs* with a final anecdote, in which he once again mentioned his guns, in the context of an explanation of his choosing the name Ten Gables for his home. Hearing noises late at night during periodic Santa Barbara wind storms, he claimed to hear "footsteps, laughter, chatter and sinister noises." Attributing these to the presence of ghosts in his attic, he counted the various parts of the home within which he heard the noises and found that they emanated from ten different locations. Counting ten hips and gables on the roof the following morning, he concluded that his home was being shared with ghosts, all of whom seemed to be happy and non-threatening. Being apprehensive about being approached from his rear because of total deafness on one side, he began locking his bedroom door at night when Edoli was out of the house and putting his loaded pistol on his desk. "I had settled in my mind that anyone coming upon me unexpectedly would be someone who had no business entering. I would not shoot anyone with pleasure, but a man's home is his castle, and he has a right to defend it and himself from intrusion. I love my ghosts and gables."

The circumstances of RN's death in January of 1965 are not clear. One descendant has him dying at the luncheon table with Edoli in his presence. Another remembers being told that RN was in the bathroom preparing for his noon meal and, when he failed to come to the table, Edoli went to investigate and found him.

A life of almost 87 years had ended. Fittingly, he selected for the final words of his *Memoirs*, the last stanza of a poem by American poet Edgar Albert Guest, *Courage, Courage, Courage!*

Never changed is the battle by curse or regret,
Though you whimper and whine, still the end must be met.
And the fight is a good fight, though you struggle in vain
You shall have many a victory to pay for your pain.
So take your reverses as part of the plan
Which God has devised for creating a man.

***

RN on horseback in Santa Barbara at age eighty-five.
Courtesy Burgess Family collection.

*RN in 1964 with his first great
grandchild and oldest granddaughter.
Courtesy Burgess Family collection.*

EPILOGUE

What the Puritans gave the world was not thought but action.
—Wendel Phillips

On a cold winter day in Walnut Creek, California, in early 1948 a seven-year old boy lost his dog. A new arrival the previous Christmas, the terrier was named Meggy and had disappeared a day or so earlier. The boy searched his neighborhood, calling the dog's name, but without luck. The search eventually took the boy to his grandfather's home, the Homestead, and there on the expansive front lawn he found his dog. Running wildly and yipping as young, highly strung terriers are wont to do, the dog was occupied with tantalizing another, larger dog, a boxer named Beau, who was constrained by a metal leash attached to an overhead dog run. Just out of reach of the bigger animal, Meggy was enjoying herself badgering and barking to her heart's content. Her fun was interrupted by the arrival of an older man, the boy's grandfather, who strode out on the lawn with the purpose and conviction of a man on a mission. Upon seeing and recognizing the young boy, the older man reached into his coat pocket and retrieved a pistol, a small, black and shiny revolver. He told the boy that if he ever saw the terrier on his property again, he would not hesitate to use the gun. Chastened by this admonishment, the boy took his dog and went home and as far as can be remembered, the terrier never returned to the Homestead. The boy, of course, was your author, and the memory is one of my earliest of my grandfather.

What kind of man was Robert Noble Burgess? Obviously, a man of tremendous ambition with native talent to match it, he was driven all of his life to accomplishment. After an impressive beginning during which he parlayed an eighth-grade education into business and investment successes which ingratiated him with the elite members of San Francisco's banking and financial communities and provided a lifestyle accordingly rich, he fell from grace. The years that followed were characterized by the employment of all of his talents in an effort to replicate what he had achieved earlier in his life, almost all without any measurable success. Not until his late sixties and early seventies was he able to regain some measure of his earlier financial security and proudly announce, in his *Memoirs*, that his personal wealth had finally grown to a level that exceeded that of his deceased wife.

Character can be thought of as the behavior one assumes when one has decided what kind of man one wants to be. In thinking of RN Burgess, I've been drawn to three facets of his being, the physiological, the emotional, and the intellectual that bring the question of his character into focus for me. I've looked at him through these three prisms as I've studied the words he left in the *Memoirs* to arrive at my conclusions.

Physiologically, RN was not a large man. From distant memory, but primarily from photographs, I've concluded he was perhaps five feet, six inches tall. His relative lack of physical stature may well have played a role in what we have seen was an aggressive personality, at least in his younger years. He was handsome as a young man and was possessed of a winning personality when it was in his interest to employ it. In particular, in his early relations with older men, he was able to generate the trust and confidence which resulted in financial assistance when he needed it.

Emotionally, he was volatile and easily pushed into confrontation. He could be combative and relentless in his pursuit of what he felt was a fair outcome to a conflict. At least in his own mind, he was a bit of a Galahad, rushing to the rescue of innocent victims wronged by the circumstances they found themselves in. He had a high need to achieve in the sense that that term is employed by Harvard psychologist, David McClelland in his Expected Value

Theory of Motivation. [1] RN simply had a strong drive to build and accomplish and this implied earning enough money to live the good life as he saw it. It meant having a fine home or homes, automobiles, fine clothes, and other indicia of wealthy living. It also meant being thought to be among the highest segments of his society and peer group. Social status was extremely important to him, particularly in his younger days. He told one of his grandsons that he had known life as a poor boy and never wanted to experience that condition again.

In RN's case, achievement centered on his need to make something of himself, to become an established and recognized man of accomplishment in his financial milieu. This drive was so strong that it sometimes subsumed other ends as was demonstrated during his financial collapse. He had a combative side, and could be quick to take offense, evidenced on numerous occasions during his life. Certainly, in his younger days, the combative part of him often overrode other behavior which might have been more appropriate and helpful under the circumstances. More than anything else, his *Memoirs* speak to his need to be perceived as belonging to a level in society that was consistent with his view of himself as a successful, prosperous and competent man.

Intellectually, he was far smarter than his average schoolmate in his brief school career. He had a natural affinity for numbers and for economic concepts. It is known that he did not study economics or marketing, as these disciplines were not in the curriculum of late 19th century California grammar schools. Yet his business successes, in particular in the first half of his life, drew heavily upon these disciplines and he displayed talents in both areas far in excess of many of his peers. He was not an intellectual, however, in the sense that Richard Hofstadter defined the term.[2] He was far too utilitarian to be interested in ideas for their sake alone. His

---

[1] Stead, B. (1972). Berlo's Communication Process Model as Applied to the Behavioral Theories of Mazlo, Herzberg, and McGregor." The Academy of Management Journal (15 ed.) 3: 804.

[2] Richard Hofstadter, Anti-Intellectualism in American Life, (New York, Vintage Books, 1962-63), 24-29.

cognitive processes were always directed at an end, an objective consistent with whatever goal he was pursuing at the time.

Was he a man of his times? His time was long and much change happened during the 87 years that he lived. In coming to California from Canada, he came into an America rocked by the changes attendant to industrialization in the last third of the 19th century. He left a mid-20th-century America different in almost all respects from what he knew in childhood. In some ways, his brains and drive put him ahead of his time; his skill as a marketing man anticipated intellectual work on that subject that would not be done until 1960. He died before the sexual revolution and just as the civil rights movement was beginning to gain traction and his writing expresses that reality in its references to minorities and women, so it is possible to think of him as old fashioned in current terms. But above all, he was a man whose approach to his business affairs, his mechanisms for accomplishment, reflected his times and the tough-minded approach implied by the application of Darwin's theories to the human sphere.

What role did religion play in his character? His father, a Presbyterian minister, does not come through in the *Memoirs* as a strong or domineering influence in his life. Rather, he seems almost passive in some of the interactions RN described, such as when he left home at age seventeen. Did RN reject his father's religion? Was it not believable to one so preoccupied with the more secular goals of getting established in business and finance? He was unquestionably a prodigious worker. Active until the last months of his life, his lifelong routine expressed the Puritan notion of hard work as a mechanism for gaining salvation, though it is hard to believe that this was high in his calculus of priorities.

RN Burgess was a man of great strengths and great flaws who personified the ethos of his early years as they were spent in late nineteenth and early twentieth century America. His rise in his economic world was meteoric, his fall almost as abrupt. His legacy, unfortunately, was inextricably wound up in the events and conditions of his undoing, deriving in no small part from the upheaval caused by the First World War. He was very much a man of his times.

ABOOKS

ALIVE Book Publishing and ALIVE Publishing Group
are imprints of Advanced Publishing LLC,
3200 A Danville Blvd., Suite 204, Alamo, California 94507

Telephone: 925.837.7303 Fax: 925.837.6951
www.alivebookpublishing.com

CPSIA information can be obtained
at www.ICGtesting.com
Printed in the USA
FSHW012012290619
59497FS